Prague

Prague

Andrew Beattie

Interlink Books

An imprint of Interlink Publishing Group, Inc.
Northampton, Massachusetts

First published in 2014 by
INTERLINK BOOKS
An imprint of Interlink Publishing Group, Inc.
46 Crosby Street, Northampton, Massachusetts 01060
www.interlinkbooks.com

Library of Congress Cataloging-in-Publication Data
Beattie, Andrew.
Prague / Andrew Beattie.
    pages cm
Includes bibliographical references and index.
ISBN 978-1-56656-956-9
1. Prague (Czech Republic)—Description and travel. 2. Prague (Czech
Republic)—Intellectual life. 3. Prague (Czech Republic)—Social life and
customs. 4. Prague (Czech Republic—History. I. Title.
DB2614.B43 2014
943.71'2--dc23

                            2014002406

Printed and bound in the United States of America

To request our 48-page, full-color catalog, please call us toll free at 1-800-
238-LINK, visit our website: www.interlinkbooks.com, or send us an email:
info@interlinkbooks.com

Contents

Introduction

In 1591 the artist Johannes Putsch created a remarkable allegorical map of Europe. It portrayed the continent as a reclining empress, with Hispania as her head, Italy, and Denmark as her arms, and Bohemia as her heart. Putsch depicted Bohemia by means of a multitude of spires that represented the city of Prague. At that time—the late sixteenth century—Prague was one of the greatest centers of Renaissance learning in Europe, thanks to the Holy Roman Emperor Rudolf II acting as patron to an extraordinarily diverse group of artists and scientists who flocked to his magnificent court. History was to prove Rudolf to be one of the city's most remarkable rulers. But he was not the instigator of Prague's greatness. By Rudolf's time the city had been a vital metropolis for over five centuries, flourishing on the trade that passed along the River Vltava and on the silver that was mined nearby in Kutná Hora.

Along with this greatness, however, there was a dark and mystical side to the city, of which Johannes Putsch would have been well aware. It was made apparent by the legends of the Jewish Quarter and by the alchemists whom Rudolf II attached to his court, and in ensuing centuries Prague's dark side revealed itself to have a political dimension too, as the struggle for independence from the Austro-Hungarian Empire bizarrely saw three defenestrations—the throwing of individuals out of windows—define the city's destiny. Yet throughout centuries of turbulence Prague's medieval and Baroque heart remained gloriously intact, undiminished by war or by the rapid suburban growth that came later on with the industrial revolution. By the turn of the twentieth century the French poet Guillaume Apollinaire, swept up by the drama of the ancient skyline, was still able to describe the city as "a golden ship sailing majestically on the Vltava," while Franz Kafka, the city's most famous literary offspring, wrote in a letter to his friend Oskar Pollack in 1902 that "Prague does not let go, either of you or of me. This little mother has claws. There is nothing for it but to give in." The writer and journalist Egon Erwin Kisch, Kafka's contemporary, was of a similar mindset. "Prague is magic, something that ties you down and holds you and always brings you back," he wrote. "You can never forget it."

The remarkable allegorical map of Europe created by Johannes Putsch in 1591, portraying the continent as a reclining empress with Bohemia as her heart

On the first floor of the City of Prague Museum, located on the outskirts of central Prague, beside the main bus station, visitors peer through glass at a vast model of the city that spreads luxuriously across a single room. The model is fashioned from cardboard and was the work of an early nineteenth-century artist named Antonín Langweil, who took over twenty years to painstakingly construct his masterpiece. Every detail is clear, from the ornate decorations on the Renaissance houses in the Old Town Square to the curving buttresses on St. Vitus' Cathedral. What is remarkable about the model is how little in Prague has changed in the two hundred years since Langweil began work on it. The cathedral has been completed (its entire western portion dates entirely from the 1870s) and the Jewish Quarter has been remodeled, but in the model, Prague looks substantially as it does today: a Baroque city occupying a medieval ground plan, with distinctive neighborhoods and a castle overlooking it all from a spectacular eyrie above the river. No wonder that since the era of the model's construction the city has drawn writers and tourists in their droves. Even in communist times the place was a magnet for visitors: in her 1968 book *Your Guide to Czechoslovakia*, Nina Nelson wrote that there was a branch of Čedok, the Czechoslovak state tourist agency, on Oxford Street in London, and that Čedok agents could sell tourists a two-week bus tour of Czechoslovakia (including flights) for just £77. That was the year, of course, when political affairs in the country made headlines all around the world, as Warsaw Pact forces intervened to crush the reform movement known as the Prague Spring. In those days tourists were relatively few in number (and most came from East Germany). But since the coming of democracy in 1990 Prague has earned a reputation for being one of the great tourist cities of the world, with tour groups clogging the major squares and thoroughfares throughout the year.

Some people lament that the place has become a giant theme park, a Disneyworld vision of olde-worlde Europe. Yet despite the crowds the city's painful history, its literary and musical associations, its legends, and its glorious architecture still charm even the most cynical: and when that happens, as Kafka himself said, there is nothing for it but to give in, and let this extraordinary place dig its claws into you as it has so many others before.

Old Town. Unlike the Old Town and the Lesser Quarter, which grew organically, the New Town, the Nové Město, was planned from scratch, and its chief designer was Charles IV, the builder of the Charles Bridge and the instigator of St. Vitus' Cathedral in its current form. According to Alois Jirásek's rendering of a Czech legend, Charles founded the New Town after a prophesy that the Old Town would be inundated in a flood and the Lesser Quarter would be consumed by fire. "He personally staked out its boundaries and laid the cornerstones for its fortifications," Jirásek recounts in *Old Bohemian Tales.* "He determined the location of its squares and market places... he spoke to many a bricklayer and labourer, and rewarded each one whose work pleased him."

At the heart of the new district was Wenceslas Square (Václavské náměstí), which is something of a foreshortened boulevard rather than a square in the conventional sense; to its south was another expansive square named Charles Square (Karlovo náměstí) after the monarch himself. It is said that Charles laid out the district so as to represent the New Jerusalem on earth as described in the Bible. What he certainly did when his New Town was founded was turn Prague into one of the largest cities in medieval Europe. Nowadays most of the buildings in the New Town date from the late nineteenth and early twentieth century, including the elegant stretch of *fin-de-siècle* apartment blocks that lines the Vltava and is the most visible aspect of the district that can be seen from the Charles Bridge. The New Town is home to nightclubs, shops, two main railway stations, and a good number of the city's hotels and restaurants. In fact this was the part of the city that embraced western capitalism fastest and most chaotically—perhaps appropriately, as Wenceslas Square played host to the biggest demonstrations associated with the Velvet Revolution in November 1989.

The final two districts that officially make up Prague are Vyšehrad, to the south of the Old Town, clearly visible from Charles Bridge and distinguished by the twin spires of the neo-Gothic Church of St. Peter and St. Paul; and the district of Josefov, the former Jewish ghetto home to a number of medieval and Baroque synagogues and community buildings, which is tucked into the northern part of the Old Town. The dark history of Prague's Jewish community is covered later. As far as the actual district of Josefov is concerned, Jews have lived here since the twelfth century when the community reformed itself following the pogrom and expulsion of 1096; prior to this date there had been communities of Jews living in both the Lesser Quarter and on the Hradčany hill. During the Middle Ages the main area of the ghetto grew up along a road then known as "Inter Judaeos" (Among the Jews) but which is now (after several name changes) called Široká street. From the Middle Ages until the end of the nineteenth century this street widened in its middle part to form an elongated square where the business life of the community could be conducted. "The houses were smaller, built of wood rather than of masonry… the streets were short and narrow, crooked, unpaved and neglected," was how Alois Jirásek described the ghetto in his book *Old Bohemian Tales*. Later on, a wall was built around the district bisected by six gates; Jews could leave the ghetto to conduct their business in the city but Christians could not enter it. In the late eighteenth century the reforms made by Emperor Joseph II (after whom the district was eventually named) allowed wealthy Jews to live outside the ghetto. This resulted in the area slowly becoming a slum, afflicted by poverty, epidemics, and high mortality, and frequently flooded by the river. In 1889 the city council held a competition to select a plan for the area's reconstruction, and ten years later the winding lanes of the ghetto were replaced by a broad, straight avenue known as Pařížská that linked the north-western corner of the Old Town Square with the Čechův bridge over the river. Only the oldest monuments remained such as the synagogues, the district's Town Hall, and the Old Jewish Cemetery, nowadays one of the must-see tourist sights of Prague. These can now be found in the tortuous network of lanes that open up from the intersection of Pařížská and Široká. Although the various Jewish monuments remain, the razing of the ghetto at the turn of the century, compounded by catastrophe that befell the Jewish community during the Holocaust, means that this is a district of Prague that is harder to pin down than the others, with nineteenth-century buildings such as the Applied Art Museum as well as later buildings like the 1970s brown-brick Intercontinental Hotel overwhelming the tiny synagogues and the cramped and walled-in cemetery.

Connections

Industrial suburbs grew during the nineteenth century so a way had to be found of linking them, and this came in the form of Prague's intricate and comprehensive tram network, begun in the 1890s. Nowadays there are few other cities in the world where trams seem such an integral and vital part of the city: rather than just a means of getting around the red-and-cream trams are an iconic feature of Prague like a red double-decker bus is an iconic feature of London. Few places in the center of the city are out of earshot of the familiar electric hum and whining screech of tramcars, some of which are sleek, streamlined, modern vehicles, others of which seem as old as Prague itself. All of the vehicles are the product of the famous Škoda works in the west Bohemian industrial city of Plzeň. As far as visitors are concerned, the most iconic tram route is number 22, which runs along Národní, the great New Town thoroughfare, past the National Theatre, over the river via the Most Legií (affording great views of the Charles Bridge), and then through the squares and lanes of the Lesser Quarter and up the Hradčany hill to disgorge passengers into the northern gate of Prague Castle. But the 22, like all Prague's tram routes, heads deep into the suburbs at either end of its route; some routes, like those along the highway known as Evropská, seem to finish up almost in the countryside.

Though efficient, busy, and extensive the tram network has suffered from lack of investment (and even some route closures) since the 1970s, when Prague's metro system began to take shape. The first suggestion that Prague should have an underground railway came from Ladislav Rott, who lived in one of central Prague's most distinctive dwellings, the so-called Rott Haus whose richly-illustrated façade overlooks Malé náměstí in the Old Town. Extensive plans for a system were drawn up either side of the Second World War but building did not start until 1967, when the concept was essentially that of an underground tramway; the Soviet invasion in 1968 that crushed the reform movement known as the

Prague Spring led to an influx of Soviet advisers who redesigned the system as a proper underground railway like that of Moscow or St. Petersburg. The Soviet influence can still be seen clearly at Anděl station (known as Moskevská, Moscow Station, until 1990) where kitschy pieces of propaganda art promoting Soviet-Czechoslovak friendship still remain. The whole system is sleek and efficient but somehow the greyness of the Soviet design keeps seeping through; the stations on the recent extensions such as the 2008 extension of Line C to Letňany are much brighter and more welcoming than those on the original network (which started operation in 1974). Tourists love using the metro and for many visitors to Prague the system's trademark closing-doors public address announcement is often the first clear line of Czech they hear: "Ukončete, prosím, výstup a nástup, dveře se zavírají"—which translates as "Please finish boarding and alighting, the doors are closing."

The metro carries one and a half million passengers each day on its three lines, A (green), B (yellow), and C (red) and is the most-used in the world when the number of daily users is measured against the population of the city served; the escalator at Náměstí Miru station is reputedly the longest in Europe. Plans are in place for a new line (Line D) out to the southern suburbs and an extension of Line A out to Ruzyně airport in the west, which itself dates from the 1930s and played a part in both the Nazi and Soviet occupations of Prague in 1938 and 1968 respectively.

Hand-in-hand with the construction of the metro was the building of a new concourse for Hlavní nádraží, Prague's main railway station. The new concourse opened in 1980 but the station itself originally opened in 1909 (as the Franz-Josef I Bahnhof) and in 1919 was renamed after President Woodrow Wilson, who promoted the creation of an independent Czechoslovakia after the First World War. In 1990 President George Bush Senior unveiled a plaque in the station that carries a quote from Wilson in Czech and English reading "The world must be made safe for democracy." No one, however, refers to the station by its official name of "Wilsonovo nádraží," although the fast highway outside the old front door of the station (actually built above the new concourse) is always known as

Wilsonova. This road was one of a number of new urban freeways built in the 1960s and 1970s that aimed to solve Prague's chronic traffic congestion; the urban planners managed in the process to leave the National Museum cut off from the rest of Wenceslas Square by the creation of another fast road beside its front door, and also forced pedestrians walking between the museum and the station into a labyrinth of unappealing underpasses that are dank and dirty and dangerous after dark—not a great introduction to Prague for those who choose to leave the station on foot.

Hlavní nádraží was actually the second station built in Prague; the first, built in 1845, was the terminus of the first railway line to Prague, which (of course) linked this outpost of the Austrian Empire with Vienna. This station is now known as Masarykovo nádraží (after the first president of Czechoslovakia, T. G. Masaryk) and still serves as the terminus for some short-distance commuter trains to various centers in Bohemia. Despite its long history it is a somewhat lifeless and dingy place whose prime city-center location (a minute's walk from the Powder Tower) makes it vulnerable to plans for redevelopment into new retail and business space—a threat that has meant that station has lacked any real investment in its facilities for some years now.

3 | **Landmarks**
Buildings and Styles

No single building serves as a symbol of Prague. The city has no equivalent of the Eiffel Tower or the Acropolis or Big Ben or the Statue of Liberty. There *is*, however, an iconic view, familiar to most even if they have never visited the city. It is the view across the River Vltava towards the Hradčany: the arches of the Charles Bridge curve across the foreground, while the castle buildings rise in the background on the summit of the low hill, the soft pastel colors of the Baroque palace forming a harmonious accompaniment to the extravagant Gothic spires of the cathedral. It is the one photograph that every tourist takes—as evidenced by the camera-clicking hordes who gather by the café just outside the Smetana Museum every day, which is the best place from which to appreciate this classic view. And in this single vista Prague's architectural eclecticism is made gloriously apparent: this is a medieval city, to be sure, crammed full of churches and defensive towers from the Gothic era, but it is a Baroque city too, the two styles creating an architectural whole of symphonic proportions—not to mention an extraordinary profusion of spires.

And yet the city is more than medieval and Baroque, and more than the cathedral and the castle, too: the handsome nineteenth century boulevards in the New Town lined with florid *art nouveau* mansions still provide more than a hint of *fin-de-siècle* Paris, while in the twentieth century architects working in the cubist, functionalist and socialist-realist styles have all contributed to the city's more contemporary architectural heritage. Despite all the battles that have raged through the city—from the Hussite conflicts of the fifteenth century, through the Thirty Years War to the catastrophe of the Second World War—Prague has been miraculously spared from devastation. In the communist era effort was expended on preserving the ancient buildings. But work was often painstakingly slow,

The Gothic towers of the Týn Church form an attractive backdrop to the
Old Town Square

and many churches and palaces remained shrouded in scaffolding and tarpaulins for years—and even now many need a good scrub, their stonework blackened by decades of soot from smoke-belching suburban factories and pollution-heavy fumes from Škoda exhausts.

Medieval Architecture

Prague's foundation in the ninth century came shortly before the construction of some of Europe's most remarkable Romanesque monuments. But the city boasts no great Romanesque cathedral. The first church to be built in Prague was dedicated to the Virgin Mary and was founded on the Hradčany hill in 882 by Bořivoj, the first of Bohemia's Přemyslid dynasty of rulers. Destroyed by fire in the Middle Ages, the building consists today of a sorry jumble of knee-high ruins visible behind glass in a corner of the castle district; the administrative wings of the castle are built directly above it and the ruins are neglected by visitors making for St. Vitus' Cathedral, a few steps away. To see Romanesque architecture in its "purest" form in Prague it is necessary to head three hundred yards east from here to the Basilica of St. George, in the far east of the castle district, which bears the classic hallmarks of the building style that dominated Europe in the tenth and eleventh centuries. Peeping over a russet-red Baroque façade like mischievous children are two identical stone towers whose tiny round arched windows provide an immediate clue as to the building's origins.

The church was founded in the early tenth century by Vratislav I, Bořivoj's grandson, as the burial place of the Přemyslid rulers, and as the abbey church of a long-dissolved adjacent nunnery. Inside, the building is gloomy and austere, with solid, virtually window-less walls rising to a flat, unadorned ceiling, and arched arcades dividing the side aisles from the main nave. At the east end of the church, the apse is semi-circular—a typical feature of Romanesque churches—but the paintings over it, and the raised chancel, reached by curving flights of steps, are both Baroque additions (as is the façade). Yet more Baroque additions were removed during a thorough renovation of the church in the late nineteenth century, whose aim was to return the building to its original Romanesque appearance. As a result,

St. George's is far from being the genuine Romanesque article. But it is the best there is in Prague. Otherwise, there is only the odd pepper-pot-shaped round church, such as the heavily restored St. Martin's Rotunda that stands proudly in a glade of trees in the Vyšehrad fortress, or the graffiti-covered St. Longin's Rotunda, neglected in a scruffy park in the New Town, that provide any tangible architectural link to the early Middle Ages.

Plenty of Prague's churches have Romanesque features, however, obscured to a greater or lesser extent by later accretions; they include the Church of St. Martin in the Walls in the Old Town (now used solely as a concert venue), whose south wall was incorporated into the city's long-vanished medieval wall, and the Church of St. Lawrence on Petřín Hill, founded on a site of pagan sacrifice in 991, whose Romanesque origin is apparent in the curved apse of the predominantly Baroque church. St. Vitus' Cathedral—which is given a section of its own in this chapter, so varied and eclectic is its architecture—also has Romanesque foundations that are still just about visible in its cellars. Away from ecclesiastical buildings, the House of the Lords of Kunštát and Poděbrady in the Old Town, which in the Middle Ages was a luxurious palatial residence (of the future King George of Poděbrady among others), has an intact Romanesque lower floor that is occasionally used for exhibitions.

In the late twelfth century the Romanesque style gave way to the Gothic. The oldest example of this style in Prague is the Old Town's Convent of St. Agnes, a nunnery founded by Václav I in 1233. This religious house is named after Václav's sister Agnes, the first abbess, who was briefly engaged to King Henry III of England as a child, and who as an adult lived on a diet consisting solely of onions and fruit. Agnes was canonized in 1989, only five days before the start of the Velvet Revolution—a case of either fortuitous coincidence or divine providence, according to one's point of view. But the order of the Poor Clares (a female version of the Franciscans) who occupied the building were given their marching orders in 1782, and their former home became a place where the poor of the city could set up workshops and businesses; now the complex is an appropriate setting for the medieval collections of the Czech National Gallery.

The most striking Gothic element within the building is the old chapel, the final resting place of King Václav I of Bohemia (died 1253) among others, which is entered through medieval cloisters that open up from the museum's reception area. On entering the chapel the eye is forced immediately upwards to the high pointed windows and the ribbed vaulting that are hallmarks of the Gothic style; the overall effect, just like in St. George's Basilica, is austere and gloomy, and this is enhanced by the fact that the church has been stripped bare of any furnishings or decoration.

In the late thirteenth century the architects and builders of St. Agnes' Convent were given a very different commission some four hundred yards to the west of the convent. Jews were not allowed to work as builders or architects so the "Old-New" Synagogue in Josefov had to be constructed by Christian workmen. Backing onto Pařížská, the grand avenue running from the Old Town Square to the Vltava, the synagogue is one of the oldest buildings in Prague and serves as a unique reminder of a specific type of medieval twin-nave synagogue; similar buildings in Worms, Regensburg, and Cracow have all fallen victim to the scourges of fire or pogrom.

The origins of the building's name are obscure: it was probably simply the oldest of the "new" synagogues built in this quarter of Prague during the late Middle Ages, but another explanation is that in German it is known as Altneu, a similar sounding word to the Hebrew *al-tenai*, which means "under the condition." The phrase points to the mythical foundation of the building: according to legend, the stones used in the synagogue's construction were those of the destroyed Temple in Jerusalem and were brought to Prague by angels under the condition that they would be returned when the Temple was rebuilt.

The synagogue—described by a nineteenth-century Baedeker guide as "a strange-looking, gloomy pile"—takes the form of a rectangular hall topped by a high, pointed, saddle-like roof of red tiles. Slit-like windows poke out from the thick masonry walls and from under the steep lines of tiles. Entering the building involves descending a flight of stone steps, the intention being to instil humility in worshippers, followed by a dive into a dim and stuffy interior.

The most obvious Gothic element in the interior is the vaulting, here arranged so that five ribs always intersect, and there is never any hint of a Christian cross. In the middle part of the room is a raised platform with a lectern for reading aloud the Torah, the five books of Moses that form the basis of Judaism. The scrolls on which the Torah is written are kept in the Holy Ark situated within a niche on the eastern wall, approached by a flight of carpeted steps and covered by a hanging curtain of deep blue velvet and surrounded by gold embroidery. Motifs of vegetation abound; on the capitals and vaulting joints, and above the tympanum of the Holy Ark a vine spirals to produce twelve grapes, a symbol of the twelve tribes of Israel. Hanging from the ceiling is a russet red banner that commemorates the granting of rights for Prague Jews by Charles IV in 1357. Although the building has been restored a number of times throughout the centuries, its original Gothic structure remains intact—and the fact that it is Europe's oldest functioning synagogue makes it one of the most intimate and moving medieval buildings in the city.

Yet it is neither the Convent of St. Agnes nor even the Old-New Synagogue that claims the crown as Prague's most famous Gothic monument. That prize is shared by two buildings constructed in the following century, namely St. Vitus' Cathedral and the Charles Bridge (Karlův most). The latter structure links the Old Town to the Lesser Quarter (and thence the castle) and takes center stage in any tourist's mental map of Prague. The first bridge across the Vltava at this site was constructed in 1160, but it was made from wood and was quickly destroyed by floods, and its successor, also made from wood and known as the Judith Bridge after the wife of King Vladislav II, was destroyed by ice in 1342. Fifteen years later Charles IV, King of Bohemia and Holy Roman Emperor, ordered the replacement that still stands today.

Its architect was a twenty-three-year-old German named Peter Parler, who reused the original bridgeheads of the Judith Bridge for his new construction (which is why the bridge is not quite straight). Aside from that he probably used the famous twelfth-century bridge across the Danube at Regensburg as his inspiration. Parler was desperate to ensure that his new bridge did not meet the fate of the two earlier bridges, and he instructed his builders to mix egg, wine, and cheese with the mortar (villages outside the city helpfully contributed to the mix by sending in eggs that had been hard boiled). Knowing—or hoping—that his bridge would last for centuries, Parler also designed a fine tower to overlook the eastern (Old Town) end of the structure. The eastern façade of this tower features statues of St. Adalbert and the Emperor Sigismund, while beneath them is St. Vitus, the patron saint of the bridge, who gazes down benevolently at the throngs passing through the archway below. St. Vitus is flanked by Charles IV and Wenceslas IV, both of them enthroned and clutching orbs, while around the three figures are heraldic emblems of the lands controlled from Prague.

The confidence and certitude of Charles's new regime, and of Prague's new-found role as an imperial capital, is visible in every stone and statue of the tower and every curving arch of the bridge. The confidence, in fact, had a heavenly provenance: Charles ensured that the cornerstone of the tower was laid in 1357, to be precise on July 9 at 5.31p.m., a propitious date and time that follows the satisfying numerical pattern of 135797531 and reflected the ruler's interest in codes and numerical symbolism. At the time of its construction the bridge was known simply as the Prague Bridge; its current name did not come into use until 1870 and has allowed for the name of this great emperor to become attached to one of the most famous bridges in the world.

Charles IV's vision for Prague was that it should be a great imperial city, and he endowed his capital with many more Gothic monuments beyond the cathedral and the bridge. When Charles founded the New Town on the Vltava's east bank, he ordered the construction of a great coronation church known as the Panna Maria Sněžná, the Church of Our Lady of the Snow. But the money ran out as the building was being constructed, which is why the church, standing on a secluded square where Wenceslas Square meets Národní, is rather too high for the squat lengthwise proportion of the nave. These days the church has a bright, airy, spacious if ill-proportioned interior, dominated by a high Baroque altarpiece fashioned from black marble.

In the Old Town the Týn Church, another of Charles' foundations, has retained more of its original Gothic splendor. The twin spires of the church, fussily photogenic and bristling with turrets and adorned with baubles, are one of the dominating features of Prague's skyline, while above the north portal are extraordinary sculptures from Peter Parler's workshop depicting Christ's arrest and Crucifixion. The interior of the church boasts a pulpit and a font that are medieval originals from the time of Charles IV. A hundred yards to the south, an oriel window overlooking a narrow lane that runs alongside the Estates Theatre is another Gothic gem with a direct connection to Charles IV. It is an original feature of the Karolinum, the university that Charles founded in 1348, and comes with a picturesque collection of heralds and gargoyles, though most are replacements of the ones that were damaged by the Nazis.

Charles not only contributed to the intellectual and religious life of Prague. He also ensured that the city's poor had work to do, providing a curious foretaste of the communist maxim that there should be employment for all, even if that employment was not particularly gainful. His "Hunger Wall" crosses Petřín Hill and was commissioned solely to provide work for the city's poor. According to Alois Jirásek, the nineteenth-century author of *Old Bohemian Tales*, Charles

> often came to Petřín and supervised the project, saying the working people were his family. Thousands blessed him and prayed for him morning and night. Since their work provided them with food, the wall which they built was popularly called "The Hunger Wall"… as a wall it served no useful purpose. The story goes that Charles had the top of it made uneven or jagged to resemble teeth, reminding the poor that its building gave them bread to chew.

The wall remains to this day, a crenulated streak across the green hill of Petřín, and a jagged addition to street maps of western Prague.

Aside from commissioning the construction of St. Vitus' Cathedral in its current Gothic form, Charles made no real additions to the surrounding buildings of the Royal Palace. These came a century or so later, with the completion of the Vladislav Hall in 1500. This appropriately grand ceremonial hall, named after King Vladislav Jagiello, is by far the most impressive late Gothic building in Prague. It was built for the feasts and dances that followed the coronation of a King of Bohemia in the adjacent cathedral; a riders' staircase at the east end allowed men on horseback to enter the hall for jousting tournaments.

The first coronation feast that took place here honored the crowning of the three-year-old Louis Jagiellon in 1509; the last was that of Ferdinand I and V in 1836. The hall's most striking aspect is the elegant ribbed vaulting that stretches almost to the floor and seems to embrace the entire space, the intersections forming a graceful web which includes ovals, diamonds, and triangles. One of the best views of it can be seen in an engraving from 1607 by the Antwerp artist Aegidius Sadeler in which the vaulting takes up three-quarters of the frame, dwarfing the courtiers in the hall (who are pictured buying *objets d'art* from stalls). In his book *A Time of Gifts* Patrick Leigh Fermor described the vaulting as creating a "sinuous mobility [that] entranced the eye... It was amazing and marvellous. I had never seen anything like it." Visitors marvel at it still to this day, and they marvel too at the adjacent rooms, the Hall of the Diet, which is the work of the same architect, Benedict Reid, and the Chancellery Room, the scene of Prague's most famous defenestration (see p. 69). Renaissance touches abound in these rooms, as they do in the great hall itself (most notably in its enormous windows and grandiose eastern portal), and it is clear that even as the Vladislav Hall was nearing completion another major new architectural revolution was already under way.

Still more secular buildings from the late Gothic era can be found around the castle district and in the Old Town. Both areas have their own Powder Towers, so named as these small, self-contained forts were used at one time in their long and busy lives for storing gunpowder. The former (Prašná věž) is tucked away behind St. Vitus' Cathedral and once housed the workshops of Rudolf II's alchemists; nowadays it is used to house a display of uniforms worn by the castle's guards, which does not exactly pull in the crowds. The fort is one of a series of towers that were built along the northern wall of the castle in the fifteenth century; the others contain motley displays of medieval torture instruments or alchemical apparatus. Just like the Powder Tower in the Old Town (Prašná brána), they were never put to the test in battle. But the Prašná brána has a more illustrious history. Its foundation stone was laid in 1475 by Vladislav II and it was situated next to his royal palace, of which no trace now remains. Its design echoes that of the Old Town bridge tower and takes the form of a tall square box built above a triumphal archway. Vladislav intended the tower to be part of the Coronation Way, which led from his palace through the Old Town Square, across the Charles Bridge, and up to the castle. But almost as soon as it was finished the building's function was made redundant. Rioting in the Old Town caused by public furore over royal expenses sent the Bohemian monarchs scurrying back to the castle. In the late nineteenth century the near-collapsing tower was given a neo-Gothic makeover by the architect Josef Mocker, whose restorative hand is also present in other medieval buildings such as Karlštejn Castle just outside Prague. Nowadays most people climb the steep staircases of the Powder Tower for the stupendous view over the Old Town, although exhibitions are also held on the building's upper floors. Surrounding the Powder Tower are buildings in the functionalist and *art nouveau* styles—the latter, the Obecní dům, is built on the site of Vladislav's long-vanished palace—in a chaotic jumble of styles that is apparent in no other area of the city.

Renaissance Prague

Over the course of the fifteenth century a new architectural fashion began to spread across Europe from its original birthplace in Florence. Renaissance architects liked to emphasize symmetry, proportion, geometry, and regularity in their designs, and their rich legacy is best seen in the stunning collection of buildings surrounding the Old Town Square. Most of the elegant town houses that line this beautiful plaza are medieval structures that were given a Renaissance facelift (although many also have later Baroque embellishments). One house, in the south-west corner of the square, was purchased from a merchant by the city burghers in 1338 to serve as a meeting place and as a venue for civic ceremonies. The Old Town Hall (Staroměstská radnice) continues to fulfill these roles to this day: during weekdays the city council meets in a room whose centerpiece is a Renaissance ceiling, while at weekends the building acts as Prague's most stylish venue for wedding receptions. But the Old Town Hall is really a potpourri of styles and it is a difficult building to pin down architecturally. Thorough bouts of restoration and reconstruction, some arising from the considerable damage caused during the Second World War, complicate the issue of declaring the structure to be Gothic or Renaissance or neo-Gothic or neo-Renaissance—as it is, in fact, all of these. In the Town Hall's basement are the Gothic cellars of the houses that make up the complex, while a small chapel on the first floor, dating from the time of Charles IV, comes complete with ribbed vaulting and fragments of medieval wall paintings. But much of the chapel, and the building's tower, are post-war reconstructions—and so is much of the building's most famous adornment, its extraordinary astronomical clock, which is at least Renaissance in its conception, if not in its actual contemporary appearance.

The *Orloj* was installed on the exterior south wall of the Town Hall in 1410 and is the oldest working astronomical clock in the world. In its original incarnation the clock consisted of a mechanical timepiece with an astronomical dial showing the progress of the sun and moon across the heavens. These instruments were the work of, respectively, a clockmaker named Mikuláš of Kadaň and a Professor of Mathematics and Astronomy at the Charles University named Jan Šandel. The device was essentially a mechanical astrolabe—used in medieval astronomy—but it can also be seen as a primitive planetarium, depicting the current state of the universe to any onlooker who can decipher its complex arrangements of dials and pointers.

A lower dial, intended as a calendar rather than a timepiece, was added in 1490, along with allegorical sculptures representing philosophy, history, astronomy, and religion, while the mechanical figures that so engage onlookers today were added either side of the upper dial in the seventeenth century. They spring into action on the hour, every hour: the motley collection comprises a skeleton who tugs on a small string to ring a bell, a Jew who waves a bag of money, a figure gazing into a looking glass who represents vanity and a turbaned Turk who shakes his head throughout the performance. All are in fact modern replacements of the seventeenth-century originals that were lost when the Nazis fired at the Town Hall on 8 May 1945, hoping to silence the loudspeaker broadcasters inside who were agitating the people of Prague to rise up against the German occupation. (The figure of the Jew was refashioned without the stereotypical beard.) The figures of the twelve apostles that appear at the doorways at the top of the clock date from the 1860s and were also subject to much restoration work after the war. The calendar dial was replaced in the following decade and now takes the form of a disk whose centerpiece is a stylized coat of arms of the city of Prague, and whose perimeter is marked by paintings depicting activities pertinent to each month of the year.

The dial was the work of Josef Mánes, a noted Czech landscape painter of the nineteenth century, but it too was damaged in the war and the current dial is a post-war replacement (the nineteenth-century original is in the Museum of the City of Prague). The upper dial—the actual clock—is more complex. It comprises icons on long stalks representing the moon and sun which are moved over an appropriate background: black to indicate night, reddish-brown to show dusk or dawn, and blue to represent day. During the day the sun icon hovers over the blue portion of the clock face while during the night it moves over the black portion; the moon does the opposite, and both sit over the red portion of the background as the night begins and ends. An arrangement of zodiac signs and arcane numerals showing old Czech time make up the clock's inner and outer dials, both of which rotate to indicate the time of the day and the astrological part of the year, respectively.

Not surprisingly many tales and legends have attached themselves to the astronomical clock over the centuries. The most famous of these revolves around a historical falsehood. When clockmaker Jan Taborský repaired the clock in 1552 he also wrote a report on it in which he maintained that the clock had been built in 1490 by a fellow clockmaker named Jan Růže, who was also known as Hanuš. Taborský managed to get both the date of the clock's installation and the name of the clockmaker wrong, and for many centuries it was believed that the clock was manufactured in 1490, rather than 1410, and by Clockmaker Hanuš rather than Clockmaker Mikuláš. Alois Jirásek picked up this falsehood and recounts in his book *Old Bohemian Tales* that when the elders of Prague saw the beautiful work of Master Hanuš they concluded that nothing to compete with the clock should ever be fashioned again. To this end, "they decided to commit a terrible deed" and had Master Hanuš blinded. But the clockmaker got his revenge. He broke into the tower, climbed up to the room housing the clock's mechanism, and by groping around in a state of sightlessness he managed to stop the clock from working. "In his mind [the maker] kept hearing the words of one of the criminals on that fateful night," recounts Jirásek. "Well, now you won't build any more such clocks!" Unfortunately the tale is a flight of fancy and a man named Hanuš was never involved in the building of the clock.

These days there are websites (and even iphone and ipad apps) explaining how the complex dials of the clock can be read, and how the hourly show—when the bell chimes, the figures move, and the apostles parade above the clock—can be interpreted. The show is easily the most popular free attraction in Prague, attracting onlookers in their hundreds in the summer. But after putting on its show, this Renaissance masterpiece is affronted by having to share the stage with one of Prague's most shameless examples of faux-medieval hokum. Following the chiming of the bells, a trumpet call from the Town Hall Tower sounds across the roofs of the Old Town, played by a trumpeter dressed in medieval garb—as a rule, a red and yellow smock. The trumpet call draws delighted whoops of applause from the assembled crowd when it draws to a close. It has a vague cousin in the hourly call that sounds from the tower of St. Mary's Church in Cracow, but that, at least, has a claim to historical resonance. The trumpet call from the Town Hall Tower in

Prague has no historical pedigree at all, and has been introduced in recent years solely as a side-show for tourists.

Further examples of Prague's Renaissance architectural heritage can be found in every district of the city. In the 1580s Rudolf II had an entire wing of the castle built, grandly conceived and spacious, including the Spanish Hall to house his statues and the Rudolfine Gallery to accommodate his paintings; both are now private administrative wings of the castle and were much altered in later centuries (somewhat incongruously the Politburo used to hold its meetings in the second room during the communist era). The Martinický Palace on Hradčanské náměsti, just outside the entrance to the castle, was constructed in 1620 following a great fire that devastated the district. It has rich sgraffito decoration (showing Biblical scenes) that was discovered only in the 1970s when the building was being restored. Down the hill from here, the Town Hall of the Lesser Quarter is slightly earlier, and is used nowadays for theater, jazz, and for cultural displays. Beside the modernist Mánes Exhibition Hall on the Vltava's east bank is the Šitek water tower, a square-box affair from the fifteenth century (with a much later Baroque roof) whose original purpose was to house crude pumping devices.

Over in the Jewish Quarter, the Pinkas Synagogue was built in 1535 by Aharon Meshullam Horowitz, a prominent member of the Jewish community, and was named after his grandson, Rabbi Pinkas Horowitz. As with many buildings of the time, it is something of a palimpsest of styles: in the cellars are the remains of a medieval ritual bath, while the body of the synagogue contains late Gothic vaulting in addition to Renaissance decoration such as the pilasters decorated with fluting; the wrought-iron grille around the *bimah*, from where sermons would be delivered, is rococo. The building now serves as a moving memorial to the Czech victims of the Holocaust and is discussed further in Chapter 11.

But none of these monuments can match two further secular buildings in the city, the Belvedere Palace and the Hvězda, for pure Renaissance style. They were both commissioned during the reign of the Emperor Ferdinand I (1526-64), which saw the architectural style reach its zenith. The former is a delightful and intimate star-shaped building (*hvězda* means "star" in Czech) built as a hunting lodge by the emperor's son the Archduke Ferdinand, who ruled Bohemia in his father's stead (the older Ferdinand spent most of his time in Vienna). Situated on the western fringes of Prague, the Hvězda is surrounded by peaceful woodland that was once the royal hunting grounds, and which now makes up one of the city's quietest parks. The ceilings of the building are decorated with pure-white stucco so delicate that it could be icing on a wedding cake; the rooms of the Hvězda now house fairly mundane exhibitions about the Battle of Bílá Hora, fought close by, but also offer an attractive venue for chamber concerts. Even more exquisite is the Belvedere Palace, situated at the far end of the Royal Gardens overlooking the castle from the north, and commissioned by the Emperor Ferdinand for his wife, Anna. The building was designed by Paolo della Stella, a Genovese architect who settled in Prague, and takes the form of a spacious and airy hall surrounded by colonnades of graceful whitewashed arches covering loggias open to the sunlight. Sitting in the shadow of the brooding medieval castle it must have felt decidedly new and foreign when it was built. Today it comes across as a noble and charming building, deliciously fresh and light after all the dark, heavily medieval architecture of Prague. Decorations on the colonnades show motifs from Greek mythology and Ferdinand I presenting his wife with a flower, while in front of the building is a self-contained garden that in Ferdinand's time gave access to greenhouses growing oranges, figs, and lemons.

Baroque Churches

By 1700 Prague's church architects, like those in most of Europe, had become converts to the Baroque fashion, with its drama and extravagance and tendency towards excess. In many cases formerly Gothic and Renaissance buildings were pulled down to make way for those in the new style. These included the Břevnov Monastery in the city's western suburbs, whose Romanesque chapel was wholly destroyed to make way for the imposing Baroque behemoth that occupies the site today. This monster was built by the father and son

on Sunday mornings but otherwise the church is in the care of the National Museum, which organized its move to Prague in 1929 in four specially customized railway wagons.

More Baroque: Synagogues, Statues, Palaces, and Gardens

As Baroque architects were refashioning Prague's churches, so the same style was influencing the construction of the city's other houses of worship. In 1689 the High Synagogue in Josefov was destroyed by fire, and its Baroque reconstruction saw the Holy Ark surrounded by an extravagant profusion of red and brown marble tiling. The Klausen Synagogue, founded like the High Synagogue in the sixteenth century by Mordecai Maisel and also destroyed in the 1689 fire, features an even more exuberant three-tiered Holy Ark: this one comprises square and round columns fashioned from russet-red, black, and gold marble and forms the centerpiece of the "purest" Baroque synagogue in Prague. A later fire, in 1754, also destroyed the Town Hall of Josefov, resulting in the construction of the current building with its rich pink and white icing sugar façade. The most notable features of the Town Hall are its two small clock towers, one of which sports a clock that has Hebrew numerals and hands that run counterclockwise. Both are operated by the same mechanism built in 1764 by Sebastian Laudensperger, watchmaker to the Czech royal court. Inside there is a kosher restaurant on the ground floor and a meeting room on the first, decorated with wood panelling. The building remains the headquarters of all the Jewish communities in the Czech Republic and also accommodates a library and a publishing house.

As the Town Hall rose above the ghetto dwellings of Josefov a rather more monumental complex was under construction in the Old Town. The Klementinum was built by the Jesuits for the purposes of education, prayer, and administration, and its construction necessitated demolishing a whole district of the Old Town that lay just east of the Charles Bridge. Its spectacular library drips with a predictable array of drapery and saints and its ceiling frescoes depict both classical and biblical learning. In the same complex is the so-called Astronomical Tower, originally built as a look-out tower for defensive purposes but which gradually became used by Prague University students for star-gazing. Nowadays the tower provides a superb view over Prague's Old Town; the rest of the building is now part of the Czech Republic's State Library. Two more great Baroque libraries were also built in the Strahov Monastery, a twelfth century foundation at the top of Petřín hill that was substantially reconstructed in the eighteenth century. The library is housed in two barrel-like rooms, the Theological Hall with its frescoes depicting wisdom being rooted in the knowledge of God, and the Philosophical Hall, where the frescoes take as their grand subject matter the intellectual history of humankind.

The statues of saints that line the length of the Charles Bridge, glaring loftily over the continuous stream of tourists, hawkers, street artists, and buskers, are also a product of the Baroque era and were added between 1683 and 1714. Most of those seen today are in fact copies of those Baroque statues; the originals are in the National Museum's Sculpture Gallery in Vyšehrad and in the Lapidarium in the Výstaviště exhibition grounds. By far the most famous statue is that of St. John of Nepomuk, who according to tradition was thrown off the bridge by the henchmen of King Václav IV after refusing, under torture, to betray a confessional secret of Václav's wife, Queen Sophia. His body then apparently floated downstream under a ring of stars; it was later fished out of the water and interred in St. Vitus' Cathedral. In *A Time of Gifts* Patrick Leigh Fermor dubbed the event "the only case of depontification" in a city notorious for its defenestrations.

Special significance is attached to the saint's tongue, which had refused to betray Queen Sophia: in 1719, when John's tomb was opened, the tongue was found to be the only part of his body that had not decayed, and the organ now takes pride of place on the saint's monstrously overwrought tomb in St. Vitus' Cathedral, where it is pointed out by a silver cherub. The truth surrounding John's death, however, is actually somewhat more prosaic: Johann of Pomuk, as the lawyer and church official from Pomuk in south-western Bohemia was actually known, was caught up in a dispute over the appointment of a new abbot of Kladruby Abbey and died under torture, whereupon his body was secretly dumped in the river (a fact admitted by the Vatican in 1961). Nowadays his statue has a ring of gold stars for a halo—although the saint's body has slowly turned green as it is the only statue on the bridge to have been fashioned from bronze rather than stone. Touching the figure of John on a relief below his statue supposedly brings good luck, and it certainly receives a regular stream of devotees who have made the image worn and shiny through constant contact. As for the other statues, probably the most striking is that of Bruncvik, a knight who stands on his own ornamental pedestal on the south side of the bridge. The knight's sword is walled up in the bridge and tradition has it that the sword can be retrieved and used to defend the city should it find itself in peril.

The final legacy of the Baroque era in Prague comprises the palaces and gardens that can be found in many quarters of the city, most notably the Lesser Quarter and the Hradčany. The most notable—though certainly not the finest—example of palatial architecture is Nicolò Pacassi's Royal Palace, the complex of buildings making up most of Prague Castle and which provides the "skirting" that surrounds St. Vitus' Cathedral. Pacassi was court architect to the Empress Maria Theresa, who commissioned the palace from him in the 1750s; Hilaire Belloc hated it and dubbed it nothing more than an "immense unbroken sheer blank wall," while George Eliot in her diary from 1858 called it "an ugly straight-lined building" but admitted that it was "grand in effect from its magnificent site." Today most of the palace houses function rooms used by the Czech president that are not on public view.

Rather more elegant than the palace, and considerably earlier, is the gateway between the castle's first and second courtyards, commissioned by the Emperor Matthias in 1614 and incorporated into Pacassi's palace buildings. To the west of the castle entrance, around the great square Hradčanské náměsti and beyond it, are more Baroque palaces, including the Sternberg Palace which houses the main parts of the National Gallery, and the monumental Černín Palace, now a government ministry. Easier on the eye is the Archbishop's Palace standing outside the entrance to the castle, whose creamy façade is embellished by elegant rococo lintels and rooftop adornments. Down the hill in the Lesser Quarter are the palaces built by the noblemen who craved the prestige of living so close to the castle. Largest of these is the Valdštejnský palác, built by the military commander Albrecht von Waldstein (Wallenstein in Schiller's play of the same title), where frescoed rooms provide a meeting place for the members of the upper house of the Czech parliament. Waldstein earned his reputation during the Thirty Years War when he famously put his Catholic army at the disposal of the Emperor Ferdinand II on the condition that he could plunder at will; by the end of the war he owned a quarter of Bohemia and was the owner of the largest of all the ostentatious palaces in the Lesser Quarter. Ferdinand, however, was jealous of his general's tireless ambition and had him murdered in 1634. The interior of the palace is open on occasions, but most visitors are happy enough with the gardens, which include an enormous *sala terrena* that consists of a pompous, overbearing, and out of proportion loggia with frescoes and reliefs showing scenes from the Trojan Wars. The statues in the gardens are replicas of those carried off by the Swedes as war booty and now in the royal gardens in Drottningholm Castle near Stockholm.

An antidote to this bombast is the Vrtbovská Garden in the southern part of the Lesser Quarter, an Italian terraced garden built for the Earl of Vrtba, the highest chancellor of Prague Castle, between 1715 and 1720. Gracefully curving walls and staircases link each terrace, while porticoes covered in frescoes and pools surrounded by statuary abound; broad, dense flowerbeds, carefully manicured hedges, and walls covered in ivy complete the picture, and the views over the Lesser Quarter from the upper terrace are as sumptuous as the gardens themselves.

The greatest secular Baroque building in Prague is the Italian-style chateau built on the banks of the Vltava for Vojtěch, Count of Šternberk, and known as the Troja Palace. The red and cream chateau sits among its own formal gardens around two miles north of the center of Prague, beside the city's popular zoo. The building was constructed between 1678 and 1685 by the architect Jean-Baptiste Mathey; the origins of its name ("Troy") are obscure but may come from the array of mythical statues on the grand external staircase that leads down to the formal gardens. Inside, most of the rooms are simply a repository for some Baroque furnishings and indifferent landscape paintings from the Czech National Gallery. However, the extraordinary Great Hall, an exercise in unrestrained Baroque excess, is an exception. The eye-wateringly vast fresco here is the work of two Italian-trained brothers from Antwerp, Abraham and Isaac Godin, and was painted in the 1690s. It covers 15,000 square feet and celebrates the victory of the Habsburgs over the Turks at the siege of Vienna; the tone is gloating and sycophantic, with moustachioed and turbaned Turks coming to grief and being led off as prisoners in one scene. The Sternberg family had important connections with the Habsburgs and the Emperor Leopold I actually appears in the painting in a coach pulled by horses, surveying his victory spoils. Outside, parts of the formal gardens are laid out in the shape of a star to honor the Sternberg family, and there is also a minor-league labyrinth to one side.

The Nineteenth Century

During the early nineteenth century a profound sense of an awakening Czech national identity began to spread through Bohemia and Moravia. The intellectual springboard for this new nationalism was the renaissance of the Czech language later dubbed the "Czech National Revival" or *národní obrození*; Josef Dobrovský's Czech grammar book of 1809 and Josef Jungmann's five-volume Czech-German dictionary published between 1834 and 1839 were milestones in this revival of written Czech following two centuries of vigorous "Germanization" wrought by the Habsburgs. The Revival went hand-in-hand with the emergence of cultural nationalism that was intensifying through the various peoples of Europe, and both led to a desire for greater political self-determination among Czechs. The nascent Czech independence movement was brutally put down by the Habsburgs in 1848, and in 1867 Czech hopes of the Austrian Empire splitting into three—with capitals in Vienna, Budapest, and Prague—were dashed when a dual monarchy (of Austria-Hungary) was created rather than a tripartite one. In response, Czechs began to champion their own culture as a prelude to longed-for independence from Austria: in the late nineteenth century this mood of awakening nationalism began to exert a profound influence on politicians, writers, artists, and composers—and architects.

The area of Prague where nineteenth-century nationalism resonates most clearly is Vyšehrad, the hill to the south of the New Town that overlooks the east bank of the Vltava. It was from here that Libuše, Prague's legendary founder, had supposedly ruled in the ninth century. In the mid-seventeenth century the Austrians turned the entire hilltop into a heavily fortified military base. By the 1880s, when the area was reclaimed for Czech nationhood, the base had been abandoned and all there was here was a park surrounded by sturdy red-brick Austrian fortifications. The first building to go up, on the site of a former Romanesque basilica, was the neo-Gothic Church of St. Peter and St. Paul, the work of Joseph Mocker. Mocker was a champion of neo-Gothic architecture and also rebuilt Karlštejn Castle and the Powder Tower in the Old Town. The twin towers of his church are surmounted by tall spires whose open latticework and fussy turrets are a neo-Gothic hallmark and can be seen right across Prague. The interior of the church is covered in rich polychrome decorations illuminated by light streaming in through colorful stained glass windows; the exterior overlooks the Vyšehrad cemetery, which was established here at the same time as the church as a burial place for the artists, writers, and composers who had contributed to the reawakening of Czech culture. The church and the cemetery continue to dominate Vyšehrad to this day: the rest of the site consists of parkland surrounded by the old Austrian fortifications, while the nationalistic flavor is reinforced by the presence of four colossal statues that formerly graced a nearby bridge, Palackého most, and which were moved here when the bridge was widened. The statues depict figures from Czech mythology including Libuše and her husband Přemysl, along with Záboj and Slavoj, two legendary warriors. The figures overlook the scant archaeological remains of a Romanesque church, dedicated to St. Martin, forming the only reminder of the days when the medieval ruler Vratislav II (1061-92) chose briefly to rule from here rather than from the castle.

A slew of buildings in central Prague also have their origins in late nineteenth-century nationalistic fervor. The Rudolfinum, beside the river, was built as a concert hall and is one again today, although many come here not to listen to music but to have tea in its grand café; in 1918, when the newly-formed Czechoslovak Republic had finally freed itself from Austrian rule, the building was chosen as home for the country's first parliament. The setting is appropriately grand: stone lions and sphinxes guard the entrance while statues of composers gaze out from the roof.

The Rudolfinum is just one of a number of buildings in Prague that championed Czech culture and were consciously designed to emulate the grand civic buildings of Paris and Vienna. Others include the Applied Art Museum, very close by, and the National Museum, both of which date from the 1890s and were the work of the architect Josef Schutz. Standing right at the head of Wenceslas Square, with a gilded glass cupola and grandiose façade, the National Museum is easily mistaken for a parliament building— and indeed was in 1968, when Soviet tank commanders fired at it assuming it was exactly that. Inside, the marble entrance hall is watched over by statues of national worthies, but the didactic collections beyond it—medals, stuffed animals, and cases and cases of rocks—fail to win plaudits from even the most enthusiastic of guidebooks. However, in 2011 the museum closed its doors for a four-year overhaul and all this may change by the time it reopens again. Contemporaneous with the National Museum, and another work of Josef Schutz, is the riverside Czech National Theatre (Národní divadlo), which theater-goers enter under the gaze of yet more triumphant allegorical figures; its opening in 1883 can be very much attributed to the flourishing of Czech culture that came in the wake of the *národní obrození*.

Stylistically the late nineteenth century saw architects harking back to previous eras of building design; this was the heyday of the neo-Gothic, the neo-Renaissance, the neo-Romanesque, and the neo-Rococo. Josef Mocker's neo-Gothic buildings have already been mentioned. A less well-known example of neo-Gothic architecture in Prague is the Maisel Synagogue in Josefov, whose reconstruction in the 1890s saw the addition of ribbed vaulting that curls across the ceiling in imitation of the Vladislav Hall and other great Gothic buildings of the city. The most visible examples of the neo-Renaissance style are the Rudolfinum and the National Theatre, with their grand external staircases and their glazed-in arcades, but the style can also be seen in Storch's House on the Old Town Square. The façade of this building sports an eye-catching painting (by Mikoláš Aleš) depicting a blond-haired St. Wenceslas riding a white steed and clutching a lance, while the hand of God emerges from a cloud above him to confer divine blessing. A short walk away from Storch's House, in Josefov, is the so-called Spanish Synagogue, decorated in Moorish style with colorful arabesque motifs in green, red, and blue, hence its name; the architect Vojtěch Ignác Ullmann added some neo-Renaissance touches too, such as the cupola rising from the domed roof. In the same district is one of Prague's few neo-Romanesque buildings, namely the ceremonial hall of the Jewish Burial Society, which was constructed beside the Old Jewish Cemetery in 1908; it was deliberately built using argillite, the building stone of Prague's medieval structures such as Charles IV's Hunger Wall.

Finally the neo-Rococo style gets a look-in in the interior of the Neues Deutches Theater, built beside the railway station by the Viennese architects Ferdinand Fellner and Hermann Helmer in the 1880s. The theater, originally intended for Prague's German-speaking community, is now home to the Prague State Opera, a body that stages a huge amount of Verdi in a sumptuous interior of velvet and gold.

A few more structures deserve a mention in a round-up of notable Prague buildings dating from the nineteenth and late eighteenth centuries. The Estates Theatre (Stavovské divadlo) in the Old Town is the finest neoclassical building in the city, its symmetry and simplicity redolent of that style that was so popular in the 1780s when the theater was commissioned by a German aristocrat, Count Nostitz, as a place where plays would be presented in German. Now the theater where Mozart's *Don Giovanni* was premiered offers a mixture of opera, theater, and ballet to audiences of both Czechs

Stylistically, Cubism rejected the calm, orderly spaces created by vertical and horizontal lines and instead favored oblique angles that created pyramids, triangles, and prisms, lending buildings (and sculptures and paintings) a far more dramatic edge. The most famous Cubist building in Prague is located a few steps away from the Obecní dům and is known as the House at the Black Madonna (Dům u Černé Matky Boží). It was built as a department store in 1912 by Josef Gočár; now it serves as the city's Museum of Czech Cubism, with a stylish café on the first floor and galleries crammed with Cubist paintings, sculptures, and furniture. Gočár's most obvious touches are the strangely angular bay windows and the balcony (now the café terrace) where all the railings intersect at oblique angles. Josef Chocol, meanwhile, designed a number of tenement blocks below Vyšehrad in the new style such as the whitewashed block at Neklanova 30 with its prism reliefs beneath each window and its corner balconies that take the shape of triangles. Nearby, beside the Vltava, the Kovařovicova villa sports a garden with a triangular ground plan, diamond latticework in the windows, and angular railings similar to those in the House at the Black Madonna. After the First World War the style evolved into "Rondocubism," with softer lines, semi-circular motifs, and folkloric influences which are seen to best effect in the Palác Adria, a fancy office block built for an Italian insurance company on Narodní, where the façade incorporates florid sculptural embellishments by the Cubist sculptor Otto Gutfreund.

As Cubism burned and then faded as a stylistic influence, so Functionalism became all the rage. The most distinctive Functionalist building in Prague is the Veletržní Palace, built in 1928 in the suburb of Holešovice to host trade fairs, and now an appropriate home for the modern art collections of the National Gallery. The building incorporates all the stylistic hallmarks of Functionalism: a plain box-like exterior and an interior designed with purpose rather than aesthetic considerations to the fore, with harsh, straight edges and stark, whitewashed walls. This is very much a building of the industrial era: alienating and functional though never oppressive. The style can also be seen in the Bať'a shoe shop and the Hotel Juliš on Wenceslas Square; in the building of the Czechoslovak State Bank, across the road from the Powder Tower and the Obecní dům, whose bold façade set on a gentle curve with long, thin windows is such a contrast to the Gothic and *art nouveau* ensemble opposite; and in the Mánes Exhibition Hall beside the Vltava, a modern art gallery that comprises a blunt, unembellished whitewashed pavilion built partly over the water.

Prague's growing suburbs also provided something of an outdoor arena for the city's Functionalist architects. In the northern neighborhood of Baba are thirty-three villas designed by Pavel Janák, and nearby is the Müllerova villa, designed by Adolf Loos, an uncompromising box-shaped living space with a striking open-plan interior. Another of Janák's works is a Hussite church in the eastern suburb of Vinohrady, whose square, whitewashed, stripped-bare belfry is capped by a copper chalice, the symbol of the Hussite movement.

A few blocks away from Janák's Hussite church, and situated in the center of náměsti Jiřího z Podébrad, Vinohrady's expansive main square, is Prague's most striking modernist church. Dedicated to the Most Sacred Heart of Our Lord and built in 1928 by the Slovene architect Josip Plečnik, the enormous church features an exterior that seems to be made from white and dark chocolate, with a neoclassical roof and a chunky tower that incorporates a see-through clock imitating a Gothic rose window. Plečnik was born in Ljubljana and was responsible for an architectural remodeling of that city. His distinctively modernist buildings intrigued and dismayed his contemporaries in equal measure, but Plečnik was a favorite of T. G. Masaryk, Czechoslovakia's first president, who also commissioned him to remodel parts of the castle. Much of this work is hidden away in the castle's private rooms, but the blunt, unadorned granite obelisk that stands in the third courtyard beside a corner of St. Vitus' Cathedral is visible to all.

Prague's largest modernist building lies half a mile to the north of Plečnik's church and smothers the summit of Žižkov hill, which was the site of a glorious Hussite victory against the forces of the Holy Roman Emperor in 1420. The Žižkov or National Monument is an overblown celebration of that victory, planned in the 1870s and constructed slowly over the course of the 1920s and 1930s. But the monument was still not complete by the time of the Nazi invasion and its current appearance is the result of modifications made by the communist regime which finally declared the monument finished in 1950. It is the modifications made by the communists that ensure that a sense of brooding totalitarianism still pervades the place. The bulk of the structure consists of gargantuan but gloomy halls and chambers lined with shiny rust-colored marble (one of which houses the Tomb of the Unknown Soldier). Later a wing of the monument was used to inter Klement Gottwald and other communist leaders but their bodies were moved to the Olšany cemetery in 1990, and nowadays much of the building is used by the National Museum for its exhibitions on twentieth-century Prague. The rest of the structure, empty, severe, and lifeless, is a vainglorious memorial to eras that have long passed. The only real sign of life is the café on the roof, which provides a view over the tenement blocks of the working-class suburb of Žižkov, deliberately turning its back on more traditional and predictable views of the castle and the Old Town.

Post-War Architecture

On Letná, a hill that rises above the Vltava to the northeast of the Hradčany hill, is one of Prague's most distinctive structures—a giant metronome whose beam sways backwards and forwards twenty-four hours a day, marking the passing of time. The ticking metronome is surrounded by a scruffy park, but a series of platforms at different elevations (now often purloined by youths for some energetic skate-boarding) suggest that another structure once stood here. This was the colossal Stalin Monument, a hundred-foot high granite behemoth that depicted the Generalissimo leading a line of Czechs and Russians towards the idyll of international socialism. Construction began in 1950 and the monument was unveiled on 1 May 1955. Shortly afterwards Khrushchev denounced his predecessor and the memorial was destroyed in a series of explosions in 1962. Brutal and grey, in its time this was the largest monument to Stalin in the world; Stalin held one hand in his overcoat and clutched a book (*Das Kapital*, perhaps) in the other, while live models were used for the solid-looking figures behind him. Some lackeys complained that the proletarians were the same height as their glorious leader; most just observed that the crush of people looked like a bread queue. "From this day onward the age-old struggle of the Czechoslovak people for their national existence and their independence can be considered as victoriously completed," read the inscription underneath, next to a hammer and sickle. At the unveiling ceremony Václav Kopecký, the Czechoslovak Minister for Information, declared "Glory to the Soviet Liberators of Our Country... Glory for ever to the memory of Generalissimo Josef Vissarionovich Stalin!"

One of the sculpture's designers, Otakar Švec, committed suicide after the monument was finished and gave all his money to a school for blind children, since they at least would not have to look at his creation. Underneath the statue was a nuclear bunker, intended for the communist elite, which is now a nightclub. Above it the machinery that controls David Černý's symbolic metronome whirrs and plonks, and the few onlookers who make it here enjoy the view across the river straight along Pařížská towards the Old Town Square, as the granite Stalin himself once did.

The Stalin Monument was the most notorious socialist-realist structure built in Prague during communist times. This style— monumental, simplistic, and deliberately rejecting of any form of interpretation—was imposed on all state-sponsored architects and artists during the early years of the totalitarian era. Today, with the Stalin memorial gone, it is most apparent in the building of the Crowne Plaza Hotel in the north-western suburb of Dejvice. This may be a plush five-star hotel inside but outside its forbidding, dun-colored, Stalinist wedding-cake design remains gloriously intact, with socialist reliefs of victorious workers and peasants still abounding. The whole thing (known as the Hotel International when it opened) bears a remarkable resemblance to the hated Palace of Culture in Warsaw. Prague also has its own Palace of Culture, located in Vyšehrad, which is supremely ugly but not nearly as offensive as its Polish cousin. ("The Soviet people must have had a production line for these gifts, dropping them like monstrous dog turds across their slice of Europe," mused David Brierley in his 1995 novel *On Leaving a Prague Window*. "When they were at last persuaded to go home they neglected to take their concrete gifts with them.")

In fact not all the communist-era buildings in Prague are as nasty as the Crowne Plaza Hotel, though most are characteristically graceless and monolithic. The 1948 Federal Assembly building was one of the first to go up. It consists of a slab of offices with bronze-tinted glass in the windows sitting on top of the old Prague stock exchange. Built by Karel Prager, its sleek black marble stilts and polished grey flagstones are not actually too crass, although the building's purpose—to show the triumph of the new regime over capitalism—is clear to all. The building's current purpose seems uncertain; at the moment it is used for temporary exhibitions of the National Museum, whose main neo-Renaissance building is next door. Just along from the Federal Assembly building is the modernized concourse of the main railway station, opened in 1980 and not much different to a grey 1970s airport terminal with its low ceiling, lack of natural light, and flickering neon strip-lighting. Three years later Karel Prager added the Nová scéna (New Stage) to the National Theatre, a box on stilts wrapped in opaque glass tiles with a sculpture outside called *My Socialist Country* consisting of a lump of fluid, curling molten rock.

The audience for the plays presented here mostly lived in bleak high-rise housing developments in the suburbs, in grim apartment blocks known as *paneláky* which were constructed throughout the communist era. The official Olympia guide to Prague published in the 1980s proudly listed all these estates and noted the number of housing units and people living in each one. Nowadays the blocks are often painted pastel colors but this does little to soften the brutalizing effect.

Although the people living in the *paneláky* were encouraged to absorb the socialist-realist dramas playing in the Nová scéna, what they were not supposed to be doing was watching Austrian or West German television, and to this end construction work began on the giant television tower in Žižkov, whose main purpose was to jam these unwelcome signals. The tower's space-age outline makes a distinctive addition to the Prague skyline, and at over seven hundred feet it is by far the tallest building in the city; there is a viewing gallery and café two-thirds of the way up. The lower portion of the tower consists of three whitewashed cylindrical legs that give the whole thing the impression of being some sort of rocket launcher, while the business end of the tower (the top third) is a more conventional white and red stalk bristling with satellite dishes. In recent years the artist David Černý has added some alarming sculptures of babies to this futuristic work: some crawl up the legs like insects, while others peep over the curling roof of the viewing galleries. The sculptures are even more disturbing up close, for their faces are blank and featureless or even consist of a smashed-in rectangle. (The same hideous creatures can also be seen crawling around on a patch of grass on Kampa Island, outside the Museum Kampa.) Černý's controversial but eye-catching sculptures are a hallmark of post-communist Prague, but they are sculptures, not structures. As far as buildings are concerned, the extraordinary Tančící dům ("Dancing House") beside the Vltava is by far the most distinctive example of post-1990 architecture in the city. Designed by the Canadian architect Frank Gehry, the office block consists of two cylindrical buildings that lean into the other like Fred and Ginger, with one of the balconies resembling a dancer's arm draped loosely against the other.

Czech religious reformer Jan Hus is burned to death at the stake in
Constance in 1415; an illustration from the Spiezer Bilder-Chronik produced
in Switzerland in 1485

4 | Rulers and Ruled
A Brief Social and Political History

The great German chancellor Otto von Bismarck once commented that "whoever controls Prague controls mid-Europe," and over the course of the city's twelve hundred-year history a succession of imperial powers have taken this to heart: the Kings of Sweden, Hungary, and Poland, the Habsburg and Holy Roman Empires, Nazi Germany, and the Soviet Union have all acted as political puppet masters in Prague at one time or another. In 1938, with Nazi invasion imminent, the great Czech writer Karel Čapek remarked adroitly that "to be anchored in the very heart of Europe is not merely a geographical location, but it means the very fate of the land and of the nation that inhabits it." For only two short periods in the city's history—during the First Republic from 1918 to 1938, when Čapek was writing, and then again from 1989 to the present day—can Prague be said to have been truly in control of its own destiny.

No wonder that a sense of melancholy pervades the history of the place. In his elusive 1979 work *The Book of Laughter and Forgetting*, émigré Czech novelist Milan Kundera noted gloomily that the history of the Czechs, "an endless story of rebellions against the stronger, a succession of glorious defeats that launched [Czech] history and led to ruin the very people who had done the launching," is a story of *litost*, "a state of torment created by the sudden sight of one's own misery." Heda Margolius Kovály, who survived the Nazi occupation of Prague only to see her husband executed during the Stalinist show-trials of the early 1950s, echoes these sentiments in her memoir *Prague Farewell*. To Kovály, Prague "lives in the lives of her people, and they repay her with the love we usually reserve for other human beings... Prague is alive, sad and brave, and when she smiles with spring, her smile glistens like a tear."

Yet throughout the centuries Czech nationalism has rarely lain dormant. In the later Middle Ages it found a mouthpiece in the religious reformer Jan Hus, and in the late nineteenth century a surge of nationalistic fervor that found expression in politics, architecture, literature, and art eventually led to the creation of an independent Czechoslovak state, with Prague as its capital, in October 1918. But this freedom was short-lived: the history of Prague in the last hundred years has been particularly dark as the vicious currents and counter-currents of Nazi and Soviet empire building have washed over Central Europe, submerging Prague in their wake.

Medieval Prague (850-1378): The City Established

As the first chapter in this book recounts, the origins of the city of Prague lie shrouded in mists thicker than those that gather along the deep valley of the Vltava on an autumn morning. The first Czech rulers to whom a name can be ascribed were the Přemyslids, a tribe that in the middle of the ninth century emerged victorious from a bloody power struggle with another Slavic tribe, the Slavniks. Around 852 AD the Přemyslid leader Duke Bořivoj established the seat of his tribal government in Levý Hradec, on the Vltava just beyond the modern-day fringes of northern Prague. There he built Bohemia's first church and dedicated it to St. Clemens. Thirty years later Bořivoj moved the seat of the Bohemian rulers six miles south to a hill overlooking the Vltava, later named Hradčany, where pagan gods had been worshipped and where Bořivoj wanted now to build his mausoleum. This was where the first incarnation of Prague Castle began to rise, and around the castle the city of Prague began to grow.

One Přemyslid ruler has seeped into modern consciousness both inside and outside the Czech lands, namely Bořivoj's grandson Václav I, better known as Wenceslas to English speakers. Václav was born in 907 and ascended the Bohemian ducal throne as a boy of just thirteen. Hard historical evidence relating to much of his life is difficult to come by, but according to tradition Václav's Christian grandmother, Ludmila, was appointed regent, which drew the ire of Drahomíra, the boy's pagan mother, who had the older woman strangled with her own scarf to release Václav from her Christian influence. But Ludmila's work was done before she was murdered: when he came of age Václav vowed to spread Christianity among the heathen people of his dukedom. Yet it was the same pagan agitators who had killed Václav's mother who also did for Václav: according to one version of the story, on September 20 in the year 929 Václav's pagan brother Boleslav stabbed the young duke to death outside a church near Prague, partly because of Václav's political alliance with the Saxons and partly because of his Christian proselytizing.

The martyred Václav was later immortalized in John Mason Neale's Christmas carol as "Good King Wenceslas," but Neale's words, written in 1853 (to a thirteenth-century dance tune) and adapted from a poem by Václav Alois Svoboda, play fast and loose with tradition never mind historical truth. St. Agnes Fountain, by which "yonder peasant dwelt" according to the carol's second verse, was constructed some three centuries after Václav's death, and Václav was never a king, he was only a duke (although the Holy Roman Emperor Otto I posthumously conferred on him the dignity and title of king). "English carol singers [have] promoted him in rank," the writer Patrick Leigh Fermor concluded in his *A Time of Gifts*, after visiting the richly decorated tomb of Václav in St. Vitus' Cathedral, and Leigh Fermor goes on to say that confronting the effigy of the "mild medieval sovereign" was like "a meeting with Jack the Giant Killer, or Old King Cole."

The instigator of Václav's extraordinary tomb, admired to this day by swarms of visitors to the cathedral, was none other than his murderer Boleslav, who repented after his deed and buried his dead brother's remains in a shrine on Hradčany hill that later became the centerpiece of the cathedral. This encouraged the rapid adoption of Christianity by the nascent city: in 973, during the rule of Boleslav II, Prague became a bishopric subordinate to the Archbishop of Mainz, who appointed a cleric named Vojtěch as the first Bishop of Prague. Vojtěch was canonized as St. Adalbert in 999 and to this day is revered as a patron saint of Czechs, Hungarians, and Poles. In 993 Vojtěch and Boleslav founded Bohemia's first monastery at Břevnov, at that time in remote countryside beyond Prague Castle but nowadays in the city's western suburbs on the road to the airport. After being used as administrative offices in the communist period, the building was returned to the Benedictine Order in 1993, exactly a thousand years after the institution's foundation (although much of the place is now a hotel sitting in the shadow of the monastery's hulking Baroque abbey).

The submission of the Bishop of Prague to the Archbishop of Mainz—historically the most important cleric in the Holy Roman Empire—is reflective of the relationship between Prague and the great empire of German states to the west. Historical documents record that in the year 806, six years after Charlemagne was crowned the first Holy Roman Emperor, Bohemian dukes were forced to pay a yearly tribute of 500 pieces of silver and 120 oxen to the emperor, an act of submission that the Nazis maintained demonstrated rightful German hegemony over the Czech lands. In 950 Emperor Otto I of the Saxon dynasty of emperors went one stage further, subjugating Bohemia by military means.

But over the ensuing centuries Přemyslid rule grew in confidence and prestige. Notable Přemyslids included Vratislav II, who abandoned Prague Castle and ruled from Vyšehrad and who was given the title King of Bohemia in 1085; Soběslav I (1125-40), who undid Vratislav's work and returned the seat of government to the castle, where it has been ever since; and Otakar I, who in 1212 obtained a formal edict from the emperor, styled the Golden Bull of Sicily, which made him the first of a hereditary line of Bohemian kings.

The real zenith of Přemyslid power came in the 1270s. By then Otakar's grandson King Otakar II, the "Iron and Golden King," ruled a swathe of territory that stretched from the Baltic to the Adriatic, garnered through decisive military conquest and shrewd marriage alliances. Otakar's territorial possessions meant that for the first and only time in its long history Bohemia could make some sort of claim to having direct access to the sea. In fact Leigh Fermor wonders in *A Time of Gifts* whether it was Otakar's rule of the Istrian Peninsula (now part of the coast of Croatia) that led Shakespeare to give his play *The Winter's Tale* the impossible geographical setting of "the seacoast of Bohemia." Whether or not this is true, Otakar certainly elevated Prague to the status of a great European city, and is overshadowed only by Charles IV and Rudolf II in the pantheon of great Czech monarchs. According to the Colmar Chronicles, written by a monastery scribe in Alsace, this notable and often overlooked ruler was "a handsome youth… broad chest, full lips, vivacious and wise." But disaster was just around the corner. In 1278, at Dürnkrut on the Moravian-Austrian border, Otakar was killed on the field of battle by Rudolf of Habsburg, the scion of an upstart family of south German nobles; when Otakar's tomb in St. Vitus' Cathedral was opened in 1976 the gash from the blow that killed him was still visible on his skull.

The Přemyslid dynasty died out less than thirty years later, the line ending with the teenaged Václav III who lasted under a year before his murder in 1306. The unfortunate Václav had no heirs, so the Bohemian nobles elected a series of weak Habsburg monarchs whose rule turned out to be nothing more than a four-year stopgap: Albert I (killed by his own nephew), Rudolf I, and Henry of Carinthia provided a foretaste of four hundred years of Habsburg rule that was to come much later. They ruled in an era that was dominated not only by political instability but by invasion (by Otto of Brandenburg), occupation, anarchy, revolt, hunger, and disease, with vast ditches being constructed around the city to bury the mountains of dead.

In 1310, on the death of Henry of Carinthia, the Bohemian Diet offered the Bohemian throne to the German-born nobleman John of Luxembourg. John's eligibility came from his marriage to Eliška Přemyslovna, who was the sister of the last Přemyslid king. Despite going blind in later life John spent much of his time fighting foreign wars and in 1346 he was killed in the Battle of Crécy, in which his son Charles was also wounded. Charles's survival turned out to be something of a miracle, for his reign was destined to be the most glorious in Czech history. As Charles IV he presided over Prague's first "golden age," transforming the city into an imperial capital. A Renaissance man before the Renaissance had even got properly under way in Central Europe, Karel (as Czechs knew him) was fluent in five languages and by the time of his death in 1378 he had founded a university (the Charles University, still in existence today), promoted Czech as Prague's official language alongside German, made the city an archbishopric independent of Mainz and launched major building projects such as the Charles Bridge and St. Vitus' Cathedral which provide modern Prague with its breathtaking Gothic splendor. He also revolutionized the somewhat chaotic political structure of the Holy Roman Empire: according to Charles' Bull of 1356, the emperor was to be chosen (at a special ceremony in the sandstone-red St. Bartholomew's Church in Frankfurt) by seven electors including the ruler of Bohemia. So great was Charles' fame that according to Alois Jirásek in *Old Bohemian Tales* the bell that tolled in St. Vitus' Cathedral to announce the king's death was ringing out even as the great man took his final gasps. On hearing the bell, Charles cried out from his deathbed "Hear Ye! God is Calling me! The Lord be with you forever!"—whereupon he promptly died. Meanwhile the official bell-ringer, hastening towards the bell tower and wondering who could be ringing the great bell, discovered the tower to be locked—which was remarkable, given that he was the only key holder. The bell had clearly been announcing the passing of the great Czech monarch of its own accord.

Jan Hus and the Czech Reformation (1378-1419)

There was no way that Charles' successor Václav IV (1378-1419) could ever live up to his father's reputation. Known to Germans as Wenzel "der Faule"—Wenceslas the Idle—he was an incompetent drunkard, and the unfortunate monarch was imprisoned twice, firstly by his own nobles (in Konopiště Castle, now a popular excursion from Prague) and then by his stepbrother the Emperor Sigismund. (Another famous tale told about Václav is that he had to be rescued from the ire of his barons by a masseuse named Susanna, who rowed him to safety across the Vltava.) Never liking Prague Castle, Václav established a brand new royal palace in the Old Town, on the site of the present-day Obecní dům, which was to remain the seat of Czech kings for the next one hundred years. In 1400 Václav was deposed as Holy Roman Emperor but he lived on in his new palace as King of Bohemia for a further nineteen years, eventually killed off by the stress of having to deal with the burgeoning Bohemian Reformation.

There had been religious reformers in Prague before the time of the unfortunate Václav IV. One of the most noted had been Jan Milíč of Kroměříž, who preached fiery sermons at the Týn Church in the Old Town in which he railed against corrupt church practices. (He also refused to wash, slept on a wooden board, lived off a diet of peas and beans, and accused Charles IV of being the antichrist at a sermon at which the monarch was present.) But Jan Hus, who appeared on the scene at the turn of the fifteenth century, was charismatic and persuasive enough to influence Bohemian history for the next two hundred years.

Hus was heavily influenced by the English reformer John Wycliffe, who was writing his last great works in Oxford at the same time as Hus was growing up in Husinec, a tiny village in the beautiful Šumava Hills of southern Bohemia. Wycliffe's translation of the Bible into English, the anti-clerical stance of his Lollard followers, and his insistence on a purely scriptural-based theology made him a key figure in the early Protestant Reformation. His works became known in Bohemia through a link forged by Václav IV's sister Anne, who was married to King Richard II, and to this day the largest collection of Wycliffe's original works anywhere in the world is in the part of the Czech State Library that is housed in the Klementinum in Prague's Old Town. By the year 1400, when Hus began preaching at the Betlémské kaple (Bethlehem Chapel) in the south of the Old Town, Wycliffe's works were being fiercely debated in the Charles University, of which Hus was soon appointed rector. Lined up against Hus and his growing band of supporters was Zbyněk Zajíc, the Archbishop of Prague, who staged public burnings of Wycliffe's books, including the *Trialogus*, which attacked monasticism and the power of the popes and which Hus had translated into Czech. (The burnings took place despite taunts from university students that Zbyněk was probably illiterate and had no idea what the books said.)

As the conflict intensified Václav IV, who bore a grudge against Pope Gregory XII for relieving him of the title of Holy Roman

Emperor, and a second grudge against Archbishop Zbyněk for supporting Gregory, came out in support of Hus and through the 1409 Edict of Kutná Hora rigged the votes within the university to favor the Hussite faction. In doing so Václav caused a huge exodus of Catholic (and mainly German-speaking) students and academics from Prague, who moved north and founded a new university in Leipzig, depriving Charles's university of its international standing. With that bastion of Catholic theology and teaching gone, Václav seemed to be on the verge of turning his kingdom into Europe's first Protestant state.

In 1411, however, the relationship between Hus and Václav broke down when Hus began to speak out against the sale of indulgences. An indulgence bought the purchaser a remission of time in purgatory; they were sold by the Church to raise funds for the war between Pope Gregory XII and the Avignon-based "antipope" John XXIII during the great papal schism. Václav received a percentage of the sale of indulgences and fearing a loss of revenue turned against Hus, who was summoned to the Council of Constance by the Emperor Sigismund. Devoid of royal protection in Bohemia and initially promised safe conduct by the emperor, Hus felt he had no option but to head for the city by Lake Constance in southern Germany. Yet after engaging in long theological disputes with council members, Hus was at last formally arrested and put on trial. A month of hearings followed, conducted in the city's cathedral, but the verdict and punishment were never in doubt. Hus, branded by the council "a veritable and manifest heretic," had a hat placed on his head depicting devils seizing people's souls and was handed over to the secular authorities of the city of Constance; he was then burned at the stake on a road just outside the city on July 6, 1415. When he was dead, his bones were broken, his heart was taken out and given a final "roasting" on the end of a stick, and his ashes were thrown into the River Rhine.

When news of the death of Hus reached Prague it brought rioters onto the streets, for Hus was revered as a Czech nationalist as well as a religious reformer. (He is remembered for a number of other achievements too, such as introducing diacritics into written Czech, particularly the use of the *haček* over the letter "c.") He remains highly venerated to this day. The anniversary of his death is a national holiday, and July 6, 1915, the four hundredth anniversary of his burning at the stake, saw the official dedication of the Hus memorial that dominates Prague's Old Town Square; Hus is its central stark figure, a champion for the repressed, ensuring the monument's prominence during upheavals such as the Nazi invasion in 1938 and the Soviet invasion that brought an end to the 1968 Prague Spring. But the most visible symbol of the esteem in which Hus is still held, nearly five centuries after his death, can be seen in the restoration work carried out on the Bethlehem Chapel in Prague's Old Town, where he preached. In the centuries following the death of Hus this remarkable building continued to attract radical reformers, in particular Thomas Müntzer, the leader of the German Peasants' Revolt, who preached here in 1521. Gradually, however, the chapel fell into disuse and in the ensuing centuries the barn-like structure was converted into a warehouse and then divided up into apartments. But communist ideology celebrated Hus and Müntzer as early socialists (Hus, for example, spoke out against the concentration of wealth in the hands of the Church) and in 1962 the chapel was restored and a museum installed in part of the building where Hus once worked.

Unfortunately only the outer walls of the building remained from Hus' time and the rest of the chapel had to be reconstructed around them, with the faux-medieval wall paintings showing Hus being burned at the stake created in the 1960s. Fragments of medieval inscriptions on the walls provide the single genuine link with Hus. But even in its restored state the church offers a remarkable link to the ideas of the reformer. When the church was originally built in 1391 it was the largest in Bohemia, capable of holding three thousand worshippers, and its monumental size remains striking to this day. Nowadays this extraordinary building, rich in history, simple and austere, is looked after by those who cherish Hus and his memory, and functions as the ceremonial hall of the Prague Technical University where degree ceremonies are held.

Religious Strife (1419-1526)

Four years after the death of Hus, in 1419, Prague once again reverberated to the noise and clash of rioters as preachers throughout the city denounced Hus to their congregations. One radical Hussite preacher, Jan Želivský, was so incensed by the inflammatory sermons that on July 30 he led his congregation from the Church of St. Mary of the Snow to the Town Hall in the New Town where some Hussites were being held prisoner. Someone threw a stone at Želivský from the Town Hall and the enraged mob reacted by storming the building and throwing fifteen Catholic councilors out of an upper-floor window. The men were impaled on the pikes of the Hussite mob assembled in Charles Square below, and the event became infamous as the first of Prague's historic "defenestrations." According to the legend recounted by Alois Jirásek, it was this event that finally brought the end for King Václav. "When the king heard this news he grew pale, his eyes flashed, he trembled with fury," Jirásek wrote. "He could not speak. Then suddenly he gave a lion-like roar and fell to the floor. He had suffered a stroke and died soon thereafter." Želivský, meanwhile, paid for his actions by having his head cut off in the courtyard of the Old Town Hall, after being tricked into the building by being told that the city burghers wanted to speak with him. Just as Želivský started speaking, the doors of the council chamber—where councillors meet to this day—were flung open and the city executioner was standing before him. Around eight or ten other Hussites died with Želivský on the same day. In communist times a plaque commemorating the event was placed on the wall of the Old Town Hall by the authorities claiming Želivský and his followers to be "victims of the bourgeoisie."

The Hussites were the definite underdogs in the religious wars that erupted after the death of Václav and Želivský. But the opening battle of the conflict, fought in 1420, brought them an unexpected victory. The fighting raged over a steep-sided hill called Vítkov that rises nowadays from Prague's inner suburbs and which later became known as Žižkov hill after the one-eyed Hussite general Jan Žižka who led his vastly outnumbered peasant army to victory against a

Catholic force led by the Emperor Sigismund. Now a gargantuan equestrian statue of Žižka, one of the largest in the world, forms the centerpiece of the hilltop monument, which is twenty minutes on foot from the Old Town Square and was later used as a mausoleum for deceased communist leaders. The triumph of Vítkov, however, was short lived: the Hussites soon split into two warring camps, the radical Táborites, named after the town in South Bohemia that became their stronghold, and the more moderate Utraquists, so-called because they administered communion *sub utraque specie* ("in both kinds")—meaning that along with bread, wine was also given to worshippers, leading to the chalice being adopted as the Hussite symbol. In 1433, at the Council of Basel, the pope reached a compromise with the Utraquists in return for peace. The following year the Utraquists joined forces with the Catholics to defeat the Táborites at the Battle of Lipany, and at last the Emperor Sigismund claimed the throne of Bohemia—only to die three years later and bring an end to the Luxembourg line of kings.

Nearly a century of comparative calm followed the death of Sigismund. His successors included the first and only Hussite king, George of Poděbrady, who was elected to the Bohemian throne in 1458 by an increasingly Protestant nobility. That he was elected in the Old Town Hall rather than in the castle was indicative of the subtle shift of power from the former to the latter that took place during the course of the fifteenth century. The burghers of the Old Town saw Protestantism as a mixed blessing: by adopting the religion they managed to wrest some influence and control from the monarch—and yet they did not want the Hussites to become too powerful, hence their execution of Jan Želivský.

George of Poděbrady, though, was a wise choice of monarch. He is seen in Czech history as a pragmatic and tolerant ruler (although his rule was marred by another papal crusade, led this time by the great Hungarian king Matthias Corvinus, who set himself up as a "rival" King of Bohemia). During his reign a large gilded chalice, the symbol of the Hussite movement, was placed on the façade of the Týn Church in the Old Town to represent George's

Utraquist beliefs—and this chalice became emblematic of the shifting religious fortunes of fifteenth-century Prague. George died heirless in 1471 and the Bohemian Diet passed the crown over to the Catholic Jagiellonian dynasty of kings who also ruled Poland, Lithuania, Hungary, and Belarus, and who melted down George's chalice to provide a new golden halo for a statue of the Virgin Mary in the same church. In the end, though, only two Jagiellonian kings ruled in Prague: the first, Vladislav II, was followed by Louis II of Hungary, who was killed in 1526 at the Battle of Mohács on the Hungarian Danube, crushed in a ditch by his falling horse as he and his ragtag army fled from the advancing Turks.

Habsburg Prague (1526-1918)

The death of King Louis meant that once again the Bohemian nobility had to search for a new monarch. The man they chose to rule over them was Ferdinand of Habsburg, related by marriage to the Jagiellonian dynasty and the brother of the great Holy Roman Emperor Charles V. With his election, power moved firmly across the river and back to the castle. One of Ferdinand's first acts was to demand a mobilization of troops to fight the powerful Schmalkaldik League of Protestant German states. His demands brought riots in Prague that were dealt with in a trial held in the castle's great Vladislav Hall, in which Ferdinand acted as both prosecutor and judge, handing down death sentences that led to four beheadings on Hradčany Square. Other sentences included exile, public whippings, and the seizure of property. In many ways Ferdinand's brutal quashing of dissent set the tone for the heavy-handed Habsburg rule that was to last until the end of the First World War.

In 1583 Ferdinand's successor Rudolf II responded to the Turkish threat to Vienna by moving the imperial capital to Prague. It was not only the threat of siege and occupation that sent him scurrying to Bohemia: Rudolf was a frail and melancholic introvert, and the austerity of Prague Castle appealed to him more than the frivolity and extravagance of Vienna—and he was away from the intrigue of the Habsburg court that upset him so much. His decision ushered in the city's second "golden age."

Rudolf, one of the most remarkable rulers of Bohemia, was prone to bouts of depression and was possibly insane; he kept a pet lion, recruited the English alchemists Edward Kelly and Dr. John Dee to his court, and made Prague the greatest center for the studying of astronomy and astrology in Europe. (His eccentricities are described in detail in Chapter 11.) Yet Rudolf transcended the sectarian differences between Catholics and Protestants and in July 1609 he signed the celebrated "Letter of Majesty" that allowed complete religious freedom to the people of Bohemia. Such a level of tolerance was unheard of anywhere else in Europe. But in the end his behavior could no longer be tolerated by the Habsburg family, and in 1611 Rudolf was forced to abdicate by his brother Matthias. Rudolf had no heirs (he had been warned by an astrologer that his legitimate heir would rob him of the throne) so the throne of Bohemia passed to his scheming brother. This was despite the intervention of a military force led by Rudolf's ambitious cousin, Archduke Leopold V, the Bishop of Passau, in support of the ailing ruler. Rudolf died the following year, three days after his beloved lion, which had been a present from the Sultan of Turkey; Rudolf and his lion shared similar horoscopes and Tycho Brahe, his official astrologer, had read in the stars that they would die within days of each other. After Rudolf's death his brother Matthias ruled for the next six years.

In 1617 Bohemian nobles elected the avowedly Catholic Ferdinand of Styria as successor to Matthias. In the same year a dispute blew up over the construction of Protestant chapels on land over which Prague's Roman Catholic clergy claimed ownership. The tense relationship between the Protestant nobles and the Catholic Church finally came to a boil on May 23 the following year when a group of over a hundred seething Protestants led by the German Lutheran Count Thurn bribed their way into Prague Castle and threw two of the city's Catholic governors, Vilém Slavata and Jaroslav Martinitz, along with their secretary Philip Fabricius, out of the third-floor window of the Bohemian Chancellery. (These days the Chancellery and the window concerned are a busy pausing-place for tour groups traipsing round the Renaissance parts of the castle.) The Catholic governors had been appointed by Ferdinand and had treated the Protestant estates with contempt. A contemporary account indicates that the three defenestrated men desperately clutched hold of the window ledge after their ejection, kicking their legs in the air behind them, but Thurn beat their knuckles with the hilt of his sword until they were forced to let go. All three survived after a fall of seventy feet and a soggy landing in a heap of manure. (Philip Fabricius was later granted the title Baron von Hohenfall—literally, "Baron of Highfall"—by the emperor.) This was Prague's second (or possibly third) defenestration—depending on whether another window-ejection of 1483 is counted—and is certainly *the* defenestration of Prague, sparking off as it did the continental-wide conflict that came to be known as the Thirty Years War. (Jerome K. Jerome once remarked that "half Prague's troubles, one imagines, might have been saved to it had it possessed windows less large and temptingly convenient.")

The Bohemian Diet fired the opening political salvo of this dynastic and religious war by electing the Protestant Frederick of the Palatinate, the so-called "winter king," to the throne of Bohemia. Frederick cut quite a dash on the throne of Bohemia. His wife Elizabeth was a sister of the English King Charles I and shocked polite society in Prague with her outré fashion sense and daringly modern hairdos. (She was, according to the diarist Samuel Pepys, "a debonair but plain woman," although John Donne wrote an appreciative poem about her.) Their son the Prince Rupert was to become a military commander in both the Thirty Years War and the English Civil War, as commander of his uncle Charles I's cavalry, while their daughter Sophia was destined to be the mother of King George I of Great Britain. But Ferdinand of Styria, whom Frederick supplanted, had no time for this upstart from the new religion, and on November 8, 1620 Frederick's Protestant forces found themselves facing Fedinand's rival Catholic army at Bílá Hora (White Mountain), a battle fought (like Žižkov) within Prague's modern-day city limits. In fact nowadays the battle site can be found in the far western suburbs of the city, at the end of a couple of tram routes. A rough patch of open ground surrounded by middle-class villas marks the spot; it is hardly a mountain, but it is raised above the sur- rounding countryside with a commanding view over Prague's outer sprawl where the city meets the countryside and bland retail parks line highways leading out to the airport.

It was at this strategic viewpoint that the army of 21,000 Czech, Hungarian, and German Protestants gathered on the morning of the battle, facing the larger force of Catholics who occupied the ground below. The only memorial here is a cairn of stones nestling beneath a glade of trees—a far cry from the overblown monument that marks the battle site at Žižkov. But the low-key nature of the memorial at Bílá Hora is hardly surprising, for here the Protestant cause met with disaster and ignominious defeat and, some might argue, the cause of Czech nationhood was similarly vanquished, although it was actually German-speaking nobles who formed the Protestant vanguard. A respectful distance away from the memorial, on the main road just along from the tram turning circle, stands a Catholic pilgrimage church dedicated to Panna Maria Vítězná— St. Mary the Victorious—whose intercession was believed to have brought about the Catholic victory.

The battle commenced with a devastating Catholic advance and lasted less than an hour. When it was clear that all was lost the Protestant commander Christian von Anhalt rushed to Prague Castle and informed Prince Frederick, who was having lunch with the British Ambassador, that he had to flee Prague. The flight of the royal couple across the Charles Bridge is gloatingly portrayed in a crude wood carving that was made shortly afterwards and now hangs in the chancel of St. Vitus' Cathedral. After their victory at Bílá Hora, Catholic troops (whose number included the philoso- pher René Descartes) went on the rampage through Prague, burn- ing and looting any Protestant churches and property they could find. The revenge continued the following year when twenty-six Protestant nobles (and one Catholic noble) were executed on the Old Town Square on June 21 in an orgy of beheading and hanging that started at dawn and went on for four hours. The exact position of the platform built for the executions is marked to this day by twenty-seven white crosses set in the paving outside the Old Town

Hall. "An atrocious spectacle," the poet Dačický later remarked: black scaffold, black dress, black masks. It is said that every year on the eve of their execution the ghosts of those killed still gather at the place of their death and then process into the Týn Church, where they kneel by the altar rail for communion in the Protestant manner.

In 1648 the Thirty Years War ended in the very city in which it had begun: the last skirmish was fought on the Charles Bridge itself between the Swedish army, which had seized Prague's Lesser Quarter, and a force made up of Jews and students from the Old Town, who held the bridge and prevented the Swedes from occupying the river's east bank. Sweden, whose armies had rampaged around Europe during the second part of this catastrophic conflict, spreading fear, violence, plague, and famine wherever they went, saw itself as the upholder of the Protestant cause in Europe and wanted to liberate Prague from its Catholic oppressors. But Habsburg policies of re-Catholicization were already well entrenched by the time the Swedish army (which mostly consisted of mercenaries, particularly from Scotland) occupied the Lesser Quarter. Prague had moved on from its early seventeenth-century Protestantism and was a predominantly Catholic city. The Swedes battled on with their hopeless cause, however, and during the fighting the troops managed to wreck the west side of the east tower of the Charles Bridge, leaving it unadorned to this day (except for a plaque commemorating the event). To honor Prague's Jews for their help in defending Prague the Emperor Ferdinand III allowed members of the community to incorporate a Swedish cap in the middle of the Star of David as their new emblem; it can be seen today on banners hanging in the Old-New Synagogue in Prague's Jewish quarter.

The Peace of Westphalia that finally brought an end to the Thirty Years War saw the remaining property of Protestant Bohemian nobles handed over to Catholic families who had proven their loyalty to the Habsburgs. Protestantism in all its forms was outlawed and Ferdinand of Styria's successor, Ferdinand III, asked the Jesuit order to return Bohemia to the Catholic fold. The religious order promptly pulled down a quarter of the Old Town for their vast new complex, the Klementinum, whose high walls now tower over Karlova between the Old Town Square and the Charles Bridge. And the Jesuits flooded the rest of the city with churches and statues. In his novel *The Book of Laughter and Forgetting* Milan Kundera wrote that the order "swamped Prague with the splendour of Baroque Cathedrals" after this decisive defeat of the Czech Reformation, and that "the thousands of petrified saints gazing at you from all sides and threatening you [in Prague], spying on you, hypnotizing you, are the frenzied occupation army that invaded Bohemia three hundred and fifty years ago to tear the people's faith and language out of its soul." The gradual draining of Prague's soul continued in the ensuing centuries. In 1741 Prague was briefly occupied by French, Prussian, and Bavarian troops in a war over Habsburg rule in Silesia; the English historian Thomas Carlyle described how the invading soldiers scaled the walls of Vyšehrad by imaginatively extending their short ladders by the addition of gallows. In the following decade the city came under Prussian bombardment during the Seven Years War between the Prussians (under Frederick the Great) and the Habsburgs. During this war in 1757 a cannonball fired at Vyšehrad army barracks lodged itself in the walls of St. Martin's Rotunda, from which it still protrudes to this day.

In 1780 Emperor Joseph II became the first Habsburg monarch not to bother holding a coronation in Prague. Meanwhile calls for Bohemian and Moravian independence began to form into a focused resistance movement, which reached a highpoint during the revolutionary fervor of June 1848, when a joint National Guard of Czech and German citizens manned barricades throughout Prague. The Habsburgs sent Alfred, Prince Windisch-Grätz, to the city to quell the revolt, which the commander did with brute force (and an army of 100,000 ranged against 1,200 barricade fighters) after his wife was killed by a stray bullet fired by a protestor. Prince Alfred declared martial law throughout Bohemia and then bombarded Prague into submission from gun emplacements on Hradčany hill.

Two decades later, in 1867, the Habsburg Empire became a dual monarchy, and Bohemia found itself in the Austrian sphere of the new Austro-Hungarian Empire. It was now a thousand years since the first incarnation of Prague Castle had risen on Hradčany hill, yet Czechs continued to be ruled by foreigners, and the castle now served as little more than a barracks, its paintings and treasures sold off by Habsburg monarchs to make way for ammunition stores. Yet as the nineteenth century drew to a close a new spirit of optimism and nationalism began to gain momentum: architects endowed Prague with distinctive buildings such as the National Theatre while Czech culture and history was celebrated by composers such as Smetana and Dvořák. Ordinary people, on the other hand, took to wearing Czech national costume and smoking cigarettes rolled out of red, white, and blue paper—the Czech national colors. In 1904 the last heir to the throne of Austria-Hungary, Archduke Franz Ferdinand, married a Czech noblewoman, Sophie von Chotek, and made his home at Konopiště Castle, a grand residence situated deep in the wooded countryside just south of Prague. It seemed for a time as if Bohemia's years as a political backwater were nearing an end: Franz Ferdinand was in favor of converting the dual monarchy into a triple one, with the Czech lands separated (if not divorced) from Vienna and afforded the same status as Hungary. But the archduke was assassinated in Sarajevo in 1914 and it was the world war that his assassination sparked which finally brought an end to Habsburg rule of central Europe—and of Prague.

During the war the campaign for an independent Czechoslovak state gained worldwide attention. Its figurehead was a former professor at Prague University named Tomáš Garrigue Masaryk, who had founded his Realist Party in 1900 on the back of the movement for political change known as the Young Czechs. Masaryk traveled to the United States to gain support for a new state while his deputies Edvard Beneš and the Slovak Milan Štefánik did the same in Britain and France. Their efforts paid off. A provisional government was created as the war drew to a close, and a new state of Czechoslovakia was declared in Prague's *art nouveau* concert hall, the Obecní dům, on October 28, 1918 as the last embers of the Habsburg Empire fizzled and died in Europe.

Democracy and Occupation (1918-45)

On independence Czechoslovakia was a land of huge potential: four-fifths of the industrial economy of Austria-Hungary was situated within its borders, and in 1920 the country was listed as the world's tenth largest economy. But the period from 1918 to 1938 turned out to be no more than a brief window of independence and democracy between the autocracy of Habsburg rule and the catastrophe of Nazi occupation and then communism.

The early years of democracy saw Czechoslovakia flourish. The 1920 elections brought a five-party coalition into power, and the party leaders known as *Pětka* or "the Five" played an important part in creating public policy through their frequent meetings with the Czechoslovak president. As the 1920s progressed the newly independent country seemed to be forging a definite path to political prominence on the European scene. Indeed, historians have argued that the Czechoslovak Republic under President Masaryk was the most successful parliamentary republic in Central and Eastern Europe between the two world wars.

But the Wall Street Crash in 1929 brought severe economic pressures. The Sudeten German Party (SdP), led by a charismatic former PE teacher named Konrad Henlein, began to receive funding from the Nazis as it campaigned for the rights of German-speakers living in Czechoslovakia. After the annexation of Austria by Germany, Hitler personally asked Henlein to call for outright autonomy of the Sudetenland, the area of Czechoslovakia that bordered Germany and where most German-speaking Czechoslovaks lived.

Hitler's claims on the Sudetenland raised the political temperature across Europe. But Britain and France were determined not to go to war over the issue. On September 30, 1938 the two European powers met Hitler at Munich and acquiesced to his demands. "We will not go to war because of a quarrel in a far-away country between people of whom we know nothing," Neville Chamberlain famously announced, brandishing the document that he claimed brought "peace in our time." By now Edvard Beneš, Masaryk's former foreign minister, had succeeded him as president. Beneš played no part in the discussions at Munich over his homeland and resigned five days after Chamberlain's announcement. Within two weeks German forces were marching into the Sudetenland. As they did, the Catholic Primate of Bohemia ordered a special prayer to be read out in Catholic churches across the country. "The land of St. Wenceslas has just been invaded by foreign armies and the thousand-year-old frontier has been violated," the prayer began. "This sacrifice has been imposed on the nation of St. Wenceslas by our ally, France, and our friend, Britain. The Primate of the ancient Kingdom of Bohemia is praying to God Almighty... to forgive all those who impose this injustice on the people of Czechoslovakia." In Protestant churches the same prayer was offered, with the name of St. Wenceslas substituted by that of Jan Hus.

After the unchallenged invasion of the Sudetenland the governance of what was left of Czechoslovakia fell into the hands of a well-respected lawyer named Emil Hácha. Dr. Hácha was something of an intellectual—he had translated *Three Men in a Boat* by Jerome K. Jerome into Czech—but he was unworldly, small and rather sickly, and on March 14 the following year he found himself embroiled in one of Hitler's most cruelly-executed military schemes. Summoned to Berlin, Hácha was kept waiting by Hitler until gone midnight while the Führer finished watching an escapist romantic comedy entitled *Ein Hoffnungsloser Fall* (*A Hopeless Case*) that had been recommended to him by Goebbels. When Hitler was finally ready Hácha was treated to one of the Führer's famously intimidating tirades, delivered to him in the grandiose surroundings of the Vice Chancellery. Hitler informed a stony-faced Hácha that his troops were already mobilized and were about to invade Czechoslovakia. Hermann Göring, also present at the meeting, announced that his Luftwaffe would be bombing Prague at dawn if Hácha did not order his country's forces to capitulate. At this, Hácha actually fainted; after he was revived by Dr. Morrell, Hitler's personal physician, the browbeaten president telephoned Prague and passed on the order that Czech troops were to offer the invading Germans no resistance. By that time, according to the French Ambassador to

Germany, Robert Coulondre, Hácha was in "a state of total collapse, and kept going only by means of injections."

The first Nazi units entered the Czech capital at 9 a.m., slowed slightly by icy roads, the faces of the troops reddened with cold and frost; a few hours later Hitler himself traveled by train and motorcade through the late winter snow and was organizing his new Nazi Protectorate of Bohemia and Moravia from Prague Castle that evening. (He also ensured that an independent Slovakia would be governed by the pro-Nazi Slovak Peoples Party.) With Hitler was Wilhelm Stuckart, a lackey from Germany's interior ministry, and together the two of them drafted a new constitution for the protectorate in which they justified the Nazi invasion by claiming that Bohemia and Moravia had for a millennium been part of the *Lebensraum* of the German people, emphasizing the alliances that Prince Václav I had struck with the Saxon kings some thousand years previously. In his novel *Mendelssohn is on the Roof* Jiří Weil sardonically captured this moment by quoting the words of the Sudeten poet Mally. The poet describes Prague as a city "whose statues and palaces spoke of its glorious German past" and writes that the Führer occupied "the seat of Czech kings now belonging to the Reich, whose eagle eyes surveyed the splendour that had returned after thousands of years to the hard but merciful hands of Germany."

Hitler only spent one night in Prague. The day after the invasion he was back in Berlin, leaving the Nazi standard fluttering from the castle's ancient towers. The comparatively moderate Baron Konstantin von Neurath was appointed Reichsprotektor of Bohemia and Moravia; his deputy was a Sudeten German with a glass eye named Karl Hermann Frank who before the war had been a bookseller in Karlovy Vary. President Hácha remained in office and his government maintained a small militia and a relatively intact public administration system. But Hácha's power was exercised "in conformity with the political, military and economic rights of the Reich," which meant that in effect he was little more than a puppet.

In October 1939 the Nazis faced the first serious challenge to their rule when Jan Opletal, a Czech medical student, was fatally wounded during the police break-up of a demonstration in Prague. A funeral wake was held for Opletal by students in the U Fleků pub, igniting further disturbances on the streets of the capital. As a reprisal nine student representatives were executed and many more students and academics were sent to concentration camps in Germany, while Prague University was closed. But the nascent Czech resistance movement fought back, organizing a series of strikes, and these coupled with intrigues against von Neurath among senior Nazis in Prague led Hitler to appoint the prominent Nazi Reinhard Heydrich as the new Acting Reichsprotektor on September 27, 1941.

Hitler chose Heydrich carefully: he was a former security police chief and had a well-earned reputation as an iron-fisted thug—the perfect man to stamp out resistance. Heydrich quickly gained the nickname "The Hangman" among Czechs and was viewed by the Allies as a possible successor to Hitler should the Führer die. (Jiří Weil's *Mendelssohn is on the Roof* is partly narrated by Heydrich, who muses on the failure of the "cowardly fat puppet Neurath [who had] messed things up... what a lot of filth [there was] to get rid of around here.") Among his first actions were the declaration of martial law and the arrest and execution of Alois Eliáš, who was prime minister in President Hácha's puppet government. A few months after his appointment, in early 1942, Heydrich presided over the bureaucratic confirmation of the Final Solution at the Wannsee Conference, by which time the deportation of Jews from Prague was well under way.

Back in Prague, Heydrich made plans to "Germanize" half the Czech population and deport the rest—presumably the "filth" in Weil's novel—to the areas of Russia beyond the eastern borders of the expanding Reich. But his plans came to nothing: in May 1942 Heydrich was assassinated by Czech freedom fighters as his motorcade passed through the Libeň district of northern Prague. The events surrounding the assassination, and Hitler's reprisals for it, are dealt with in Chapter 11, as is the dreadful fate of Prague's Jews during the Nazi occupation.

As a city behind enemy lines Prague was subject to bombing raids by the Allies during the war. The most serious came in on the afternoon of St. Valentine's Day 1945 and resulted in nearly two thousand people killed or injured. One of the few historic buildings to be damaged by bombs was the Emauzy monastery, situated a mile south of the Old Town Square, whose Gothic spire was toppled by a stray bomb allegedly dropped by an Allied pilot who thought he was over Dresden. As a result the monastery's Gothic abbey now supports two very twentieth-century-looking intertwining concrete spires, looking like a hare's ears and built in 1965 as a replacement for the original tower that dated to Charles IV's foundation of the institution. A later raid on March 25 saw American bombers target the Böhmen und Mähren engine works, which manufactured guns for the Nazis, leaving 500 Prague residents dead. But overall the bombing raids in Prague were light compared to those suffered by cities such as Dresden and Berlin.

Prague was also spared the sort of barbarous destruction wrought by the Nazis on Warsaw; the damage to the back of the Old Town Hall, which can still be seen today, was caused by a Nazi fireball that was supposed to engulf the whole city but which fortunately never got going. However, the Nazi occupiers of Prague proved themselves a tenacious foe. Nazi-controlled Prague Radio condemned Grand Admiral Dönitz's announcement of the unconditional surrender of all German troops on May 7, 1945 as an "Allied propaganda trick" and urged Germans to keep on fighting. Four days later, when German forces in Prague finally did capitulate, the city was the last in central Europe to remain under Nazi control, and its surrender to the Red Army came nearly two weeks after Hitler's suicide in Berlin.

The people of Prague greeted the Soviet soldiers with genuine delight, drinking, dancing, singing, decorating the gun turrets of tanks with flowers, and flying the red, white, and blue flag of Czechoslovakia next to the hammer and sickle. The unfortunate Emil Hácha was arrested by the Soviets three days after the Nazi capitulation and was transferred to a prison hospital where he died the following month—by which time Edvard Beneš (whom Hácha had secretly co-operated with during the occupation) had resumed the presidency, governing with a coalition hastily assembled during the closing months of the war. His new government was one in which the Communist Party played a vitally important role.

Under Stalin's Gaze (1945-68)

As the war drew to a close it became clear that President Beneš was looking to the USSR as the political guarantor of a stable post-war Eastern Europe. "We are Slavs and we are neighbors of the Soviet Union, a predominantly Slav state," he maintained in March 1945 as he formed his provisional government in Košice, the first major town in Slovakia to be liberated by the Red Army. "It is natural that its socialist structure has an influence on us." Beneš saw the USSR as the natural protector of Czechoslovakia against a possibly resurgent Germany, yet he could never reconcile this with his wish for a democratic Czechoslovakia. Once Prague was liberated and Beneš was installed in the presidential apartments in the castle he appeased socialist agitators by appointing Klement Gottwald to the post of prime minister. Gottwald had been the leader of the Czechoslovak Communist Party (KSČ) when it was exiled in Moscow during the war and had led something of a rival government-in-exile to that of Beneš in England. Now Beneš hoped that Gottwald's appointment would sow the seeds for a united post-war government in which socialist policy was present, but not dominant.

Gottwald was a communist through and through. "We are more than a political party," he declaimed as he took office. "We are a vanguard of the new life." With Gottwald in the prime minister's chair the Communist Party moved quickly to gain as much influence as it could. Communist activists took control of the armed militias that had emerged from the confusion of the Nazi retreat, while brigades from Moscow began to whip up support for the party as they swept through the country in the wake of the liberating Red Army. Once victory over the Nazis was secure the communists also hastened the expulsion of German speakers from Czechoslovakia (which had been agreed to by the victorious Allies at the Potsdam Conference in July/August 1945), ensuring that confiscated German property was distributed to KSČ supporters.

No wonder, then, that when Czechoslovakia held its first full post-war elections in May 1946 the KSČ garnered 38 percent of the vote and became the largest party in the new coalition government; the party's victory came from its promise to nationalize the heavy industry on which the Czechoslovak economy depended but it was also a reward from the Czechoslovak people for Stalin's opposition to the Munich agreement and of course for the liberation of the country by the Soviets.

Soon after the elections, however, the wheels of the communist juggernaut appeared to be coming loose. Rumours of corruption within the Ministry of the Interior and a severe drought resulted in wavering support for the Party. Czechoslovakia was invited to send a representative to the Paris peace conference that was organizing the distribution of American Marshall aid; but at the last moment the Soviets prevented the representative from attending, fearing that, as the wartime alliances finally collapsed in 1947, Czechoslovakia would end up in the western sphere of a politically divided Europe. The coalition government was soon tearing itself apart over the political direction the country should take. In February 1948 twelve non-communist cabinet ministers resigned, hoping their action would force Beneš to dismiss Gottwald and hold new elections. Stalin, eyeing the situation with alarm from Moscow, bridled at the potential loss of one of his buffer states and ordered Soviet troops to mass along the Hungarian border, ready to mount an invasion. Gottwald refused to allow the Soviet troops to invade— the only time in his political career that he stood up to Stalin—and instead manipulated the situation by presenting Beneš with a list of suggested appointees to a new, all-communist cabinet that he said would defuse the tense military and domestic situation.

Soon the political crisis had spilled out of government offices and onto the streets of Prague. Students from Charles University marched to the castle in support of Beneš; at the top end of Nerudova they were attacked by armed communist brigades, an event commemorated now by a plaque overlooking one of the most impossibly picturesque corners of the Hradčany district. To counter the students' demonstration Gottwald ensured that a crowd of 250,000 massed in central Prague in support of the communists. Steadily gaining the upper hand he threatened to call a general strike unless Beneš capitulated. The beleaguered president, who by this time was very ill, at last waved through the list of new cabinet members, and Gottwald addressed jubilant crowds in Prague from the balcony of the Kinský Palace overlooking the Old Town Square, celebrating the bloodless communist coup that was christened the "Victorious February." The following month the foreign minister Jan Masaryk (son of the first president) was killed after falling from a bathroom window of the Černín Palace in the castle district, which then housed the Ministry of Foreign Affairs. Was he a suicide victim? Or a victim of the Soviet Secret Service? If it was the latter then his death—yet another Prague defenestration—provided a foretaste of the political violence that was yet to come. Beneš finally resigned on May 9 when parliament passed a law asserting the leading role of the Communist Party within the government, and died shortly afterwards. Gottwald immediately assumed the presidency, and political parties remaining after the May 9 legislation were either banned or merged themselves with the KSČ—and the communist takeover of Czechoslovakia was complete.

These days the Kinský Palace, the work of the great architect of the Baroque era Kilian Ignaz Dientzenhofer, is one of the most beautiful buildings on the Old Town Square. Its façade gleams a gorgeous creamy-yellow color while its windows are crowned by elegantly swirling decorative lintels of a rich reddish-brown stucco. The interior presently houses the Mediterranean and Asian collections of the Czech National Gallery, with everything from Korean tapestries to Greek vases on display. Gottwald's address from the palace balcony on that snowy February morning in 1948 has proved rich inspiration for the novelist Milan Kundera, who describes the incident at least twice in his novels. In *Life is Elsewhere* he remarks with a characteristically sardonic tone that the crowd "gathered in the Old Town Square had launched [that day's] date into the skies, where it would shine like a star for centuries," and in *The Book of Laughter and Forgetting*, in which Gottwald's address forms the opening scene, the satire is even more biting. The coup was, according to Kundera, "a great turning point in the history of Bohemia… a fateful event of the kind that occurs only once or twice in a millennium." The opposition, he maintained, "had no great dream, only some tiresome and threadbare moral principles, with which they tried to patch the torn trousers of the established order," whereas the communists presented the people of Czechoslovakia with a socialist idyll that promised "justice for all." That socialist idyll would endure in Czechoslovakia for just over forty years.

Gottwald himself had a reputation as a drunkard and a womanizer. During the five years of his presidency he transformed Czechoslovakia into one of the most hardline communist states, relegating Beneš and Masaryk to mere footnotes in history while heavy industry was championed, agriculture was collectivized, and the economy was subjected to the full rigors of Stalinization. Gottwald also had a reputation for political ruthlessness that grew out of his dictator's natural paranoia. Thousands were arrested during his presidency. Heda Margolius Kovály writes in *Prague Farewell* that Thursdays and Fridays were "the worst days for arrests" because the Central Committee met on a Thursday and "whenever a doorbell rang on those evenings, everyone turned pale." Many of those arrested were sent to Czechoslovakia's version of the Soviet gulags, usually prison work camps established around coal or metal ore mines.

Yet in many ways the people who ended up victims of the Czechoslovak gulag were the lucky ones. The first purge came in 1950 when thirteen supposed anti-communists were tried for sedition and received either long prison sentences or the death penalty. By far the best-known victim was Milada Horáková, a former Prague city councillor and member of parliament who had also been a prominent figure in Beneš' party and a noted campaigner for women's and human rights. She defended her position at her trial with great courage even though she knew this would increase the severity of her sentence. She was hanged on June 27 in the notorious Pankrác Prison in Prague's dreary southern suburbs, and since 2004 the date has marked the Czech Republic's Commemoration Day of the Victims of Communism. (In 2008 the prosecutor at her trial, a woman named Ludmila Brožová-Polednová, then aged eighty-seven, was sentenced to six years in prison for her part in Horáková's conviction.)

The trial that saw Horáková hang was just a prelude. In November, 1952 fourteen politburo members—holders of key posts in the government and the Communist Party—were arrested on Gottwald's orders in a mass purge. After a brief trial held in the courthouse attached to Pankrác Prison all were convicted: three were given long prison sentences and eleven were hanged. (The ashes from the cremated bodies were later used to grit icy roads.) The "crimes" of the defendants included ideological adherence to Trotskyism, Titoism, and Zionism (eleven of the fourteen were Jewish), along with plotting to remove Gottwald from office and forging links with the west. The trial was the biggest "show trial" ever staged in the Soviet bloc. The high number of victims can be attributed to the size of the pre-war Czechoslovak Communist Party and that fact that its members had fought in Spain and traveled in the west, making them ideologically suspect in the eyes of Gottwald's Stalinist faction. Like the previous show trials in Albania, Bulgaria, and Hungary, the trial was fueled by Tito's rebellion against Stalin, by the growing chill of the Cold War, and by the need for the revolution to be seen to be continually turning, liquidating its enemies.

In his book *The Report on the Murder of the General Secretary*, the exiled Czech historian Karel Kaplan maintains that the prosecutors knew from the outset that all the charges were false and that the defendants had confessed only after the application of brutal psychological pressure and physical violence. The "General Secretary" of Kaplan's title was Rudolf Slánský, the head of the Central Committee of the Czechoslovak Communist Party, effectively the second most important political player in the country after Gottwald and the most high-profile victim of the purge. He had dared to criticize the Soviet Union in the 1930s and in the pressure-cooker atmosphere of the early 1950s Stalin felt he could not be trusted. Slánský was one of those who faced the hangman in Pankrác Prison on the bright, chilly morning of December 3, as was Vladimír Clementis, the former foreign minister, who had taken off his hat and given it to Gottwald during the famous balcony speech of February 1948, and who was later airbrushed out of photos of the event—except his hat, of course, which remained perched resolutely on the head of his victorious comrade.

Gottwald's death in 1953 came shortly after that of Stalin, his political mentor in Moscow. According to popular legend, Gottwald caught flu while attending the Soviet dictator's funeral, but in all probability the actual cause of his death was syphilis. By then Gottwald's personality cult dominated the country. His statue overlooked town squares, many of which were named after him; both a metro station in Prague (now Vyšehrad) and a town in Moravia (now Zlín, as it was in pre-communist days) carried the name Gottwaldov; and his face stared out from banknotes. The great man was embalmed—as was Lenin—and the monument on Žižkov hill to the dead of the First World War, with its overblown totalitarian aesthetics, was chosen as his mausoleum. But in 1963 Gottwald's corpse was damaged by fire and the body had to be cremated; in 1990 the ashes were moved from Žižkov and interred in the Olšany cemetery in eastern Prague. The complex machinery that once monitored the temperature and humidity of the air around his embalmed corpse can still be seen in the basement of the Žižkov memorial, where later presidents and other major communist functionaries were also buried.

Antonín Zápotocký succeeded Gottwald as president. A few weeks after he had moved into the president's apartments in Prague Castle Zápotocký was forced to implement a severe currency devaluation that reduced wages, raised prices, and robbed many of their savings. Riots broke out in response throughout Prague and Zápotocký ordered a brutal police clampdown. It was clear that the new president was not going to show any sign of veering from the Stalinist course. "De-Stalinization is a synonym for the idea of weakening and giving way to the forces of reaction," he claimed before commissioning the construction of the colossal granite statue of Stalin that began to rise above the Vltava on the Letná Plain. The grotesque sculpture, which dominated the Prague skyline when it was at last completed, was a distinctly unwelcome reminder of the dominance of Moscow in Czechoslovak affairs: the Soviet dictator was depicted glowering across the river and straight down the broad avenue Pařížská at anyone in the Old Town Square.

Czechoslovakia remained resolutely Stalinist even as the political wind from Moscow began to lose its chill. Zápotocký's successor Antonín Novotný was repeatedly dogged by pleas for economic, social, and cultural reform, and according to Milan Kundera in *The Unbearable Lightness of Being* he developed the longest finger of anyone in Central Europe because of all the pointing he did, jabbing his finger in the direction of those who demanded change. But even Novotný could only hold out for so long. At last in 1965 he created a new model for the economy and two years later he ordered the release of those imprisoned in the show-trials of the 1950s. Even so, the pace of reform was slower than in the rest of Eastern Europe until Alexander Dubček replaced Novotný as first secretary of the Communist Party in January 1968, and Ludvík Svoboda succeeded him as President of the Republic in March, setting the scene for the start of the reform movement known as the Prague Spring.

The Prague Spring and the Velvet Revolution (1968-89)

It was in February 1968, in a speech commemorating the twentieth anniversary of Gottwald's famous "victorious February" address, that Dubček announced his credentials as a radical reformer. He maintained that he wanted to create "a socialism that corresponds to the historical democratic traditions of Czechoslovakia." Within weeks his plans for "socialism with a human face" had taken the form of a ten-year plan that would see the introduction of democracy and private enterprise, allow greater freedom to travel, abolish censorship, cultivate better relations with the west, and create an economy based on science and technology rather than heavy industry. (His sentiments had actually been around for some time, championed by a faction of the ruling oligarchy since the early 1960s; in fact, the reformers were those whom Novotný had spent so much time jabbing his finger at.) The Soviet bloc became understandably jittery: on March 23, delegations from the USSR, East Germany, Bulgaria,

Poland, and Hungary met in Dresden and openly questioned the path that Czechoslovakia was taking.

But the momentum for reform was unstoppable. On June 26 censorship was abolished and the following day *Two Thousand Words*, the manifesto of the reform movement, was published by the author and journalist Ludvík Vaculík. Relaxation was introduced on foreign travel. In *Prague Farewell* Heda Margolius Kovály writes that

> the spring of 1968 had all the intensity, anxiety and unreality of a dream come true. People flooded the narrow streets of Prague's Old Town and the courtyards of Hradčany castle and stayed out long into the night. If anyone set out for a walk alone, he would soon join a group of others to chat or tell a joke, and we would all listen with relief as the ancient walls echoed with the sound of laughter... groups of students would sit around the Jan Hus monument in the Old Town Square playing their guitars and singing till dawn. Tourists from abroad and our own people would join them, listening, and pondering those beautiful, deceitful words carved into the stone: Truth Prevails.

The dissident and playwright Václav Havel used the loosening of travel restrictions to travel to London, where he told the journalist Joan Bakewell on the BBC program *Late Night Line Up* that "the ice began to melt and windows began to open."

Dubček, however, denounced *Two Thousand Words* as a step too far. Already backtracking, he was summoned to a meeting with the Soviets at the tiny Slovak village of Čierna nad Tisou, hard by the Soviet border. The meeting was held in the Railwaymen's Club and each night the Soviet delegation's train crossed back into the USSR, to emerge again in the morning. At this meeting, and at a further meeting in Bratislava at the beginning of August, Dubček agreed to slow down the pace of reform. But less than three weeks after the Bratislava meeting, on August 21, the Soviets turned Warsaw Pact military exercises in Czechoslovakia into a full-blown invasion to crush the reform movement. Precisely why they did, after Dubček had agreed on such a large-scale retreat, remains unclear: it may simply be that Brezhnev had run out of patience with the Soviet Union's errant neighbor.

The invasion force that took part in "Operation Danube" consisted of two hundred thousand troops and two thousand tanks, drawn from all countries of the Warsaw Pact except Romania. Letters appeared in the press claiming that the government had requested the invasion but this was immediately denied (although more recent evidence suggests that some conservative elements within the Czechoslovak government did indeed ask for it). Ruzyně airport outside Prague was occupied and more troops were flown in by air. Resistance to the invasion in the capital was coordinated by Radio Prague, which asked protestors to change road signs to confuse the invaders. But the protestors had little chance against phalanxes of Soviet tanks and within days the reform movement had been brutally and decisively crushed.

Their invasion successful and largely uncontested, the Soviets took Dubček to Moscow and then to a remote military base in the Ukrainian mountains. He was threatened with execution—the fate that had befallen the Hungarian reformist leader Imre Nagy in 1956—but he capitulated to Soviet demands and was brought back to Prague. Milan Kundera describes what happened next in *The Unbearable Lightness of Being*: "When Dubček returned to Prague he gave a speech over the radio. He was so devastated after his six day detention he could hardly talk; he kept stuttering and gasping for breath, making long pauses between sentences, pauses lasting nearly thirty seconds." Were the pauses because the Russians had drugged him? Or were they caused by despair or exhaustion? Clearly an agreement had been reached during Dubček's sojourn in the Ukraine. There were to be no mass deportations to Siberia. "But one thing was clear," Kundera continues. "The country had to bow to the conqueror. For ever and ever, it will stutter, stammer, gasp for air like Alexander Dubček." The poor man tottered on as first secretary for a few months, until in April 1969 Czechoslovakia beat the USSR at ice hockey and the Prague secret police cynically fomented anti-Soviet riots on the streets of the capital. This gave President Svoboda (and his Soviet puppet-masters) the excuse they needed to replace Dubček. Gustáv Husák (who the previous decade had received a prison sentence during the era of the show trials) assumed the role of first secretary and in 1975 replaced Svoboda as president.

Under Husák a period of "normalization" was ushered in, which essentially meant a return to the status quo of the mid-1960s, with one major change—Slovakia was given greater independence within a new federal arrangement, the only one of Dubček's reforms to survive. In 1987 Miloš Jakeš took over from Husák as Communist Party general secretary and cautiously introduced *přestavba,* Czechoslovakia's own version of *perestroika.* But Husák remained Czechoslovak president and *přestavba* made little headway under a regime that had been brought in, twenty years previously, to put an end to just this kind of reform. Former Soviet premier Mikhail Gorbachev later acknowledged that his reforms in the USSR had owed much to the Prague Spring; Gorbachev had been politically close to future architects of the Czechoslovak reform movement while a rising young politician in Moscow in the 1950s, and later recalled that on a visit to Czechoslovakia in 1969 he was ashamed, as a Soviet politician, of what his country had done the previous year. However, the brutal repression of the reform movement in Prague led him, some twenty years later, to introduce his own reforms in the USSR much more cautiously and gradually, fearing disaster if, like Dubček, he tried to act too quickly.

The grim repression of the 1970s and 1980s—the fate of dissidents, the stifling of political debate, the stagnation of the economy—is described in detail later in Chapter 11. Czechoslovakia remained one of the most hardline of Communist states during this time and seemed incapable of reform even as regimes in East Berlin, Warsaw, Budapest, and Sofia crumbled one by one during the summer and autumn of 1989. That fateful year had already been a tense one in Prague, with ad hoc, spontaneous demonstrations against the state breaking out in January and August. The extraordinary events that took place in other parts of Eastern Europe touched Prague directly for the first time when hundreds of East Germans crossed into Czechoslovakia and sought refuge in the West German Embassy in the Lesser Quarter (some actually climbed over the embassy wall and camped in the garden). Disoriented by the rapid pace of change, on September 30, the Czechoslovak government put the East Germans onto trains and sent them off to West Germany in a deal brokered by the foreign minister in Bonn, Hans-Dietrich Genscher. But the pressure showed no signs of abating. On November 4, one million protestors gathered in East Berlin and five days later the Berlin Wall came down.

Those events in Berlin, watched around the world by millions, provided the impetus for similar demonstrations in Prague. Through the official youth organization the SSM, a group of tough-minded students gained permission to hold a demonstration on November 17, the fiftieth anniversary of the death of Jan Opletal at the hands of the Nazis. The ceremony at the cemetery where Opletal is buried turned into a demonstration that swarmed into the city center. That was when fifty thousand students in Národní, one of the streets joining Wenceslas Square, found themselves in a stand-off against fully-armed riot police. The students placed lighted candles on the ground and handed bunches of flowers to the police—who stormed the crowd, resulting in five hundred injuries and one hundred arrests. The event has come to be known as the *masakr* (massacre), even though no one was killed; whether that was due to an unintended exaggeration or a deliberate white lie will never be known. But the event aroused public indignation, and is now commemorated by a small bronze sculpture on Národní in a gloomy arcade outside house number 16, known as Kaňka's House after its architect. The sculpture takes the form of a relief depicting multiple pairs of hands reaching out in an expression of hope and despair, a striking memorial but also one that seems rather neglected now as memories of the Revolution begin to fade. Today it is the only direct and tangible reference to the Velvet Revolution in the entire city.

d had the walls of the building's endless corridors
ith the sort of avant-garde paintings that the old
sted. Initially he continued living in the riverside
on Masarykovo nábřeži that had always been his
by his architect grandfather), and ate at the Na
nt in the New Town where a table was permanently
But then came the first elections, and Havel came
th a bump.

1990 elections Civic Forum and its Slovak sister
roti násiliu (People Against Violence) gained sixty
otes, and Havel found himself governing with a
overnment that was split as to how to manage the
arket economy: the right-wing Civic Democratic
Václav Klaus, an outspoken fan of the economic
garet Thatcher, wanted a headlong plunge into
talism, whereas Havel and the centrist and left-
vanted to adopt a more cautious approach. In
Havel spoke on Czechoslovak radio of the "social
. chaos" of the transition. "People are unsettled by
cannot see firm order," he said. "Everything has
uncertainty."

. the income of most Czechoslovaks fell by a
e sector employment quickly eclipsed that of the
s not to be forgotten: in October of that year the
as passed (from the Latin *lustrare*, which means
through sacrifice); it set up a communist witch-
r name, which aimed to bring into the public
t of the corruption and misrule of the previous
prosecute those responsible for it. And so the
—but now the original perpetrators had become
ding to David Brierley in his novel *On Leaving*
Prague became "a city of questions" during those
ocracy. "Everybody demanded to know where the
ley writes. "Under the ground, some of them, up
ing cabinets, in the shadows, in the woodwork,
were locked tight." To this day those questions

The massacre led to calls for a general strike, while students in the Charles University launched an immediate protest campaign. The calls spread from students to drama students to actors and on November 19 on the instigation of Václav Havel, who had rushed back to Prague from his farmhouse in Bohemia after hearing of the massacre, an umbrella opposition group named Občanské fórum (Civic Forum) was formed to coordinate the anti-government demonstrations. The group ran its operations from the former Magic Lantern Theatre in the basement of the Palác Adria, a century-old building originally built for an insurance company on Národní, close to Wenceslas Square. Leaders gave press conferences in the auditorium while others planned their strategy in the dressing rooms. (The set in position on the theater stage was for a play called *Minotaurus* by Dürrenmatt; speakers would emerge onto the stage through a hole in the set designed for the monster.) According to Timothy Garton Ash in his book *We the People*, the auditorium "smelt of cigarette smoke, sweat, damp coats and revolution."

Civic Forum demanded amnesties for political prisoners, the resignation of key communist leaders, and an immediate transition to democracy. Within days, according to Garton Ash, "all of Prague became a magic lantern. It was not just the great masses on Wenceslas Square. It was the improvised posters all over the city, the strike committees in factories, the Civic Forum communities that were founded in hospitals, schools and offices. It was the crowds standing in front of television sets in shop or office windows at all hours of the day or night, watching... the events of November 17 played over and over again."

The events in Berlin coupled with the *masakr* began to bring hundreds of thousands of peaceful protesters onto the streets around Wenceslas Square night after night demanding political change. After five days of demonstrations Alexander Dubček—who had been forced to work as a forester in Slovakia after the crushing of the Prague Spring, and who would later lead the Slovak Social Democratic Party—addressed a crowd of three hundred thousand people in Wenceslas Square, alongside Havel. After more speeches from a soccer player, a student, and a worker, the crowd, all 300,000 of them, made an extraordinary spontaneous gesture: they took their keys from their pockets and shook them, as if they were showing the communist leadership the door.

The growth in the movement was unstoppable: it took as its motto *Pravda Vítězí*, the old Hussite slogan also adopted by Masaryk: "Truth shall prevail." Meanwhile the Soviet Union came out on the side of the revolutionaries by publicly denouncing the 1968 invasion. On November 27, a general strike paralyzed the city while three quarters of a million people gathered in the snow in the park on Letná overlooking the Vltava's west bank. It was bitterly cold: whole sections of the crowd jumped up and down as one to keep warm. But still the government would not yield to the protestors and another general strike was announced. After that events began to gain a momentum of their own: Prime Minister Adamec was booed off the stage while addressing a demonstration and on November 29 the Federal Assembly agreed to abolish the leading role of the Communist Party in government and to remove Marxism-Leninism as the basis of education. But the strikes and protests continued unabated.

Eventually the government opened up a dialogue with Civic Forum and discussions took place in the historic surroundings of the Obecní dům, where the first democratic Czechoslovak state had been proclaimed back in 1918. As talks progressed Adamec resigned and was replaced by his deputy Marián Čalfa, and then on December 10, Čalfa and President Husák finally threw in the towel, promising multi-party elections the following June. But who would replace Husák as president? The answer was obvious: "Havel na Hrad," the protesters chanted, "Havel to the castle," and on December 29, Václav Havel was duly sworn in as president after a unanimous vote in the Federal Assembly. (Assembly members had recently elected Alexander Dubček as their speaker, a post he took as part of an agreement for not standing for president against Havel.) Soon Havel became the most internationally recognizable figurehead of the collapse of East European communism, claiming the unofficial crown held until then by the Polish trade union leader

Lech Wałęsa; not surpr[...] that were held in June 1[...]

Prague since the Ve[...]

In Poland the revolutio[...] taken ten long, hard y[...] East Germany it took[...] Revolution—whose nar[...] lution but also evokes th[...] Velvet Underground, of[...] In his 1990 New Year'[...] Havel announced: *Tvá*[...] your government has re[...] seventeenth-century Cz[...] 1918 by T. G. Masaryk i[...] of Czechoslovakia. Have[...] manager, and lead actor[...] as much as politics. But[...] very different stage.

His approach from th[...] Garton Ash, Havel was[...] and a thick body perch[...] than his fifty-three years[...] waving like twin propelle[...] corduroy jacket, only putt[...] for example when receivi[...] Havel was a Bohemian i[...] and an artist who was [...] During his first months i[...] withdrawal from Czecho[...] Sudeten Germans after th[...] quarters), organized an am[...] Frank Zappa as Czechos[...] appointed the son of exe[...] (also named Rudolf) as C[...] took to zipping from me[...]

child's scooter,[...] of power hung[...] regime had de[...] apartment bloc[...] home (designe[...] Rybárně restau[...] reserved for hi[...] down to earth[...]

In the Jur[...] party Verejnost[...] percent of the[...] broad coalition[...] transition to a[...] Party headed b[...] policies of M[...] unrestrained c[...] leaning partie[...] November 199[...] and psycholog[...] the fact that t[...] been thrown i[...]

During 1[...] third while pri[...] state. The past[...] Lustration Ac[...] to purge or pu[...] hunt by any [...] domain the e[...] four decades,[...] paranoia retur[...] the victims. A[...] *a Prague Wind*[...] early years of [...] answers lay," [...] the chimney,[...] in memories[...]

are still being answered and perpetrators are still being prosecuted as the dusty files of the old security services are pored over by researchers.

On January 1, 1993 the "Velvet Divorce" saw Slovakia gain its independence from Prague. The celebrations were, however, muted in both Prague and Bratislava by the news that Alexander Dubček had been killed in a car crash a few hours into the life of the new country. Havel, who had campaigned to keep Czechoslovakia intact, resigned as president but was immediately re-elected, with Václav Klaus as his prime minister; Klaus eventually replaced Havel as president in 2003. By then Havel's star had begun to wane: he had married an actress almost twenty years his junior less than a year after the death of his wife Olga, and he had had a public falling-out with his sister-in-law over the inheritance of the Lucerna Palace, an *art nouveau* shopping arcade just of Wenceslas Square built by his grandfather. He also began to be beleaguered by constant health problems, many of which the result of a lifetime's enjoyment of cigarettes and Moravian red wine; lung cancer, blood poisoning, pneumonia, and a series of abdominal operations conspired to keep him almost constantly in and out of hospital. It was all a far cry from the late 1990s, when Havel had been shortlisted for the Nobel Peace Prize and when Timothy Garton Ash had christened him "the moral leader of Europe" in an article in the British newspaper *The Independent.*

Nonetheless the national outpouring of grief at Havel's death in December 2011, at the age of 75, his subsequent lying in state in Prague Castle and his funeral in St. Vitus' Cathedral demonstrated the enormous respect that he still commanded in his home country, where many of the mourners were too young to remember communism; and the attendance at the funeral by luminaries such as Bill Clinton demonstrated that the world still had not forgotten 1989 or the bleak decades in Eastern Europe that had preceded it.

In May 2004 Klaus took his country into the European Union after 77 percent of Czechs voted in favor of joining in a referendum. The economy has grown since then but politics has become mired in stalemate, with inconclusive elections and coalition government the

The monument to Franz Kafka created by the Czech artist Jaroslav Rona and unveiled on the edge of Prague's Jewish Quarter in December 2003. The sculpture, depicting Kafka sitting on the shoulders of a walking head-less figure, was inspired by the writer's *Description of a Struggle*

whose 1855 work *Babička* (*Grandmother*), the tale of a Czech matriarch bringing up her children in the Bohemian countryside, is considered one of the greatest Czech novels of the nineteenth century; and the poet Karel Hynek Mácha, whose work, like that of Němcová and other writers of the era, tapped into the growing vein of Czech nationalism. These authors and others had their work published in the literary magazine *Květy* (*Blossoms*) and subsequent historians have dubbed this development of language and literature the *národní obrození* or Czech National Revival, which created a firm foundation for the flourishing of Czech writing in the second part of the nineteenth century.

Two of the most popular writers at the turn of the twentieth century retold the stories of old Bohemia that had been in circulation since the time of Cosmas and were now informing the awakening of Czech national identity. The epic poem *Vyšehrad* by Julius Zeyer (1841-1901) told the story of the legendary founding of Prague, while the most famous work written by Alois Jirásek (1851-1930) was *Old Bohemian Tales*, a prose rendition of the many legends that permeate Czech culture and have their origins in the Middle Ages (and which has again been discussed in the Chapter 2). Jirásek was a historical novelist, a playwright, a teacher at a grammar school in Prague, and also a campaigner for Czech independence; much of his work glorified the Czech past at a time when Prague was still part of the Austro-Hungarian Empire, and his tales of war, bloodshed, greed, and jealousy were often pro-Slavic and anti-German in tone. Yet at the same time as Jirásek was writing and publishing his work celebrating the rebirth of Czech patriotism, a young boy was growing up in Prague whose name would become indelibly linked with the city's literary heritage—and the language he spoke and wrote in was German.

Kafka in Prague

Foreign tourists who visit Prague would be forgiven for thinking that the city's literary tradition starts and ends with Franz Kafka. His image is everywhere, from T-shirts and mugs to statues and

A similar movement afflicted the theater: typical of government-approved plays was Otto Šafránek's *The House of Lieutenant Baker*, which tells of an American pilot who drops the A-bomb and subsequently becomes unemployed and disenchanted with capitalism. The film director Miloš Forman, who came to Prague to train as a theater director in the early 1950s, recalls in his memoir *Turnaround* how at this time "Czech theater had entered the dark period of socialist-realism. The only productions allowed by the government were by-the-numbers pieces of agitprop. Most plays were Soviet and dealt with the joys of building dams in Siberia or reforming the lumpen proletariat or surpassing the production plan." Only in small out-of-the-way theaters or through semi-legal publishing houses could plays or novels that challenged the system ever see the light of day.

The selection of writers covered in this chapter is guided partly by how easy it is to obtain their works in English translation—as well as how much their life and work was bound up with Prague. One Czech author from the early communist era whose works have been recently made readily available in English is Jiří Weil. He was born in 1900 and drew the ire of the Soviets in the 1930s when he published *From Moscow to the Border*, a political novel that grew out of his observations of Soviet totalitarianism while working in Moscow. Weil was Jewish and tried to kill himself when the Nazis entered Prague. He was believed by the authorities to be dead but he actually remained hidden throughout the occupation, mostly in the bathroom of the house of Kafka's niece Vera Saudkova. After the war Weil was made a director of the State Jewish Museum of Prague and wrote two novels, *Life with a Star* and *Mendelssohn is on the Roof* (the latter published posthumously in Czech in 1960) which documented life in occupied Prague. In recent years the American novelist Philip Roth has emerged as his champion, writing in his introduction to the English editions of Weil's books of his "ability to write about savagery and pain with a brevity that in itself seems the fiercest commentary that can be made on the worst that life has to offer."

In August 1968 Soviet tanks rolled into Prague to put an end to the liberal reform movement of Alexander Dubček known as the Prague Spring. Internationally, the writer most associated with this benighted era of Czech history is the novelist Milan Kundera, who proved such a nuisance to the authorities during the process of "normalization" after the Prague Spring that he was allowed to seek exile abroad. In 1975 he moved to Paris and since 1981 he has been a French citizen; most of his recent novels have been written in French. Kundera was born in Brno and his first novel, *The Joke*, was set in Moravia. But three subsequent novels, *Life is Elsewhere* (1973), *The Book of Laughter and Forgetting* (1978), and *The Unbearable Lightness of Being* (1984) were all set in Prague during the communist era and include memorable scenes that take place during the Soviet invasion. *The Unbearable Lightness of Being* is by far the best-known of these works. The novel concerns Tomaš, a Prague surgeon, who marries the photographer and artist Tereza while conducting an affair with another woman named Sabina; his dilemma is whether he should choose a course of life that weighs him down with responsibility or take the opposite path where actions are "as free as they are inconsequential." Tomaš' glib existence stands in stark contrast to the weight of international events that surround him, as the Soviets occupy Prague—although ironically Tomaš seems to need the oppression of the Russian invasion to give his life some sort of substance and meaning. With its non-linear narrative, philosophical digressions, and darkly comic tone, Kundera's novel is as beguiling as it is enigmatic, but it will always be known by its detractors as the work of a writer who chose exile rather than remain at home to be a thorn in the side of the authorities.

Václav Havel and the Samizdat Tradition

If Milan Kundera was the most famous émigré Czech writer during the communist era, then the most famous author to remain at home was, of course, Václav Havel—at least as far as an international readership was concerned. He was a playwright, essayist, and dissident throughout the 1960s, 1970s, and 1980s, and then served as President of Czechoslovakia and the Czech Republic from the fall of communism to 2003. Havel was born into a bourgeois family in 1936. His maternal grandfather had edited *Literární noviny*, the leading Czech literary journal, while his other grandfather had been an architect and designed the Lucerna Palace, the *art nouveau* shopping arcade on Wenceslas Square. Havel started off as a stagehand at the ABC Theatre and then moved to the Theatre on the Balustrade beside the river, which remains to this day one of the best small theaters in the city. In time he became resident playwright there; his first play performed on its fifteen-foot-wide stage was *Hitchhiking* (1961), which revealed that the fetishization of commodities was part of the Marxist as well as the capitalist tradition. Later plays were savage indictments of the socialist system. *The Garden Party* (1963) tells of the absurd encounters of an ordinary man, Hugo Pludek, with a labyrinthine bureaucracy, as he is appointed liquidator of the liquidation office and then head of the Central Committee of Initiation and Liquidation, reducing him to plastic nobody, infinitely malleable but incapable of independent decision making; *The Memorandum* (1965) creates an entire new bureaucratic language named Ptydepe that reduces its speakers to little more than robots; while *Largo Desolato* (1984) concerns a political writer who goes mad during a period of self-imposed house arrest when he fears being imprisoned.

Many of Havel's plays blend together a number of literary traditions—most particularly the metaphysical anguish of Kafka (and his purposeless but powerful bureaucracies), Hašek's lowlife clowning, and the Pinteresque whiff of violence that always lurks just below the surface of the action. Havel himself also acknowledged his love for and debt to Samuel Beckett and Eugene Ionesco. Plots are often open-ended and Havel's plays are funny but do not seek to provide easy answers; rather, they are more content to pose questions, engaging the intellect of the audience as a result. Some of Havel's plays such as *The Mountain Hotel* (1981) explore theatrical form so much that they become experiments in twisting and stretching the conventions of theater rather than something a company of actors could actually perform.

Despite being performed in tiny theaters Havel's work nonetheless began to draw the ire of the communist authorities. In

1977 his version of *The Beggar's Opera* led to his imprisonment. The play had been performed in secret in a pub-restaurant on the outskirts of Prague and its plot focused on a morally corrupt chief of police. On the second day of Havel's questioning a petition was launched in Prague by several hundred dissidents, and was given the title "Charter '77" by the novelist and playwright Pavel Kohout. In Havel's later words the charter was "a free, informal, open community of people... united by the will to strive, individually and collectively, for the respect of civic and human rights in our own country and throughout the world"; when he was released Havel became Charter '77's spokesperson. Through it the plight of writers, academics, and dissidents in communist Czechoslovakia received worldwide attention.

By the time Charter '77 was founded most of its signatories were publishing their works in *samizdat* editions, where authors were responsible for copying their own manuscripts, first on roneo machines and later on early photocopiers. There were two important *samizdat* publishing houses—Petlice (Padlock), founded by the novelist Ivan Klíma, and Expedice, founded by Havel. Both published many of the works of Bohumil Hrabal, another widely-read Czech author from the second half of the twentieth century whose most famous novel *Too Loud a Solitude* (1977) examined the life and loves of a paper crusher in a Prague paper mill. (That book was published in English translation by 68 Publishers in Toronto, a company set up by Czech émigré writer Josef Škvorecký to promote the works of leading Czech dissidents.) Many authors who published in *samizdat* editions made no money from their writing and were forced to work as stokers in the boiler rooms of dingy apartment blocks and factories, the classic occupation for dissidents who had fallen foul of government censorship. Other jobs imposed on dissidents by the state including working on public transport or cleaning the streets. "Where else [but Prague] would one find... a tram-ticket salesman who was a scholar of the Elizabethan stage?" muses a historian in Bruce Chatwin's 1988 novel *Utz*, "Or a street-sweeper who had written a philosophical commentary on the Anaximander Fragment?" "This is the way we arrange things now," the dissident theater director Bolotka informs the narrator Nathan Zuckerman in Philip Roth's novella *The Prague Orgy* (1985). Bolotka has to work as a janitor in a museum because he is viewed as an

> ideological saboteur... in my theatre, the heroes were always laughing when they should be crying, and this was a crime... The menial work is done by the writers and the teachers and the construction engineers, and the construction is run by the drunks and the crooks. Half a million people have been fired from their jobs. *Everything* is run by the drunks and the crooks. They get along better with the Russians.

His words prompt Zuckerman to imagine the New York critic Susan Sontag wrapping buns at a Broadway bakery or Gore Vidal bicycling salamis to school lunchrooms in Queens. According to the Czech Minister of Culture, who appears as a character in Roth's novel, dissidents had a "stupid, maniacal delusion" whereas the ordinary people "know how to submit decently to their historical misfortune. These are the people to whom we owe the survival of our beloved land, not to alienated, degenerate, egomaniacal artistes!"

This underground city of writers and intellectuals lasted until the fall of communism. Roth describes Prague in the 1970s as consisting of "old-time streetcars, barren shops, soot-blackened bridges, tunnelled alleys and medieval streets, the people in a state of impervious heaviness, their faces shut down by solemnity, faces that appear to be on strike against life." But as cold, grey Prague struggled on through the years, writers and intellectuals were waiting patiently in the wings ready to take to the stage when the curtain of democracy went up. Yet in 1989 Havel found himself running the country and Kundera was away from the action in Paris, so it was left to the likes of former dissidents such as Ivan Klíma to chronicle the Velvet Revolution and its aftermath. Klíma's novel *Waiting for the Dark, Waiting for the Light* is set during the revolution while *No Saints or Angels* is set in 1998, recounting the reactions to the fall of communism of characters from different political generations in Prague.

British and American Views

Prague, with its dark and macabre history and its suffering under the yoke of Nazism and communism, has proved an alluring setting for a number of British and American writers. The first of these novels was *A Stricken Field* by the American journalist Martha Gellhorn, which was published in 1940. Set in Prague during the Nazi occupation of the Sudetenland, it concerns a young American journalist's dealings with German-speaking refugees who have fled from the Nazi onslaught. As we have already seen, the tyranny of communism is examined by the American writer Philip Roth in *The Prague Orgy*, which recounts the visit in the 1970s of an American novelist, Nathan Zuckerman, to the city where he hopes to recover the unpublished manuscript of a Jewish writer. It is a scabrous, scathing portrait of a city suffering under the paranoia of late communism, with Roth spitting venom over the moral and intellectual bankruptcy that comes with totalitarianism.

Bruce Chatwin's *Utz* is in a different vein altogether. This is the account of a collector of Meissen porcelain, Kaspar Utz, who lives in a lonely apartment overlooking the Old Jewish Cemetery and whose scandalous personal history is slowly unpeeled as the novel progresses. The fear and tension of the Cold War also permeate a number of thrillers and spy novels set in communist Prague such as Len Deighton's *Funeral in Berlin* (1965), in which the city features as something out of "Hans Christian Anderson... a fairy tale of spiky spires." David Brierley's 1995 *On Leaving a Prague Window* takes a slightly different angle to many others and is set just after the Velvet Revolution in a city where many have a vested interest in not allowing the secrets of the communist era to see the light of day.

Other writers have presented a more romantic vision of the city. Chief among these is Sue Gee whose *Letters from Prague* (1993) treads a difficult path between the literary and romantic genres.

It tells the story of a London schoolteacher who travels to Prague shortly after the Velvet Revolution in search of the only man she has ever loved, Karel, whom she met twenty years previously when he came to London during the Prague Spring. Gee's Prague is

> chalk and pastel colours, gleams of gold, rippling terracotta...
> washed-out blue and faded rose, copper-green domes and dark
> slate towers... the façades of medieval houses painted in shades of
> parchment and linen, coffee and cream and ochre... It was bells,
> ringing across the city, it was string quartets in churches, it was
> Mozart, Mozart, Mozart.

In terms of drama the Anglo-Czech playwright Tom Stoppard, born in Moravia, has maintained continuous connections with his homeland throughout his writing career, championing Charter '77 and translating a number of Václav Havel's works into English. Stoppard's own plays include *Cahoot's Macbeth*, which recalls the efforts of the novelist and playwright Pavel Kohout to stage Shakespeare plays in private apartments in Prague after he had been banned from working in the theater by the communist authorities; *Professional Foul*, a BBC television play which concerns the visits of a Cambridge don and two England football fans to communist Prague, which was written in 1977 for Amnesty International's Prisoner of Conscience Year; and *Rock 'n' Roll*, again set partly in Prague, which looks at the influence of rock music in Prague under the communists. The play was premiered at the Royal Court Theatre in London in 2006 and was performed the following year in Prague's National Theatre.

6 | Images and Stages
The Visual and Performing Arts

Painting, Sculpture, Photography, and Design

From the diverse collection of paintings that can be seen in the various buildings that make up the Národní galerie (Czech National Gallery) to the avant-garde movements that flourished in art, design, and photography during the early years of the twentieth century, Prague has long been a city where art has been both collected and created. Nowadays the creation of art is most visible in Nový Svět (which literally means "New World"), a winding street in the castle district where modern-day artists create their work in public view, their windows open to the street to reveal stacks of canvases lying around their studios. As for the collection of art, that tradition was begun by the Habsburg Emperor Rudolf II (1576-1611), who gained a reputation as Renaissance Europe's greatest collector of paintings, with Dürer being a particular favorite. Rudolf crammed his rooms in Prague Castle from floor to ceiling with his extraordinary collection; Karel van Mander, the seventeenth-century art historian and critic, maintained that the eccentric emperor was "the greatest art patron in the world at this present time... [in the imperial residence] is a remarkable number of outstanding and precious, curious, unusual and priceless works." By the end of his reign Rudolf's collection numbered some three thousand paintings that were rarely seen by anyone other than him; many were gifts, such as Holbein's *Isaac Blessing Jacob* and Dürer's *Trinity*, both of which came from the Burgomaster of Nuremberg, or the Titians that came by way of the Spanish Count Khevenhiller. Guidebooks like to claim that Rudolf's collection forms the core of the Czech National Gallery's collection, but in truth many of the paintings moved from Prague to Vienna when the seat of imperial power shifted after Rudolf's death, and still more were looted by the Swedes during the Thirty Year War.

The best known painting by Giuseppe Arcimboldo, court artist to Emperor Rudolf II, is entitled *Vertumnus* and is a surrealist portrait of Rudolf himself, with his eyes depicted as cherries, his cheeks shown as apples, his hair represented by grapes, his neck by a zucchini, and a radish for the Adam's apple

Rudolf II was not only a collector; he also ensured that a community of artists was attracted to his court to create artworks specifically for him. Among these were goldsmiths and gem cutters—and a Westphalian stone cutter named Caspar Lehmann, who had the ingenious idea of applying to high-quality glass the methods he had been perfecting to cut precious stones; the result was sparkling crystal glass, and the birth of a tradition for which Bohemia became famous. Among Rudolf's court artists were Bartholomaeus Spranger and Guiseppe Arcimboldo, the latter a Milanese painter who was also Rudolf's Master of the Revels. Both were painters in the mannerist style, filling their canvases with mythological themes, arranging their subjects to create the most dramatic effect possible and washing their paintings in a wealth of allegorical and often erotic detail. The works often glorified Rudolf and were essentially imperial propaganda; but many were arcane and complex, with levels of meaning that the artist knew only Rudolf would understand.

Spranger's *Allegory of the Turkish Wars*, an enormous canvas hanging in the Prague Castle Picture Gallery, is typical of the style, full of curvaceous bodies and strangely elongated women, which Spranger knew would please the emperor's eye. In the painting a near-naked Victory stands ready to award a laurel wreath to the victors of a raging battle, while to one side a winged goddess is depicted with her foot on a struggling Turk. Arcimboldo's best-known painting, *Vertumnus*, is a surrealist portrait of Rudolf himself with his eyes depicted as cherries, his cheeks shown as apples, his hair represented by grapes, his neck by a zucchini, and a radish for the Adam's apple. The painting honors on canvas the man who brought so much art to Prague in the first place, but also provides a kind of shorthand for Rudolf's famously dysfunctional reign. Rudolf was so taken with Arcimboldo's portrait that he commissioned similar depictions of every member of his entourage, down to the cook; these paintings such as *Water*, in which the head of the subject is made out of sea creatures, and *Fire*, which features another head made from a mixture of burning faggots and firearms, are in the Kunsthistorisches Museum in Vienna, while *Vertumnus* is in the gallery of a Swedish castle named Skoklosters Slott near Uppsala. In fact Arcimboldo's pictures are rather thin on the ground in Prague, but visitors to the city's two main art galleries exhibiting paintings from before 1800 are treated to works of other artists in a wide collection amassed by Rudolf and the monarchs who followed him. These include paintings by Cranach, Rubens, and Tintoretto in the Prague Castle Picture Gallery, and work by masters such as Rembrandt, Frans Hals, and Dürer in the Šternberský palác situated just across from the main entrance to the castle. Earlier work from the medieval period, including dozens of gloomy panel paintings from Bohemian altarpieces by artists such as Master Theodoric, court artist to Emperor Charles IV, can be found in the collection of Gothic art housed in the Convent of St. Agnes in the Old Town.

Czech art really came into its own at the turn of the twentieth century. One of the standard bearers of the radical new direction that art was taking was Alfons Mucha (1860-1939), whose name is closely linked to the *art nouveau* movement in painting and design.

Mucha based himself in Paris where, in 1895, he was commissioned to design a poster advertising a new play featuring the French actress Sarah Bernhardt. His fashionable new style, featuring in colorful abundance of floral motifs, women in vaguely neoclassical robes and swirling, curling deigns that filled the edges of his frames, quickly became known as the "Style Mucha"; it really caught on when the artist's works were shown at the 1900 Universal Exhibition in Paris. Mucha himself illustrated books in the new style and also provided designs for carpets, jewelry, wallpaper, and even stamps and banknotes. He also designed two windows made from painted (not stained) glass in St. Vitus' Cathedral, one of which depicts the birth of Christ and includes characteristically colorful motifs that spiral gamely away in each corner of the design.

Mucha's most famous work was the *Slav Epic*, a series of twenty vast canvases portraying the history of the Slav people, which are now on display in a castle at Moravský Krumlov in Moravia; many of his other works can be seen in the Mucha Museum in Prague's New Town. The new style that he popularized was widely imitated and can also be seen in some of the ceramics and glassware exhibited in the Umělecko-průmyslové museum (UPM or Applied Art Museum), a rich collection of tapestries, crystal, and ceramics housed in a nineteenth-century building overlooking the Old Jewish Cemetery. Here in particular are works made by the Bohemian glass company Loetz that feature fluid curves and floral designs. Designers there were much influenced by *art nouveau* at the turn of the century, and Loetz pieces are still sold at auction and exhibited in museums all over the world.

Some twelve years after Mucha's work created such a stir at the Universal Exhibition in Paris, the work of another revolutionary Czech artist again caused tongues to wag when it was exhibited in the same city. František Kupka (1871-1957) moved to Paris in 1894 and in 1912 an exhibition at the Salon d'Automne featured two of his paintings that are now regarded as the first abstract works of art ever exhibited. *Fugue in Two Colours* is painted on an enormous square canvas half as tall again as a person, and consists of a swirl of red and blue that bursts from the top right corner of the painting, onto a background of white circles on a black void. It now hangs in the Czech National Gallery's nineteenth- and twentieth-century art collection housed in the Veletržní palác in Prague's northern suburbs. The second painting, *Warm Chromatics*, is gloomier, quieter, and more enigmatic, a swirling miasma of various shades of brown, red, purple, and grey that hangs in another Prague gallery, the Museum Kampa. This gallery is housed in a former watermill complex on the banks of the Vltava on Kampa Island and was established there by two Czech-American art collectors, Jan and Meda Mladek, to house Prague's largest private art collection. Two hundred more of Kupka's works are exhibited here including oil paintings, pencil studies, watercolors, prints, and color pastels in a gallery whose wide range of twentieth-century art and sculpture (and policy of continuous acquisition of new work) makes it a vital stop for any lovers of contemporary art visiting Prague.

At around the same time as Kupka was painting his boldly revolutionary canvases similarly avant-garde sculptures were being carved by his contemporary František Bílek (1872-1941). Bílek's work taps into a number of traditions. The melodrama and fluidity of *art nouveau* are present, and Bílek allied these with a symbolism that emphasized the mystical and the morbid, the personal, the private, and the obscure. For much of his life Bílek lived the life of an ascetic in the depths of the Bohemian countryside, but he maintained a home in Prague, known as the Bílkova villa, situated just to the northeast of the castle, which now serves as a gallery of his most famous works. Unfortunately these days the curving brick villa, which comprised several studio rooms as well as the living quarters for Bílek's family, now overlooks a busy tram and road junction, but the work on show there remains dramatic and powerful.

The most distinctive sculpture is a work entitled *Wonder* (1907) and consists of a ten-foot-high figure whose expression is simultaneously one of rapture, intense wonder, and surprise as he contemplates the beauty of the universe around him. The figure is fashioned from stained beech wood and the facial expression is one of vitality and drama, as is the case with all of Bílek's work. Another of his important works was a statue of Moses on his knees in despair at the shattered remnants of the Tablets of Law, which was placed in a small park outside the Old-New Synagogue in 1935, but which was destroyed by the Nazis; a new copy was placed there in 1948 and remains to this day. Further works include a very human wooden sculpture of the Crucifixion hanging in St. Vitus' Cathedral (1899) and a sculpture entitled *Sorrow*, incorporating Bílek's trademark grooved wood and impassioned expression, which stands above the grave of the writer Václav Beneš Třebízský in Vyšehrad cemetery.

While Kupka and Bílek worked on their paintings and sculptures yet another new style, that of Cubism, was also making an impact on art, architecture, and furniture design. Otto Gutfreund (1889-1927) emerged as the leading exponent of Czech Cubist sculpture and his work can be seen in the Museum of Cubism in the House of the Black Madonna, Prague's most noted Cubist building. Gutfreund lived for much of his professional life in Paris, like his contemporary Kupka, where he joined the French Foreign Legion; but he was later interned for insubordination and returning to Czechoslovakia he died tragically young, at the age of 38, swimming in the Vltava in Prague.

The hallmark of Cubism is a fracturing of reality to create abstract images that are ripe for reassembly and analysis; right angles are loathed and oblique angles are championed for the dramatic effect they provide. Much of Gutfreund's work such as *Don Quixote* (1911) and *Cellist* (1913) consists of contorted and twisted faces and figures that look as if they have been melted. His *Úzkost* (*Anxiety*) of 1911, which depicts a woman whose features are distorted in pain and despair, was one of the first Cubist sculptures ever created and can be seen in the Museum of Cubism. Other striking exhibits here are the examples of Cubist furniture such as the chairs by Pavel Janák and Josef Gočar that have no right angles at all but are fashioned with triangular backs and strangely-angled legs.

Gutfreund, Bílek, Mucha, and Kupka were all members of the Skupina výtvarných umělců (Group of Creative Artists), a loose collection of writers, artists, architects, and designers founded in 1911 whose creative daring made the first years of the twentieth century one of the most culturally productive in the history of Prague. Their

(*top*) Prague Castle from Petřín Hill; (*middle*) The tenements of Žižkov, one of Prague's traditionally working-class inner suburbs, once known as "Red Žižkov" on account of its support for the communists; (*left*) A page from the Chronicle of the Bohemians (early twelfth century), in which Cosmas, the dean of St. Vitus' Cathedral, recounts many of the legends of Prague's foundation

(*top left*) The Lesser Quarter (Malá Strana); (*top right*) The dome and tower of St. Nicholas' Church of the Lesser Quarter form the most imposing landmarks in the district; (*below*) Malostranské náměstí, the elegant square at the heart of the Lesser Quarter

(*top*) Bridges over the Vltava: Prague has been a vital crossing point on the river since the time of its foundation; (*middle*) The Old Town Square; (*left*) The russet-red façade of the Basilica of St. George dominates the eastern wing of the Castle

(*top*) Charles IV, the greatest of Prague's medieval monarchs; (*right*) The statue of St. John Nepomuk on the Charles Bridge; (*bottom*) The Charles Bridge with the Castle and the Cathedral rising beyond it

(*top*) Vladislav Hall in the Castle, one of Prague's most noted secular Gothic buildings; (*left*) The Old Town bridge tower of the Charles Bridge: Charles IV, St. Vitus and Václav IV gaze benevolently over the pedestrians passing below

(*above*) A contemporary woodcut illustrating the defenestration of Prague; (*left*) The astronomical clock, installed on the Town Hall in 1410

(*left*) The Baroque Břevnov monastery

(*above*) Stucco decoration on the exterior of St. James' Church in the Old Town; (*left*) The wooden Ukrainian Church on Petřín Hill was dismantled and brought to Prague in the early twentieth century

(*top*) The Church of St. Peter and St. Paul is the principal landmark of Vyšehrad; (*bottom*) The Rudolfinum concert hall, one of the principal buildings inspired by the growth of Czech nationalism in the nineteenth century

(*top left*) The Hanavský Pavilón, the first *art nouveau* building in Prague;
(*inset*) The nineteenth-century Jubilee Synagogue: Moorish arches with a flourish of *art nouveau;*
(*left*) The *art nouveau* façade of the Obecní Dům

(*above*) Reinhard Heydrich, the Nazi "butcher of Prague," whose assassination led to the destruction of the village of Lidice; (*right*) Memorial to the parachutists who assassinated Reinhard Heydrich outside the crypt of the Church of St. Cyril and St. Methodius, where they died; bullet scars still pockmark the walls around the street access to the crypt; (*below*) Memorials to the dead of Terezín

(*top*) Stalin leads a group of peasants and workers towards a socialist paradise: the giant statue that rose on the Letná plain in the 1950s and was demolished in the 1960s; (*middle*) Socialist-inspired reliefs on the façade of the Crowne Plaza Hotel (formerly the Hotel International); (*left*) Bust of Milada Horáková, one of the most high-profile victims of the communist purges

(*top*) Frank Gehry's Tančící dům (the "Dancing House") on the banks of the Vltava;
(*left*) The Television Tower in Žižkov with David Černý's "crawling babies"

(*top*) The Old Jewish Cemetery is the burial place for tens of thousands of former members of Prague's Jewish community; (*bottom*) The Hus Memorial in the Old Town Square

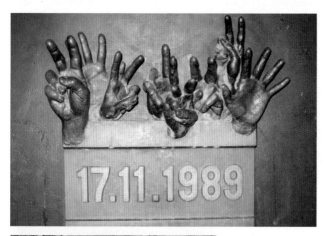

(*top*) Memorial to the "masakyr" on Národní: a decisive episode in the Velvet Revolution; (*left*) The "Lennon Wall" in the Lesser Quarter recalls the protest movements of the 1960s; (*bottom*) Václav Havel, 2008 (Martin Kósak)

(*top left*) Franz Kafka, Prague's most famous literary offspring; (*top right*) *Wonder*, one of the most famous sculptures by František Bílek; (*left*) The Bertramka, the elegant villa where Mozart often stayed during his visits to Prague; (*bottom*) The Villa Amerika, home to the Dvořák museum

(*top*) The Šárka valley, on the outskirts of Prague, makes for a popular getaway from the city; (*middle*) The market on Havelská is now the only open-air market in Prague; (*above*) The village of Karlštejn is surrounded by typical Bohemian countryside

(*left*) The expansive main square at Litoměřice, with its Baroque and Renaissance buildings; (*middle*) The River Elbe at Litoměřice; (*bottom left*) The extravagance of St. Barbara's Cathedral at Kutná Hora reflects the town's former role as a center of silver mining; (*bottom right*) The ossuary at Sedlec, Kutná Hora, is fashioned from the remains of over 40,000 people

influence was to last until the communist era and was to spread across the creative spectrum. For example, in the 1920s the new stylistic creeds of *art nouveau*, Cubism, symbolism, and modernism also begin to influence a new art form that was quickly gaining currency in Prague—that of photography. The two leading Czech photographers of the mid-twentieth century were František Drtikol and the better-known Josef Sudek. Drtikol specialized in photographing nude females whose bodies appear as silhouettes in front of stark geometric backdrops emphasizing pillars, curves, arches, and prisms, while many of the works of Sudek (1896-1976) are cycles such as *Still Life on the Window of my Studio* (1950-58), which consist of various mono shots of fruit photographed against the background of rain streaming down window panes. Sudek worked in a studio in the Lesser Quarter accessed from Karmelitská, where a tiny one-room gallery dedicated to his work has now been installed; the work of both photographers can also be seen in the UPM and the photography galleries in the Veltržní palác.

As Sudek absorbed the influences of the Group of Creative Artists so another group appeared on the Prague art scene. Group 42, created in 1942, continued the traditions of earlier artists by developing the styles of Cubism and Surrealism. Seen as decadent by the communists, the group was wound up in 1948 but its influence is plain in paintings by artists such as Mikuláš Medek (1926-74) hanging in the Veletržní palác. Medek's painting *Large Meal,* for instance, shows three figures sitting around a dinner table with spider-like limbs emerging from mannequin bodies, while *Magnetic Fish* depicts a knife plunged into a decaying fish that floats through the sky. But the work of Group 42 was to be the last gasp of an extraordinarily dynamic period in Czech art. Paintings by artists such as Medek were anathema to the socialist-realist style championed by the communists, which was blunt, monumental, and simplistic, devoid of subtext and resistant to interpretation. (In Milan Kundera's novel *The Unbearable Lightness of Being,* the artist Sabina is told that "the strictest realism [was] required of all students... Art that is not realistic saps the foundations of socialism.") Some paintings from this era are still to be found in the Veltržní palác, full of the bold, decisive, expectant faces of workers and peasants, often with hammer-and-sickle flags fluttering in the background.

Those artists who refused to be compromised by the new political creed often found themselves sharing the same fate as dissident academics and writers: in another of Kundera's novels, *Life is Elsewhere*, a painter is accused of being "an enemy of the people" for making art that is "contemptibly bourgeois" and ends up as a construction laborer. Creativity clearly struggled to find an outlet in this era—and often when it did so it was in the field of industrial design; the Veltržní palác also contains an absorbing exhibition of chunky radios and eye-catching chairs in primary colors, all of which were exhibited to great international acclaim in the Czechoslovak Pavilion of the 1958 Expo in Brussels. In the same gallery are artworks created since 1989, when artists were at last able to shed the constraints imposed on them by socialist-realism. They include the riot of glass bubbles and prismatic shapes in green, blue, and red that is the work of René Roubiček, one of the leading contemporary Czech artists, which was originally commissioned by the Czech parliament and which he donated to the gallery in 2007.

Film

Prague has been synonymous with film since the advent of talking pictures. The association dates specifically from 1933 when two enterprising brothers, Miloš and Václav Havel, opened the Barrandov Studios in a south-west suburb of Prague, ushering in an extraordinary tradition of film production that continues to this day. Miloš Havel, uncle of the future president, was openly gay and something of a dandy. By the time he became involved in the Barrandov Studios he had already made his mark in Czechoslovak films: his movie house in Prague had been the first to show talking pictures, and in 1921 he had created the country's principal film distribution outfit by merging his own American Film Distribution company with another distributor, Biografia. When his architect-developer brother Václav, the future president's father, began to create a new residential development on the outskirts of Prague, Miloš suggested that it should include a film production facility; the brothers named the development, and the studios, after Joachim Barrande, a French geologist who had worked at the site in the nineteenth century. In 1934 *Murder on Ostrovni Street* became the first film to be shot in the studios and by the outbreak of the Second World War the facilities at Barrandov were churning out over eighty films each year.

The next reel in the story of the Barrandov Studios introduces a new character, the Nazi propaganda minister Josef Goebbels. In the 1930s Goebbels had an affair with a Czech film actress named Lída Baarová, and by the time of the Nazi occupation of Prague he thought he knew a thing or two about Czech films. The propaganda minister wanted European cinema to eclipse Hollywood and recognized that Barrandov was a better equipped studio than any in Germany—so he ordered that three huge sound stages should be added to the complex. Films are still being shot on those stages today, yet in the end few German films were made here during the war. (One exception was *Tiefland*, which Hitler's favorite director Leni Riefenstahl shot in the studios in 1944.) Instead it was native Czechoslovak directors who made films at the Barrandov on the new stages. The most famous wartime film made here was *Babička* (*The Grandmother*), based on a classic nineteenth-century novel by Božena Němcová, about a Bohemian matriarch who fervently brings up her children in the countryside as Czechs at a time when Czech identity was feared to be under threat from foreigners (the story includes an episode where a Czech girl is raped by a foreign soldier). Filmmakers had to turn to historical themes because they were up against so many restrictions imposed by the Nazis: Jews could not be shown in a positive light, there was to be no depiction of student life at all and of course any suggestion of "Anti-German" activity was completely forbidden.

Yet the studios were not as securely under the thumb of the Nazis as they might have been. The day after the invasion of Prague Miloš Havel himself actually threw some Gestapo officers off the Barrandov premises, and although he was arrested and interned for a while he was never sent to a concentration camp, as some in his cultural circle were. It was a sad twist of fate that after the communist coup of 1948 Havel was accused of having collaborated with the Nazis, which had never been the case; nevertheless his film company was nationalized by the new regime and, seeing no future for himself in communist Czechoslovakia, Havel eventually escaped to Vienna with the help of American servicemen and then began a new life for himself in West Germany.

Throughout the communist era of state-subsidized film production around seventy pictures were made at the Barrandov Studios every year. The industry took its lead from the busy Soviet film production houses in Leningrad and Moscow: off the cinematic production line in Prague rolled everything from slapstick comedies to dramatizations of Czech folk tales and live-action children's films. Historical epics were popular too, of which the most enduring has been *Markéta Lazarová*, a 1967 adaptation of a novel by Vladislav Vančura that provides an up-close-and-personal depiction of the intrigue, bloodlust, and suspicion that swirls like winter mists around an aristocratic clan in thirteenth-century South Bohemia. The plot, which unfolds over a running time of nearly three hours, is almost wilfully impenetrable, but the stark monochrome cinematography, the setting amidst a landscape of frozen fields and forests, the story populated by earthy characters such as scavengers and tyrants, and the eerily evocative soundtrack gives the film a mystical, even hallucinatory quality. *Markéta Lazarová* was a purely Czechoslovak production but many films of the communist period were made in partnership with the East German state film outfit DEFA, and some were even made in conjunction with film production houses in West Germany and France. Films such as *Markéta Lazarová* were also exhibited abroad, creating a revenue stream that allowed the Barrandov Studios to develop film processing laboratories and special effects facilities including a water tank for underwater scenes.

Many of those who came to make films at Barrandov in the 1950s and 1960s were graduates of the Film and Television School of Prague's Academy of Performing Arts (FAMU). They formed an enormously influential creative community during the communist years, one that spread Czechoslovak culture abroad as well as bearing the standard for opposition to the regime at home. The most famous FAMU graduate remains Miloš Forman, who became a leading light of the Czechoslovak "new wave" in the 1960s before his defection to Hollywood.

Forman was born in a tiny village in Bohemia and attended King George of Poděbrady School in Eastern Bohemia, a boys' boarding school with Dickensian attitudes to discipline that was eventually closed by the communists; he was a dormitory monitor there when Václav Havel joined the school as an eleven-year-old fellow pupil. Forman initially trained as a theater director in Prague but then switched to studying at the film school, where the novelist Milan Kundera was one of his lecturers. He graduated just as the new wave filmmakers were beginning to find their feet. The pioneering, censor-baiting films made by Forman and others involved in the new cinematic movement were characterized by dark and often absurdist humor, by the casting of non-professional actors, by a documentary eye for detail, and by long passages of unscripted dialogue; the films were personal, fleeting, and ambiguous; and often they had the aim of making the audience collectively (though subconsciously) aware that they were participants in a system of brutalizing oppression and incompetence. Not surprisingly many new wave films were either banned or heavily cut.

One of the most notorious films of this time—which never saw the light of day—was *The Ear (Ucho)*, in which a high-ranking bureaucrat, Ludvík, returns to his home in Prague with his wife one night after a government reception in the castle to discover that the secret police have bugged the place. The action takes place over a single night and (once again) it is the striking monochrome cinematography (of the floodlit castle, in particular) that lends the piece its atmosphere and tension. (The film was at last shown at the Cannes Film Festival in 1990 and has since been distributed on DVD.) In the same bracket is Jan Němec's rather more opaque 1966 *The Party and the Guests (O slavnosti a hostech)*, which had the dubious distinction of being "banned forever" by President Novotný, who reputedly turned puce with anger when he was shown it; through its portrayal of the compliant behavior of guests at a party (staged beside a lake) the film provides an allegorical commentary on how easily people submit to dictatorship—and how the dictatorship treats dissent, when one of the guests decides he has had enough and leaves.

But not all new wave films suffered the fate of *The Ear* and *The Party and the Guests*: some dodged below the radar of the censors and made it on to cinema screens in both Czechoslovakia and Western Europe and North America. Among these were Forman's *Loves of a Blonde* (1965) and *The Firemen's Ball* (1967), both of which were nominated for Oscars for best foreign film. Both movies are predominantly set in provincial Bohemia, although the story of *Loves of a Blonde* ends in Prague where Andula—the blonde of the title, who holds down a humdrum job in a shoe factory—comes to pursue her lover Milda, a jazz pianist who tells her that "most women are round, like guitars, but you are like a guitar by Picasso." The film became the most popular Czechoslovak film ever made: melancholic and funny, its universally appealing themes transcend both time and place. (Prague itself does not appear in the film beyond the interior of the Milda's could-be-anywhere apartment.) Forman shot the film with non-professional actors, which gives the piece its rough-edged charm, and the drabness of the time, bitterly ranged against the wide-eyed expectations of Andula, is evoked with almost documentary clarity.

Forman may have garnered a reputation for being the most influential player in post-war Czechoslovak cinema, but he was not the only director making films at the Barrandov Studios during that difficult political era. Jiří Weiss was born into Prague's German-speaking Jewish community in 1913 and fled to Britain when the Nazis invaded Czechoslovakia. In London he made films such as *The Rape of Czechoslovakia* (1943) for the Crown Film Unit. Back in Prague after the war, his films such as *The Wolf Trap* (1957) and *The Coward* (1962) concerned themselves with small-town life, but *Romeo, Juliet and Darkness* (1960) was set and filmed in Prague and put Weiss on the world cinematic map for the first time, earning him the Grand Prix at the San Sebastian and Taormina Film Festivals. The background to the film is the Nazi occupation of Prague and the brutal crackdown on Czechs following the assassination of Reinhard Heydrich, the Acting Reichsprotektor of

Bohemia and Moravia; the action, taut and spare and filmed in stark monochrome, focuses on a young man, Pavel, living in a grim apartment building with his parents, who secretly provide shelter to a Jewish woman.

Another influential director of the time was Jiří Menzel, who unlike Forman actually brought an Oscar for best foreign film back to Czechoslovakia. This he won for his 1966 work *Closely Observed Trains*, a film based on a novel by Bohumil Hrabal that portrays a young man's sexual coming of age in dead-end provincial Bohemia. Menzel also worked as an actor and played a supporting role in another important new wave film, *The Cremator*. Made in 1968 by the Slovak director Juraj Herz, this visually arresting and occasionally terrifying monochrome film tells the story of a paunchy director of a Prague crematorium named Karl Kopfrkingl who finds that his increasingly deranged impulses for "liberating" souls through burning has an outlet in the Nazis' plans for Jewish extermination. Part surrealist horror and part ghoulish fantasy, this blackly comic film is chock-full of close-ups of mouths and eyes and rapid-fire images of tormented souls from medieval paintings, while the title credit sequence featuring crudely animated photographic cut-outs of bodies has a quality similar to that of the work of Monty Python animator Terry Gilliam (who has cited Czech animation among his influences).

In 1968 both Miloš Forman and Jiří Weiss defected to the United States. Weiss left Czechoslovakia (with hundreds of others) during the easing of travel restrictions that came with the liberalizing reforms of the Prague Spring; Forman was in Paris when the Soviets occupied Prague and chose not to go back. Weiss settled in Los Angeles but made no films in America, choosing instead to teach film courses. He returned to Czechoslovakia in 1989 to direct *Martha and I*, a film set in Prague during the Nazi era. The film concerns the marriage of a successful Jewish doctor, Ernst, to his housekeeper Martha, whose inevitable disappearance in the Holocaust is told through the eyes of the doctor's young nephew, Emil. The film is now almost impossible to track down; its director died in 2004 at the age of ninety-one. Forman, conversely, carved out a filmmaking career for himself in Hollywood, and nearly a decade after his defection his 1976 film *One Flew over the Cuckoo's Nest* finally brought him the Oscar recognition that his Czech films had not. Somewhat nervously Forman returned to Prague in 1984 to film his second Oscar-winner *Amadeus* at the Barrandov Studios, in the streets and palaces of the Lesser Quarter, in the eighteenth-century Estates Theatre and among the stately rooms of Prague Castle. (Forman's costume designer, Theodor Pištěk, is responsible for the uniforms worn by the sentries who guard the castle to this day.)

As an émigré, Forman was something of a persona non grata in the eyes of the communist regime, and it was only with some persuasion from the Barrandov Studios that he was able to shoot the film in his home country. In his memoir *Turnaround* the director recalls that during the filming of *Amadeus* he was kept under constant surveillance by the secret police, while his Czechoslovak cast and crew was, he suspected, full to the brim with government informers; and no word of the film appeared in the press, despite it being the biggest Western film ever shot in the country. Twenty-five years after the success of *Amadeus* Forman continues to make films: at the time of writing he was working on a project entitled *The Ghost of Munich*, which concerns a journalist's interest in an official involved in signing the infamous Munich Agreement of 1938. But this film, along with the film Forman made in 1991 with Vojtěch Jasný entitled *Why Havel?*, appears to be the closest he has come to addressing Czech themes since his move to the United States.

As émigré directors such as Forman and Weiss made their mark in Los Angeles, Prague began at last to attract filmmakers from the West who wanted to make their films in the city. Besides *Amadeus* the best-known Hollywood film shot in communist Prague was *Operation Daybreak* (1975), a rather fanciful account of the assassination by Czech freedom fighters of Reinhard Heydrich. Financed by Warner Brothers and directed by the British director Lewis Gilbert, whose credits also include *Alfie*, *Educating Rita*, and the James Bond film *Moonraker*, the film is shot in a darkly beautiful (and seemingly perpetually rainy) Prague, the buildings of the

Old Town Square decked out with swastikas and the bridges over the Vltava crossed by impressively organized phalanxes of marching Nazis. Czechoslovak actors and technicians rub shoulders with the likes of Timothy Bottoms, Anthony Andrews, and Joss Ackland, while the Barrandov Studios provided the filmmakers with indoor shooting and post-production facilities. The film itself, though, is of its time, with a synthesized soundtrack and a shoot-out at the end that is noisily unconvincing and remorselessly drawn-out. (The screenplay, by Roman Polanski's frequent collaborator Ronald Harwood, is based on a long-forgotten novel *Seven Men at Daybreak* by Alan Burgess.)

During the same era a number of other Western-financed films were set in Prague but filmed elsewhere, often because of their less than flattering portrayal of the communist regime. Most famous among these was Philip Kaufman's 1988 film adaptation of Milan Kundera's novel *The Unbearable Lightness of Being*. This remarkable film, set during and just after the crushing of the Prague Spring, stars Daniel Day Lewis as the philandering Prague doctor Tomaš, the French actress Juliette Binoche as his wife Tereza, and the sensual Swedish actress Lena Olin as his lover Sabina. With a three-hour running time and something of a Euro-pudding of accents, the film could have been a disaster but in the end Kaufman turned out one of the most memorable and striking films ever made about Prague. It is at its best during the sequences when actual footage from the Soviet invasion is interspersed with the actions of the characters, as Tereza, a professional photographer, snaps away at the tanks rolling through the streets and the bodies lying in alleyways. Despite being funded by an American studio the film is very much in the tradition of European art house movies—although much of Kundera's philosophizing (as well as a large chunk of the novel that is set in the Far East) was excised for commercial reasons.

The film's producer was Saul Zaentz, who also produced *Amadeus* and who initially offered the project to Miloš Forman—who turned it down, apparently not wanting to be involved in such a resolutely Czech project. Kundera, whose novel *The Joke* had been turned into an important Czechoslovak new wave film in 1968, reportedly did not like the film, perhaps because it tells the story in a linear fashion rather than adopting the elliptical approach to narrative of the original novel. Filming took place in the French city of Lyon whose ancient streets and squares were judged by the filmmakers to bear a passable resemblance to Prague, while the melancholic, jittery music of Czech composer Leos Janaček was used for the score. The film became an art-house favorite during the dying months of communism, and the advertising poster adorned the walls of many a 1980s student lodging. On it was plastered the film's most iconic image— Lena Olin dressed only in black lace underwear and wearing on her head her character's most notorious erotic plaything, namely a black bowler hat.

With the withdrawal of state subsidies to the film industry after the end of communism the future for the Barrandov Studios seemed bleak. But the studios bounced back as producers of television commercials and dramas began to make use of the stages and the post-production facilities. Capital was raised and in 2006 a fourth sound stage was added. It is the largest in Europe and provides over forty thousand square feet of production space. Taking advantage of decades of technical expertise and relatively cheap production costs, Hollywood films such as *Prince Caspian, Mission Impossible*, and *The Bourne Identity* have all been shot in the Barrandov Studios, which are now owned by the industrial conglomerate Moravia Steel.

Prague itself is often also used for location work by foreign filmmakers shooting at Barrandov: the city's streets have stood in for London in *Casino Royale* (2006) and the Jack-the-Ripper-themed *From Hell* (2001), and perhaps even more oddly for nineteenth-century Stockholm in the 1993 Swedish film *The Slingshot*, a coming-of-age tale in which a young boy makes slingshots out of condoms. Meanwhile FAMU remains a vital nurturing ground for cinematic talent: in August 2011 it was listed as the top film school in Europe (and seventh best in the world) by *Hollywood Reporter* magazine. Its graduates continue to make films at the Barrandov Studios although finance is much harder to come by than it was in the communist era. In fact these days Czech films rarely get seen beyond the country's borders and are often intended primarily for domestic consumption. The Nazi occupation or the events of 1968 regularly provide subject matter for these films. Typical of contemporary Czech films is *Pelíšky*, a 1999 film from director Jan Hřebejk set in the dreary suburbs of Prague during the crushing of the Prague Spring. The film's protagonist is a teenage boy named Michal who develops a crush on his anti-communist neighbor Jindřiška, much to the chagrin of his army officer father who believes that nothing the American imperialists can dream up will ever be a match for East German Tupperware.

As far as audiences outside the Czech Republic are concerned, the two most widely-seen films to have emerged from the post-communist country are *Kolya* (1996) and the very different *Czech Dream* (2004), both of which have a Prague setting. The former won an Oscar for best foreign film; set during the dying days of communism, it tells the story of a middle-aged orchestral cellist who is lumbered with a six-year-old Russian boy after his new wife—the boy's mother—defects to West Germany. The cellist, František, lives in a chaotic apartment picturesquely overlooking St. Nicholas' Church of the Lesser Quarter, and because he moonlights as a restorer of gravestone inscriptions some of the film was shot on location in Prague's vast cemeteries. Documentary footage of the demonstrations leading up to the Velvet Revolution is shoehorned into the film's closing scenes, while Prague airport, the metro, the Petřín Tower, and the police headquarters in the Old Town all feature in the film. Although *Kolya* is undeniably well-made, its essential story has been told many times before; one leading film guide calls it "obvious, obnoxious and shallow," though eventually some charm does succeed in leaking out from all the sentimentality. Much more interesting is *Czech Dream*, a mischievous but fascinating documentary made by two students at FAMU that tells the story of how Czechs reacted to the opening of a fake but convincingly advertised hypermarket that the filmmakers created in Prague's dreary suburbs, and is discussed more fully on p. 168.

Finally, in the last twenty years the Barrandov Studios, and Prague itself, have benefitted from an interest from overseas in films set in the city but not made in Czech and often not concerning

Czech characters. Instead these films are intended for foreign audiences, with Prague forming a beguiling backdrop to the storytelling. Typical is *Prague*, a Danish film from 2006 directed by Ole Christian Madsen that tells the story of a Danish couple, Christopher and Maja, who travel to Prague to confront the reality of their collapsing marriage. Prague's melancholic cityscape, its anonymous international hotels, and its dismal housing developments provide a suitable background of ennui and despair as the story of Maja's affair with an artist slowly unfolds along with the drama of Christopher's father's death. Prague comes across in the film as aged and dignified but also cold and rigid, its mentality still resolutely Eastern Bloc.

The city's more romantic side forms the background to the 1998 film *Prague Duet* (also known as *Lies and Whispers*) in which an American doctor played by Gina Gershon falls in love with a Czech writer who was a dissident in the communist period, only to have her love tested by a dark family secret from her past. The somewhat overwrought screenplay creates a tourist's-eye view of Prague, with scenes filmed in a checklist of picturesque settings in the city center as well as in the former Gestapo prison in Terezín.

In 1991, immediately after Prague opened up fully to the West, noted American *auteur* Steven Soderbergh, who had made a splash with his first film *Sex, Lies, and Videotape* two years previously, came to the city to make *Kafka*, a mystery thriller in which Jeremy Irons portrays the writer as an insurance clerk lost in a nightmare that could easily come from one of his stories. Shot mostly in stark black-and-white, Prague's skyline looks particularly moody, framing a background to a story of an all-pervasive machine-like bureaucracy that is as threatening as the leprous creatures that skulk in the shadows of gas-lit cobbled streets. Soderbergh's story provides a passing nod to elements of Kafka's work: the castle is the center of the controlling but secret organization looming above everything, while the deadening and impenetrable bureaucracy of the insurance office (run by Alec Guinness in one of his last roles) threatens to sap the soul of all who work there. The film is an uneasy mix of surrealist and absurdist comedy and conventional murder-mystery and was panned on its release in the United States. Soon after Soderberg shot his film a very different side to the city was depicted in *Not Angels but Angels*, a disturbing documentary that examined under-age male prostitution in Prague, and which is discussed more fully in Chapter 11.

Music

Just as it sometimes appears that Prague's literary tradition starts and ends with Kafka, so it can also seem that the city's musical heritage is bound up entirely with Mozart. The composer made several visits to the city between 1787 and 1791, and Prague repaid him by falling in love with his music. Mozart lodged either with Count Thun in a palace in the Lesser Quarter (at Thunovská 14, now the British Embassy), or with the Dušek family, whose house, the Bertramka, sat amidst open countryside on the south-western edge of the city. František Dušek, who owned the villa, was an accomplished pianist and music teacher, and his wife (and former pupil) Josefa was a singer. (Mozart composed the aria *Bella Mia Fiamma* for her in November 1787, which sparked inevitable rumors of an affair.) In the past two centuries the Bertramka has been swallowed up by encroaching suburbs and now the approach on foot to the two-story villa passes beneath one of Prague's nastier traffic flyovers. The villa, tucked away into a fold of a hill and surrounded by a small garden, contains a museum dedicated to Mozart's time in Prague—or rather it purports to, for at the time of writing the airy rooms were mostly bare (and devoid of visitors) as the museum was fighting a prolonged legal battle to have its exhibits returned from other institutions where they had somehow ended up. Consequently the temporary exhibits here consist of little more than facsimile scores and photographs of concert halls and opera houses where Mozart's works were performed.

The most famous piece that Mozart composed while staying in the villa was the overture to his opera *Don Giovanni*. It was famously written within hours of the opera's opening performance, and the score was put in front of the musicians with the ink barely dry and the curtain ready to go up. *Don Giovanni* received its premiere in Prague largely because of the enthusiastic reception that the city had previously afforded Mozart's operas *The Abduction from the Seraglio* and *The Marriage of Figaro*. These pieces were performed in Prague at the instigation of the community of musicians and opera impresarios who had emerged in Prague during the eighteenth century. Count Thun, for instance, had been a patron of Italian operas for years and often staged productions in his grandiose villa. Mozart was not in Prague for the *Seraglio* but brought *Figaro* here after its disastrous reception in Vienna where it survived for only nine performances (twenty performances would have constituted success). But the people of Prague loved *Figaro* when it was performed in the Nostitz Theatre (now the Estates Theatre) in the Old Town. "Here they talk about nothing but Figaro," Mozart wrote afterwards in his diary. "Nothing is played, sung or whistled except Figaro... [This is] certainly a great honour for me!" During Mozart's four week stay in the city, which began on January 11, 1787, he not only directed *The Marriage of Figaro* but also conducted a concert that included his symphony no. 38 in D major, which quickly came to be called *The Prague*. The opera impresario Pasquale Bonini was so impressed by the success of the two works that he commissioned another opera from Mozart—and this time the patrons of Prague's music scene made sure that the opera received its premiere in the city.

When Mozart returned to Prague in October the new work *Don Giovanni* was nearly—but not quite—finished. Another performance of *The Marriage of Figaro* was hastily arranged in place of the unfinished opera, which was finally performed on 29 October to tremendous acclaim. Three years later, in 1790, Mozart returned again to Prague to stage his last opera *La Clemenza di Tito* for the festivities attached to the coronation of Leopold II as King of Bohemia. The opera was commissioned by another Prague opera impresario, Domenico Guardasoni, who had originally offered the commission to Salieri, and according to legend the piece was written in eighteen days, partly as Mozart traveled by carriage to Prague from Vienna. The reception of the piece was not as rapturous as that given to *Don Giovanni*: during the premiere the newly-crowned empress, unimpressed with what was unfolding before her on the stage, was alleged to have cried "German hogwash" from the royal box.

La Clemenza di Tito turned out to be one of Mozart's final works. He abandoned Prague's adoring crowds for the cynical audiences in Vienna, and fourteen months later he was dead. His funeral in Vienna attracted only a handful of people but in Prague they still loved him: three thousand mourners squeezed in to St. Nicholas' Church in the Lesser Quarter (where Mozart had played the organ on a number of occasions) for a commemoration mass, and a similar number stood outside to pay their respects in the driving sleet. "Mozart seems to have written for the people of Bohemia," the *Prager Neue Zeitung* commented, shortly after his death. "His music is understood nowhere better than in Prague."

The composer's connection with the city continued after his death. His first biographer was his Czech friend Niemetschek, who also looked after his two surviving sons, one of whom lived in the Lesser Quarter for fifteen years before emigrating to Milan, and the second of whom died and is buried in Karlovy Vary. And almost two hundred years after the death of the composer, Miloš Forman filmed the opera scenes of *Amadeus* in the Estates Theatre, whose interior has changed little from the day when Mozart conducted *The Marriage of Figaro* and *Don Giovanni* there. In fact Forman recalls in his memoir *Turnaround* that he nearly set the theater on fire during the filming of the scenes from *Don Giovanni*.

No Czech composer can touch Mozart in terms of international appeal. Nonetheless, Bedřich Smetana (1824-84) and Antonín Dvořák (1841-1904) are towering figures in world music, and both contributed to the flowering of Czech culture in the late nineteenth century at a time when many prominent artists, writers, and architects were also producing work of a distinctly nationalistic flavor. Both composers lived and worked in Prague—indeed in the 1860s the young Dvořák played the viola in the Bohemian Theatre Orchestra, which was conducted by Smetana. And both composers are buried in the cemetery in Vyšehrad, an honor afforded only to the greatest of Czech cultural figures. Dvořák's tomb is set against the cemetery's exterior wall and his name is spelled out in gold mosaic tiles. Smetana's memorial is a harsher, plainer grave marked by an almost priapic column.

The Czechs are immensely proud of these two figures, largely because of their championing of national musical tradition—Dvořák in his *Slavonic Dances* and Smetana in his symphonic cycle *Má vlast* with its famous movement *Vltava*—and the two composers are commemorated extensively throughout Prague.

Since 1932 the Dvořak Society has maintained an almost shrine-like museum to the composer in a suburban villa named the Villa Amerika, which lies on a quiet street in the New Town. Here the composer's lush orchestral music floats through rococo rooms stuffed with exhibits such as the gown Dvořák wore when receiving an honorary doctorate at Cambridge in 1891. Even the seating plan for the degree ceremony is on show, alongside photos and mementoes from his extensive traveling—most notably to the Czech-speaking community of emigrants in Springville, Iowa, where Dvořák spent the summer of 1893, but also to Chicago, Moscow, London, New York (where he was director of the National Conservatory of Music), and Birmingham (where his Requiem was premiered). The Villa Amerika itself was designed by the famous Baroque architect Kilian Ignaz Dientzenhofer in 1717 as a home for the Michna family; the expansive ceiling paintings upstairs and the quiet garden with its sculptures make this a vastly more satisfying exhibition space than the Bertramka.

Dvořák's most famous work was, of course, his ninth symphony, *From the New World*, composed during his three-year sojourn in America in the early 1890s. But the name of the building has nothing to do with the symphony: it originates from the Amerika restaurant that occupied the villa long before Dvořák had begun work on his famous masterpiece. In fact the composer never actually even lived in this building; his home was on another street close by, and this villa was originally intended to be a museum dedicated to the works of Ignaz Dientzenhofer prior to its purchase by the Dvořák Society.

Smetana, despite being born of German-speaking parents, embraced the cause of Czech nationalism at a young age and even participated briefly in the uprising of 1848 against Habsburg rule in Bohemia. None of his works has ever achieved the worldwide popularity of what has come to be known popularly as Dvořák's *New World*, but serious musicians rate Smetana as the father of Czech music and most consider him the greater of the two composers. Patriotic themes run through Smetana's major operas *Dalibor*, which tells the story of a violin-playing nobleman imprisoned in Prague Castle in the early fifteenth century, and *Libuše*, whose central character is Prague's mythical founder. This second opera was the first production staged in the newly-opened National Theatre in 1881—a building for which Smetana himself had laid the foundation stone some thirteen years before. The same opera was also the first to be performed two years later in 1883 when the theater reopened after a disastrous fire, and it was again performed in the theater in 1945 after the liberation of Prague from Nazi occupation. The audience on that occasion included President Beneš, and the opera's closing words, sung by Libuše, carried such an extraordinary resonance that it brought the whole house to its feet: "My dear Czech people shall never die," the heroine gasps. "They will gloriously overcome the horrors of Hell."

Like Dvořák, Smetana has a museum dedicated to him in Prague, and like the Villa Amerika, the building of the Smetana Museum, housed in a converted nineteenth-century water mill beside the Vltava, had nothing to do with him when he was alive. The museum is crammed with original scores, letters, and personal effects, although there is less here to grab the imagination of non-initiates than there is in the Villa Amerika, partly because Smetana was less traveled and partly because he was less well-known outside Bohemia. Oddly the statue of Smetana outside the museum (dating from as recently as 1984) is facing away from the water, which is ironic as the river served as the inspiration for his most famous work, *Má vlast* (*My Fatherland*), with its instantly recognizable movement *Vltava*. These days the piece always opens the Prague Spring Music Festival on 12 May each year, the anniversary of Smetana's death; a procession from the composer's grave in Vyšehrad is followed by a performance of this piece in the *art nouveau* Smetana Concert Hall in the Obecní dům, which by tradition is always attended by the Czech president.

Just as there is more to music in Prague than Mozart, there is actually more to Czech music than Smetana and Dvořák. Another festival in Prague commemorates the composer Bohuslav Martinů (1890-1959), much of whose music is avant-garde in style, including his 1943 piece commemorating the victims of the Lidice tragedy. Martinů's contemporary Jaroslav Ježek (1906-42) was more of a populist figure, composing music for films and stage shows in addition to piano and chamber music, and achieving success as a jazz musician. Both composers spent most of their adult lives outside Czechoslovakia, in Paris and New York respectively. Of all the composers mentioned in this section, Ježek is the only one who was actually born in Prague—in the working-class suburb of Žižkov, to be precise—an urban childhood that led to a love of music hall and jazz rather than the rural childhoods of Smetana and Dvořák which exposed them to so much Czech folk music.

Serious music lovers will find much of the contemporary music scene in Prague unbearably kitsch. Concerts abound, held in Baroque churches or sumptuous palaces, but anything called "Music of Prague Castle" (or such like) will have nothing to do with the castle and precious little to do with Prague. Vivaldi's *Four Seasons* features highly on the menu at these concerts, as does Pachelbel's Cannon in D, and there will usually be some Mozart—though none of the compositions associated with his stay in Prague. The offerings in the major music venues such as the Obecní dům, home to the Prague Symphony Orchestra, or the Rudolfinum, the extravagant neo-Renaissance concert hall on the river bank that hosts the Czech Philharmonic, are more likely to offer programs appealing to serious music lovers.

Non-classical music, meanwhile, is gaining a reputation in the city, although it often struggles to make itself heard above all the Mozart and Dvořák. Gigs staged by live acts in pubs and clubs fill the listings sections of publications such as the *Prague Post*, while a world music festival (known as the Respect Festival) is held in the city each June. As for pop music, anyone interested in how that fared during the communist era is encouraged to travel to Bělohorská, far out in the western suburbs, and the Popmuseum. In communist times anodyne pop music was sanctioned by the regime while more avant-garde artists were considered subversive and often suppressed. Western pop music was frowned upon and in the 1980s a number of members of the influential jazz section of the Musicians' Union were arrested for distributing recordings of groups such as the Beatles. They were particularly popular; after the death of John Lennon in 1980 the wall of a former priory in the Lesser Quarter on Velkopřevorské náměstí became a canvas for graffiti artists wanting to express their admiration for the dead singer. Over time the so-called "Lennon Wall" became filled with murals, lyrics, and commemorative items, and the dogged survival of the wall during communist times led President Husák to denounce those who contributed to it as being "agents of western capitalism." The authorities used to whitewash the wall on a regular basis but since 1990 it has been left to gather murals and other artwork undisturbed. A trickle of pilgrims come here on December 8, the anniversary of Lennon's death, but nowadays the wall attracts a lot of general graffiti along with genuine paeans to John Lennon, his lyrics, and his era (such as CND symbols).

Meanwhile, the 1968 Prague Spring and its brutal crushing have provided pop musicians the world over with inspiration. The Israeli song *Prague*, performed at the Israel Song Festival in 1969, commemorated Jan Palach's self-immolation the previous month, and a song entitled *They Can't Stop the Spring*, which was Ireland's entry for the 2007 Eurovision Song Contest, was an allusion, said its composer John Waters, to Dubček's assertion that "they may crush the flowers, but they can't crush the spring."

Czech pop musicians have also been inspired to write songs about the repression experienced in their country during communism. The country's most famous pop music act of all time is the experimental rock group Plastic People of the Universe, who at the time of writing were still going strong some forty years after their first gig, although the line-up of members has changed over the years. The group formed in Prague in August 1968 just days after Soviet tanks moved into Czechoslovakia. The musicians were heavily influenced by the New York rock group Velvet Underground and by Frank Zappa, and in fact the band took its name from *Plastic People*, one of Zappa's songs.

Their style was unorthodox from the word go, with band members blending instruments such as violas and saxophones with more conventional bass and lead guitars. For a time their lead singer was Paul Wilson, a Canadian living in Prague who later translated many of Václav Havel's works into English. In 1970 the government revoked the band's licence to perform and from then on an entire underground movement grew up around the Plastics, with followers gaining the disapproving moniker *máničky* due to their long hair. In 1972 Wilson was arrested and deported to Canada and four years later the imprisonment of the band's members led directly to the creation of the human rights movement Charter '77. The band continued to perform and record their songs during the 1980s, breaking up in 1988 but reforming again in 1997 at the suggestion of President Havel. In 2001 their founder, principal songwriter and bass guitarist Milan Hlavsa died of lung cancer, and was replaced by Eva Turnová from the group Půlnoc, itself formed from former members of the Plastics. In 2006 a new play by Czech-born playwright Tom Stoppard entitled *Rock 'n' Roll* featured some of the band's music, and in January the following year the band performed in London for the first time in their history, spreading their music, and an appreciation of the muzzling of artistic freedom in communist Czechoslovakia, to an ever wider audience.

7 | **Leisure and Pleasure**
Popular Culture and Pastimes

Escape to the Country

With many Czechs working very hard—sometimes in two jobs—to make ends meet, opportunities for time spent in leisure are comparatively few, and with the center of Prague besieged by tourists for much of the year city dwellers elect to spend their free time elsewhere. Many maintain weekend homes tucked away amidst the woods and hills of the Bohemian countryside, and this was so even in communist days when owning plots in community gardens was also popular. Each allotment came with a wooden hut, a case of private property ownership that the authorities might have balked at had the produce from those allotments not gone some way to alleviating the chronic shortage of fruit and vegetables in communist Czechoslovakia.

Many citizens of Prague still own country cottages and grow their own vegetables, but it is not necessary to travel out into the wilds of Bohemia to appreciate a bit of its countryside. The pretty Šárka valley can be found right on the edge of the city in the district of Prague 6, where the apartment blocks give way to fields and woods and the tram lines end in a broad turning loop that point the trams back in the direction of the city center. On weekend afternoons in summer each new tram that rattles its way along busy Evropská—the main highway to the airport—and then grinds around the turning circle disgorges another load of trippers ready to head off into the valley.

The delights here are not exactly world-beating and they attract far more locals than foreign tourists, but on their own terms they are diverting enough. (Milan Kundera romanticizes the area somewhat in the opening of his novel *Life is Elsewhere*, in which it is described as "a romantic landscape strewn with boulders

Christmas in Prague

looming out of wildly rough terrain.") Just down from the tram stop, hidden by trees, a reservoir called Džbán offers many spots for quiet afternoons of bathing or boating. The stream that gurgles its way out of the reservoir, the Šárecký potok, then dives immediately into the twisting, thickly-wooded gorge of the Šárka valley, with limestone crags tumbling down on both sides. A paved path (good enough for biking), signposted as the Divoká Šárka, runs alongside the stream, taking walkers around a broad loop that brings them back to a tram stop on Evropská after a very pleasant and not at all taxing 45 minutes. In a couple of places the valley opens out slightly and there are more swimming pools and restaurants. Beyond one of these, Želivka, the path divides, and a route heading off to the left gives access to a further network of marked paths that wriggle picturesquely alongside the Šárecký potok stream all the way to its confluence with the Vltava in the northern suburb of Baba—a walk of some four miles. The network of paths straggles across the top left hand corner of most fold-out street maps of Prague, allowing for straightforward route finding. (The legend behind the valley's name is recounted in Chapter 1.)

May Day and Christmas

In communist times May Day was in fact three holidays spread over the first part of that month. 1 May celebrated international workers' day; 5 May commemorated the beginning of the Prague uprising, which relieved the city from Nazi rule; and 9 May marked the final liberation of Prague by the Red Army. Czechoslovak and Soviet flags would flutter happily in a show of international socialist solidarity and posters proclaimed *Zdravíme slavné májové dny*—"we greet the glorious May Days." The theme of the three days was "peace," although Václav Havel commented wryly that the word in this context meant "nothing more than an unreserved concurrency with the policy of the Soviet bloc and a uniformly negative attitude towards the west." The celebrations also saw massed displays of synchronized gymnastics staged in the enormous Strahov Stadium on Petřín hill, where the May Day processions also finished up (to the applause of Politburo members and other assembled lackeys).

These days the second and third holidays have been conflated into a single holiday on 8 May that remembers VE Day. May Day is still a holiday but instead of the military march-pasts of yore backed by enormous posters of Marx, Lenin, Engels, and Gottwald a motley collection of anarchists, skinheads, and die-hard Stalinists now seize the holiday as an opportunity to march (somewhat ineffectively) through the streets of Prague.

The weather at Christmas can often be bitingly cold but this does not prevent celebrations moving outside at least some of the time during the festive season. On the evening of December 5, the Eve of St. Nicholas, adults dressed as St. Nicholas (who wears a white robe and carries a bishop's miter), an angel, and a devil tour the streets giving sweets to good children and coal or potatoes to those who have been bad, and temporary ice rinks spring up wherever there is space (such as the islands on the Vltava). The Old Town Square becomes home to a Christmas market, inevitably fairly tourist-driven, with shoppers warming themselves up by consuming *klobasa* (sausage) and *svařák* (mulled wine). As for the Christmas celebrations themselves, December 24 is often a day of fasting, with the season's main feast appearing on tables when the first stars appear; the menu normally consists of carp, potato, schnitzel, and sweetbreads. After that, children are allowed to open their presents, which appear beneath a Christmas tree courtesy of Santa Claus. Christmas Day, by contrast, is a quieter day as it is throughout much of continental Europe. The three days of December 24-26 (the last is St. Stephen's Day) are all public holidays.

A Day Out

Others who brave Prague's bitter winter temperatures are football fans, who still come to watch Sparta Prague in their tens of thousands although the team's glory days (such as when they beat Glasgow Rangers and Marseille to reach the semi-final of the European Cup in 1992) are now reckoned to be well behind them. Sparta play in the 18,500-seat Generali Arena on Letná Plain, northeast of the castle. The team usually plays in red, a tradition dating from 1906 when their president brought a red Arsenal jersey back to Prague after a visit to London. A team named Sparta Praha is also Prague's best-known ice hockey side, playing in a stadium in the Výstaviště exhibition grounds in Holešovice, and achieving better success in ice hockey than their namesakes have in football, in both national and international competitions. The Czech Republic's national ice hockey team is one of the top five in the world, with Russia being the most historic rival; in football, by contrast, the national team languishes and has failed to qualify for the past three World Cups.

Prague's second team in both ice hockey and football is Slavia Prague. In football, Slavia's fan base is traditionally more middle-class than that of Sparta, with a noted following among expatriates living in Prague. They play in a smaller stadium that hides behind the colossal Strahov Stadium (there is a good view of both from the top of the Petřín tower). The Strahov Stadium itself seats 220,000 people and is the second largest in the world; gone, though, are the days of synchronized gymnastics from the communist period, and nowadays the stadium only fills up for huge rock concerts (George Michael played here in 2007). Other than football and ice hockey there is horse racing at Velká Chuchle, just outside the city on the main rail line to Plzeň, while the Prague marathon is run every May, with the course always routed over Charles Bridge.

In terms of indoor entertainment, newspapers such as the English-language *Prague Post* are crammed full of listings for clubs and bars that fill the city center, while rock groups playing live gigs advertise with semi-legal stickers plastered all over the metro. Theater has always been important in Czech culture—this is a country that, after all, elected a playwright as president—and the theater scene is thriving in Prague although most of the mime and puppet shows are aimed at tourists. The National Theatre by the Vltava on Národní still maintains an audience base of mainly Czech speakers, as do the more experimental theatres such as the Divadlo na zábradlí in the Old Town. And then there is the cinema, which has always been popular in Prague: art house releases and subtitled films can be seen in the city center, while multiplexes, often attached to shopping centers on the city's fringes, show the latest American blockbusters.

An Afternoon in the Park

Prague is full of parks; a glance at any map of the city will show the expansive areas of green that spread east of the New Town and west from the castle. The city's first park was the Chotkovy sady, immediately northeast of the castle, whose centerpiece is a grotto commemorating the Romantic poet Julius Zeyer fashioned from figures carved from white marble. More extensive is the woodland park that drapes itself over the slopes of Petřín hill and which is full of statues of writers. However, the funicular railway and the proximity to the Lesser Quarter mean that visitors are unlikely to have this park to themselves. For that, the Stromovka park in the north of the city, or the Hvězda park in the west, both of which were former royal hunting grounds, allow greater possibilities for lonely ambling among thick and largely undisturbed tracts of woodland.

Away from the formal gardens in the Lesser Quarter—which often charge an entrance fee—it is two islands on the Vltava that provide some of the best open space in the very center of Prague. On Slovanský ostrov pleasure-seekers are content to while away warm afternoons drinking beer and hiring rowing boats, a far cry from former times when this island was dedicated to entertainments known as *Hetzen* or *Štvanice* during which bloodhounds would tear bears, stags, and goats to pieces to the accompaniment of appreciative roars from audiences. Rather quieter is Střelecký ostrov, accessed from the Legií bridge, whose name Shooters' Island refers to its former role as an army firing range. Now outdoor theater and other live entertainments are often staged here, although for the most part this wooded island is a haunt only of dog-walkers and joggers, and bathers in the river too on hot days.

For entertainment with a little more bite, Praguers head for the Výstaviště exhibition grounds to the north of the center, originally opened for the 1891 Prague Exhibition and Trade Fair. Among the motley collection of buildings here are a planetarium, an aquarium, an open-air theater and cinema, and a rather tawdry funfair for children known as the Lunapark with a distinctly un-Disneyland collection of roller coasters and other rides. Also popular is the Křižíkova fontána, a display fountain in the center of the grounds that puts on sound and light displays which, like the rest of the attractions here, see far more Czechs than foreign tourists.

An Evening in the Pub

For those locals and visitors who do not want to spend their leisure time outside but would rather spend it inside with a glass of something to hand, there are plenty of pubs, wine bars, and cafés spread through central and suburban Prague. There is not much to distinguish between a *pivnice* (beerhouse), a *hospoda* (pub), and a *hostinec* (inn)—all three terms denote a pub of some sort, and all are ubiquitous throughout Prague and the rest of the Czech Republic. These establishments, often dark and smoky, cater for a local and often exclusively male clientele, with half-liter glasses of beer being served in copious and inexpensive quantities, and food, if there is any, consisting of the traditional Czech sort with the emphasis on pork, dumplings, and cabbage: great for washing down with the local brew. In recent years it has been harder to find these institutions in the very center of Prague—although that said, visitors do not need to wander far out of the city's commercial and tourist-driven center to come upon one where the first residential blocks start to spring up. These days the center of Prague is largely given over to establishments that are more likely to score a hit with Prague's legions of backpackers, better-heeled tourists, and business people—namely the wine bars, coffee chains, and "Irish" pubs that are indistinguishable to those found in any large European city (although some establishments such as the Café Slavia opposite the National Theatre, and long the haunt of writers and intellectuals, still retain a measure of individuality and manage to appeal to a crowd of locals as well as visitors).

Consumption of beer (*pivo*) is higher in the Czech Republic than in any other country in the world. Even so, violence and rowdiness are uncommon and emanate more often from parties of British bachelor-party weekenders than from locals. Bohemian beers are famous worldwide but the two most famous breweries producing Pilsner Urquell (Plaeňský Prazdroj) in Plzeň and Budvar in České Budějovice are located in towns outside Prague (American Budweiser has little to do with Budvar beer beyond the name). Prague's biggest brewery, producing Staropramen beer, is based in the suburb of Smíchov, south of the Lesser Quarter; indeed, the establishment of the brewery here in 1869 was responsible for the growth of that predominantly working-class suburb in the late nineteenth century. The name means "ancient spring" and the mild flavor is typical of Bohemian brews, which supposedly derives from a blend of hand-picked hops, Moravian barley, and soft local water. The head is typically thick and creamy, owing to the large amount of carbon dioxide absorbed during fermentation.

These days much of the product of the brewery is exported; following nationalization under communism the Prague Breweries Group that brews Staropramen was bought by the multinational Bass and the company is now owned by a Belgian-Brazilian conglomerate, Anheuser-Busch InBev. In the northern suburb of Holešovice the same company makes another beer, Měšťan, while other Staropramen brews include various dark, light, and "red" lagers.

At the other end of the scale some Prague *pivnice* brew their own beer—the best-known of these being the dark and syrupy Flek, which has been brewed and served at the U Fleků pub on Křemenkova in the New Town since 1499. This huge drinking and eating den seats hundreds, can get very busy with tour groups and is unlikely to offer much of an authentic Prague drinking experience. U kalicha on Na bojišti comes closer to the genuine article, with plenty of reminders on the walls that this was the pub immortalized in the opening scenes of Jaroslav Hašek's comic novel *The Good Soldier Švejk*; the location, in a fairly humdrum part of the New Town that sees few passing tourists, ensures a rather better ambience than U Fleků, although even this place is fairly tourist-oriented compared to places further out into the suburbs. But whether drinks are consumed in a city center pub on the tourist trail or a local *pivnice* down a back street, certain conventions are always followed: tables are shared with other drinkers and waiter service is the norm, with consumption of drinks being noted on a tab and payment being made when the drinker leaves.

8 | **Faith in the City**
The Religious Landscape

Despite its geographical position sandwiched between the great Catholic strongholds of Austria, Bavaria, and Poland, the Czech Republic is one of the most secular states in the world, with well over a third of its population professing atheism. This proportion is even higher in liberal-minded Prague, which is something of an irony bearing in mind the spectacular profusion of Gothic, Renaissance, and Baroque churches. One reason for Czech society being so antithetical to any form of religion is that church-going was frowned upon by the communist authorities who often put worshippers under police surveillance, while priests who became too popular sometimes found themselves defrocked and sent to work as stokers (like many writers and academics). The communists also closed a number of monasteries such as the Strahov Monastery on Petřín hill; after the Velvet Revolution these communities reformed and had their property returned to them, and the religious community of Strahov Monastery is once again thriving. But the vein of anti-clericalism among Czechs has been present since long before the communist era: back in Habsburg times the Catholic Church was seen as indissolubly allied to the hated Austrian Empire, and antipathy to the Church was essentially championed as another form of Czech nationalism—just as it had been in the days of Jan Hus in the fifteenth century.

Christian Prague

The Thirty Years War (1618-48) marked the final gasp of Bohemia's once burgeoning reformist traditions. After it was over the Jesuits, the vanguard of the Counter-Reformation, were invited into Bohemia by the Habsburgs to re-Catholicize the wayward Czechs. As a result it is not surprising that the vast majority of Christians in the Czech Republic are Roman Catholic. In Prague Catholics

The Bambino di Praga is a much-venerated object of devotion for Catholics in Prague

worship at churches such as the Panna Maria Vítězná (Church of Our Lady Victorious) in the Lesser Quarter, which is home to the revered Bambino di Praga, or the Prague Jesus (the Pražské jezulátko), a wax effigy of the infant Jesus whose ornate gown is changed on a regular basis by Carmelite nuns; they have over fifty costumes from which to choose. The figure was brought to Prague from Spain in the late eighteenth century by a noblewoman who married into a prominent Catholic family; later on, after a member of the family presented the effigy to the church, it assumed responsibility for a number of miraculous incidences of healing. As a result the figure was reverentially placed in a glass cabinet, surrounded by a glut of silvery swirls and topped by a golden starburst: a glittering sea of Catholic kitsch unmatched in Prague. In his novel *Utz* Bruce Chatwin remarks that the figure, "aureoled in an explosion of gold… seemed less the blessed babe of Bethlehem than the vengeful divinity of the counter-reformation." A small museum in the church shows off the infant's collection of vestments, many of which are gifts from Catholic organizations all around the world. Most of the costumes in which the figure is clad are brightly embroidered tapestries that dwarf its tiny head. But the Prague Jesus, like the other great Catholic pilgrimage site of Prague, the Loreto Shrine in the Hradčany district, seems almost an irrelevance now, inspected by bus loads of visitors rather than attracting regular cohorts of the faithful. Similar sites over the border in Poland and Austria seem much more relevant to their nation populations than these sideshows that cater mostly for bemused tourists.

Protestant and Orthodox churches had a much happier time than their Catholic counterparts during the communist period. Churches such as sv.Mikuláš (St. Nicholas) on the Old Town Square, plainly decorated in typical non-conformist style, serve the city's small Protestant community and are a reminder of the religious divisions that have beset Prague for long stages of its history. Czech Protestant churches affiliate themselves to the Unity of Czech Brethren national church created in 1918, and which sees itself as upholding the reformist ideals of Jan Hus; their symbol is the chalice, which was also the symbol of the Hussite church of old.

The Brethren's main church is the Kostel u Salvátora (Evangelical Church of the Savior) located just east of Pařížská in the Old Town. The movement has 120,000 followers throughout the Czech Republic (and a few in the United States too).

The Cathedral of Saints Cyril and Metoděj, tucked away along Resslova in the New Town, caters for Prague's small Orthodox community, while Uniate followers, who practice Orthodox rites but remain in communion with Rome, worship in churches such as sv.Kliment on Karlova in the Old Town. Other churches serve even smaller communities of Baptists (their church is on Vinohradská in the east of Prague) and Methodists. Following the Velvet Revolution in 1989 Prague briefly became a magnet for proselytizing Jehovah's Witnesses, although they have mostly gone now; however, the Seventh Day Adventists maintain a church on Korunní in the eastern suburb of Vinohrady.

Judaism, Islam, and Eastern Religions

The history of Prague's Jewish community, rich in legend but often dark in tone, is documented in Chapter 11. During the communist regime the number of practicing Jews totaled around a thousand and this figure has since risen to around five thousand, thanks to many Jews with a Czech background returning to Prague from the United States and Israel to give the community a new impetus following the return to democracy. Jews worship at two synagogues in the city center, the Jubilee Synagogue in the New Town and the so-called Old-New Synagogue in Josefov (the old Jewish Quarter), which is the oldest functioning synagogue in Europe. Elders of the Jewish Community are responsible for caring for the extraordinary monuments in Josefov, still the spiritual heart of Jewish Prague, even if tourists vastly outnumber those who come here to worship.

Prague's small Muslim community traces its heritage back to the Austrian annexation of Bosnia-Herzegovina in the nineteenth century, when the Habsburg Empire first gained control of a predominantly Muslim area (in the 1990s another Muslim influx originated from Bosnia-Herzegovina after the devastating civil war there). The first Muslim community in Prague was declared in 1934.

Muslims kept a very low profile in communist days but were treated well by the authorities who wanted to maintain cordial relations with various left-leaning Middle Eastern countries for political reasons. As a result of these ties a number of students (mainly from Egypt and Syria) came to study in communist Czechoslovakia in the 1970s and 1980s and many simply stayed on after the dawn of democracy. There are also a number of Czech converts to Islam.

The community maintains an Islamic prayer center and a mosque on Blatská, in Prague's eastern suburbs, close to Černý most station at the very end of metro Line B. The mosque was opened in 1999 and its Friday services attract anything up to five hundred worshippers; prayers are read in Czech, English, and Arabic. In 2009 the mosque was subjected to a wanton act of desecration when an eyeless pig's head was placed on the fence outside; gloating photos of the incident later appeared on the websites of various far-right organizations. In addition to the mosque on Blatská there is a smaller Islamic prayer room near Muzeum metro in the New Town.

Other religions represented in Prague include Buddhists, who maintain a meditation center on Dlouhá, just off the Old Town Square, and Hare Krishnas, who are a voluble group within the city but are still looking for an appropriate site for their proposed temple. But Prague is not a pluralistic city as far as religion goes, reflecting in part Czechoslovakia's long history of isolation from the world community behind the post-war Iron Curtain, and the limited immigration from regions outside Europe that has taken place in comparison with other European capitals.

Saints and Martyrs

The thirty-six statues of saints lining the sides of the Charles Bridge are among Prague's most iconic features: by day they keep silent watch over the passing locals and tourists, and by night, according to Prague folklore, they spring into life and parade through the darkened city. On these occasions, according to the poet Vítězslav Nezval, the statues leave "their suicidal pedestals" and mix "with passers-by... admiring the twelve bridges of Prague." The earliest statue on the bridge, that of the Crucifixion, was placed on the northern parapet in medieval times; that statue was demolished by a Swedish cannonball in 1648 and the replacement that remains in place to this day was erected the following decade.

The lines of saints came some fifty years later, between 1707 and 1714, although two statues are original works from the nineteenth century, and one dates from as late as 1938. Ostensibly the statues are a demonstration in stone of the Austro-Catholic power that held Prague in its grip after the defeat of the Protestant nobles at the 1620 Battle of White Mountain. Yet the reality is more complex and intriguing. The most famous saint portrayed on the bridge, St. John of Nepomuk, was originally intended as a Catholic counterweight to Jan Hus: like Hus, Nepomuk was to be a home-grown saint and the story of his martyrdom was almost wholly constructed by the Jesuits for that specific purpose. Yet a few decades after the carving of his statue, Nepomuk had been transformed into something else entirely, a cultural symbol of national distinctiveness that was attracting an annual gathering of Czechs as early as 1771. Soon Nepomuk had been adopted as a Czech martyr, and moreover one who took his place in a long tradition of saints whose cults took on a secularist and nationalist hue as well as a religious one.

The first Czech martyr was, of course, Wenceslas, whose cult was fostered in the fourteenth century by Charles IV, the builder of the bridge over which the lines of statues now gaze; Prague is full of reminders of him, but it is full of reminders of secular saints too, who owe at least some of their mystique to a tradition dating back to Wenceslas. These secular saints, martyrs of Czech nationalism, include victims of the Nazis such as Jan Opletal, a student activist who was killed in a demonstration in 1938, and victims of communism like Jan Palach, who set himself alight on Wenceslas Square in 1969 in protest at the Soviet occupation of Czechoslovakia. They are joined by the murdered villagers of Lidice (see Chapter 11), by the instigators of the Prague uprising at the end of the Second World War and by the victims of communism now celebrated in a sculpture in the Lesser Quarter.

The notion of Czech self-definition through martyrdom has attracted the attention of a number of scholars, most notably Robert

Pynsent who developed his ideas in his 1994 book *Questions of Identity: Czech and Slovak Ideas of Nationality and Personality.* Is it possible that this "martyrdom complex" of a predominantly secular, rather than religious, nature, provides the most compelling manifestation of faith in Prague? The notion of martyrdom as a secular rather than religious concept is certainly a prominent feature of many works of Czech literature and art. In fact in many instances secular martyrdom is blended with the more traditional Christian kind. In Jaroslav Hašek's classic novel *The Good Soldier Švejk* Father Katz, the chaplain, asks the hero to cut off his head and throw him in a sack into the Vltava, adding that some stars around his head should suit him well: "I should need about ten."

This blending of religious iconography and nationalistic fervor is seen most explicitly in the work of late nineteenth- and early twentieth-century artists, a number of whom adopted the Crucifixion as their theme but used it as a subliminal allegory of the political agonies of their times. Many Czech artists created self-portraits of themselves as the Crucified Christ, while the noted photographer František Drtikol took a photo of himself wearing a crown of thorns. The sculptor František Bilek wrote that he was obsessed "by the idea of Czech lands as a place of sacrifice where the greatest sacrifices burn with excitement as if on an altar"; he fashioned a piece entitled *Tilling by the Cross* in which the Crucifix becomes a plough, pulled through the soil by Czechs, a reference to the ploughman Přemysl who was the founder of the first dynasty of rulers. A number of cultural historians have maintained that perhaps nowhere else in Europe has the iconography of the Crucifixion seeped so clearly into the political consciousness of artists.

The sculptors who carved the statues on the Charles Bridge also made puppets as a sideline. Puppet shows have been popular in Prague for three and a half centuries—ever since, in fact, the strings of political power have been firmly pulled from elsewhere (Vienna, Berlin, Moscow). Now these puppet shows are often seen as merely tourist sideshows, but they are emblematic of Prague's obsession with all things mechanical—a tradition embracing the monster known as the golem that once haunted the Jewish Quarter, the mechanical figures surrounding the astronomical clock, and even Karel Čapek's play *Rossum's Universal Robots*. Martyrdom has been celebrated as a method for cutting these strings, even as, paradoxically, the cult of martyrdom stands in contrast to a rejection of violence and an internalization of rebellion that can be seen in *The Good Soldier Švejk* and in the Velvet Revolution itself. The martyrs of the Czech nation—secular, religious, or both—remain pervasive figures in the culture of Prague, and it is perhaps in this tradition that "faith in the city" is most readily apparent rather than in any row of saints, or even in any church, mosque, or temple.

9 | Changing Faces
Migration and Social Change

Religious pluralism and ethnic diversity form two sides of the same coin, at least in most European cities, and it is not surprising that a reasonably homogenous religious culture is reflected in a similarly homogenous ethnic one. Prague's German-speaking community, which formed the majority of the city's population until the nineteenth century, was expelled after the Second World War to leave a population that was almost entirely Czech. Peter Demetz, whose book *Prague in Black and Gold* is the most heartfelt and thorough biography of the city, views this lack of ethnic diversity in Prague as the complete converse of societies in North America and Western Europe. "It is sad to see that in the Old World many places of multi-ethnic traditions have, in the past generation or so, turned to the more solid enjoyments of a single national culture characterized by the policies of exclusion and a dash of xenophobia," he notes, wryly alluding to the difficulties non-whites have often experienced in contemporary Prague.

The tradition of ethnic diversity that Demetz describes goes back to the merchant communities that settled in Prague in the Middle Ages. Many of these incomers were Italians. In the seventeenth century two Italian merchants, namely Pietro della Pasquina and Francesco Cortesi, were actually elected councilors of the Old Town. Many of the itinerant laborers in medieval Prague were also Italian: builders came from impoverished villages in northern Italy and settled around St. Thomas' Church in the Lesser Quarter, while for many generations all of Prague's chimney sweeps were Italians. From the eighteenth century onwards chimney sweeps, builders and merchants all came together to worship in the Italian chapel in the Klementinum, the great Jesuit college in the Old Town. Other immigrants were more exotic and cut something of a dash: one was Georgios Deodatus from Damascus, who wore

Sapa, the market and cultural center catering for the sizeable
Vietnamese community of Prague

traditional Arab garb around the city and opened Prague's first coffee house in 1713.

The principal minorities in contemporary Prague are those from the Roma and Vietnamese communities, and these are discussed in the following sections; mention has been made in the previous chapter of those minorities with a Middle Eastern background. In addition to these groups there is a small Greek community whose forebears sought refuge in communist Czechoslovakia after the defeat of the left in the Greek Civil War of the late 1940s. Another community originating in movements of political refugees is that of Russians, the first of whom came here in 1917 after fleeing the revolution. The Soviet Red Army took many Russians back to their homeland in 1945 but since then the community has reformed, and along Bubenečská, close to Hradčanská metro station, are shops and restaurants catering for what would appear to be a sizeable present-day community.

Beyond the communities of Greeks and Russians most non-Czechs living in Prague have a heritage that goes no further than the Czech Republic's borders, with communities of Slovak-, Hungarian-, Polish-, and German-speakers all present, if numbering only a few thousand each. Most groups have their origins in the small migratory movements that nudged people across Eastern Europe during the communist era: today's German speakers, for example, are often descended from East German migrants, whereas many Russian-speakers trace their heritage back to the Soviet political domination of Czechoslovakia.

Since 1990 these communities have been joined by the same groups of foreigners that can be found in any capital city in the world—diplomats, teachers, students, business entrepreneurs, and travelers who simply pitched up one day and decided to stay. The transition to a market economy was, of course, helped by newcomers from Western Europe (particularly Germany) who grabbed hold of business opportunities when they saw them, and now that the Czech Republic is a member of the European Union citizens of the member states that make up the union are free to live and work in Prague for as long as they wish, giving the city an international character that is bolstered further by the thousands of tourists who swarm through the place each day.

The Roma Community

Forebears of the present-day Roma community moved into Eastern and Central Europe during the late Middle Ages and ultimately trace their roots back to India. They have long been the victims of both overt and covert racism. In Habsburg times Roma were considered Turkish spies and their nomadic practices were severely restricted. During communist rule the Czechoslovak government often ordered Roma caravans to be smashed and horses slaughtered to encourage the community to settle permanently, mainly in specifically designed apartment buildings. The communist authorities also initiated a sterilization program for Roma women that lasted from 1973 to 1991 (and beyond: cases of Roma women being sterilized during childbirth have been unearthed as recently as 2008). Roma were forced to integrate and all forms of cultural expression, such as the performing of traditional music, were banned.

Yet even this systemic persecution did not come close to the murderous persecution of the Holocaust, when the Nazis killed virtually the whole community of Czech Roma. After the war Roma from Slovakia moved into Bohemia and Moravia in search of work, and members of Prague's Roma community are descended from these migrants. They live now in the poorer parts of Prague such as the working-class district of Smíchov, where levels of unemployment among the community remain high. Today some ninety percent of children in special schools in the Czech Republic are Roma, and the community continues to find itself on the receiving end of racially motivated harassment from a tiny number of vocal and occasionally violent gangs of skinhead thugs who are spurred on by the utterances of far right parties both in the Czech Republic and abroad.

In August 2000 a TV documentary showed that those Czech Roma who had migrated to Canada were making a good living there, and a thousand headed across the Atlantic within weeks, with another documentary on Roma life in Britain encouraging yet more to leave. Since then the persecution of Roma communities has been largely confined to north Bohemian mining towns such as Rumburk on the German border, which was the scene of violent scuffles between Roma and young white men in August 2011, and Ústí nad Labem, where memories of a wall briefly built (and then destroyed) in 1999 by the town's authorities to separate Roma and Czech housing developments still engenders uncomfortable racial tension.

The Vietnamese

The government of communist Czechoslovakia fostered links with countries all around the world that shared its socialist ideology. As a result Prague became home to a vibrant community of Vietnamese, many of whom came to the country as guest workers. After the Velvet Revolution they stayed on (unlike the members of the much smaller North Korean community, who were brought back to their homeland by their paranoid government when democracy dawned in Prague). There are now around 61,000 Vietnamese living in the Czech Republic—a massive increase from around 17,000 in 2001—and most live in Prague. Nguyen, the most common Vietnamese surname, is now the ninth most frequent surname in the country, and in March 2011 a new television channel serving the interests of the Czech Vietnamese began broadcasting. Every September there is a day-long Vietnamese cultural festival held on the streets of central Prague, the chief attraction of which in recent years has been Le Quang Dao (also known as "Singing Noodles"), a Vietnamese chef who gives traditional Czech folk songs a decidedly Far Eastern twist.

As far as tourists are concerned the most visible presence of this minority are the cramped shops selling general provisions found on any street in the city center, which are often staffed by Vietnamese. But Praguers and expatriates know that there is far more to the community than this, and that its beating heart can be found in the southern suburb of Libuš on the edge of the city. Here, where apartment buildings give way to fields and commuter villages, is a part of the city known to Czechs as "Little Hanoi" and to Vietnamese as "Sapa," whose name recalls one of the most beautiful regions of

Vietnam. Sapa is essentially a busy market that sells an extraordinary variety of Chinese imports, from noodles to clothing, while soup stalls and restaurants cater for hungry shoppers; the whole place is a rather less intense version of Vietnam, with none of the screeching traffic, reckless motorcycles, clutter and bustle, or noise of Hanoi or Ho-Chi-Minh city, and none of the stultifying heat of the tropics either, unless it is a very unusual day in Bohemia. Much of the place seems like a giant industrial park, with the explosion of garish, colorful hoardings in Vietnamese (which uses Latin script like English) the only hint that this is somewhere unusual.

Much of the main market, selling a mundane collection of household goods, takes place under the roof of a vast shed, with wooden pallets and old cardboard boxes stacked outside, and aisles thick with clothing and detergents inside; it is a dim and cavernous market unlike anything else in Prague and provides a vibrant and alternative variation to the department stores and clothing boutiques of the city center. Services abound too in Sapa, from driving schools and hairdressers to shabby travel agencies selling discount flights to destinations in south-east Asia. Virtually all the shoppers in Sapa are from the Vietnamese community; only a few curious expats, tourists, and Czechs make their way here, traveling by bus along Libušská and getting off right outside the market, which is close to the junction of Libušská and an arterial road named Kunratická spojka. Another network of shops selling similar products exists in Prague's eastern district of Malešice, but this is less of a market and more of a wholesale retail unit for storekeepers, and it is a lot less welcoming to casual visitors.

10 | **Consuming Interests**
Trade and Consumerism

The Middle Ages: Merchants and Markets

Since its foundation Prague has been a place of buying and selling, of commerce and markets and merchants. In fact even before the first incarnation of Prague Castle began to rise on the Hradčany hill a well-established trade route crossed the Vltava where the river flowed by the foot of the slope. In 965, a hundred years or so after the city's foundation, the Moorish traveler (and possibly slave trader) Ibrahim Ibn Ya'qub passed through Prague and wrote (in Arabic) of the merchants he encountered and of the frenzied trade he saw in slaves and tin and furs and "all kinds of things" in the markets of the Lesser Quarter. The leather saddles and shields on offer were of particularly good quality, he maintained, and were paid for (remarkably) by means of linen banknotes; according to Ibn Ya'qub, Prague "was made richer by commerce" than any other city he had passed through on his long journey from his home in Tortosa in Spain.

Those early merchants were mostly Jews. In 1090 the historian Cosmas wrote that "under the castle walls of Prague... you will find Jews with the greatest abundance of gold and silver [trading in] markets where great bargains can be made." But in 1096, six years after Cosmas had recorded the bustle of merchants and bankers in the Lesser Quarter, King Vratislav II responded to the launching of the First Crusade by expelling the Jews and encouraging German merchants to take their place. Soon these merchants were controlling the trade in goods that were moved along the Vltava on floating wooden barges known as *voroplavba*. These barges were a common sight on many of the rivers of medieval Europe; on journeys downstream they would be navigated by skilled bargemen, but for the return journey upstream they were either towed from the bank or goods were simply transferred onto land and taken by packhorse.

Wenceslas Square lies at the heart of commercial Prague

(Modern descendents of these barges remained in operation along the River Vltava until as late as the 1950s.)

Since the Vltava is a tributary of the Elbe, water-borne goods from Prague could reach the important mercantile centers of Dresden, Magdeburg, and Hamburg with ease, while produce such as salted herring from the North Sea came back the other way. Heading south and west from Prague was a more difficult matter: for these journeys across the Šumava hills to Munich or Nuremberg or to the Danube at Passau, traders had to resort to packhorses, and by the late Middle Ages well-trodden roads reached right across Bohemia and linked Prague with cities as far away as Warsaw, Vienna, Venice, and Kiev—and so on into Asia. By this time items on sale in Prague's busy markets included Flemish cloth, Bavarian linen, French wine and figs, and almonds from Venice and the Middle East.

The Old Town was officially designated a district of Prague in the mid-thirteenth century. But by then it, like the Lesser Quarter, had been home to communities of merchants and craftsmen for nearly three hundred years. The Old Town Square was laid out as a market square in around 1100, and soon afterwards visiting merchants were provided with a house where they could stay while they traded. Documentary evidence from the year 1212 attests to the services of a man named Blažej who looked after the affairs of the merchants and the markets for the king, and it is likely that the cemetery that has been unearthed close to Bartolomějská was specifically intended as the burial place for merchants of the Old Town. With official town status conferred on the district in 1234 yet more merchants moved in, such as those from France who made their home around Malé Náměstí, a square just a few steps away from the Old Town Square, while a Florentine also opened Prague's first pharmacy on this square in 1353.

The Lesser Quarter nevertheless remained home to the most powerful merchants, and it was they who in 1260 took control of the trade in silver mined at Kutná Hora to the east of Prague, and watched greedily over the next three hundred years as those mines became the most productive in Europe. By the end of the Middle

Ages silver had come to be the most valuable commodity traded in the city, and the merchants who took their cut grew to be the wealthiest burghers in Prague. In later centuries yet more minerals and precious stones were found under the rich soils of Bohemia. "Here are found a greater quantity of agates and topazes than in any other part of the world," wrote the French writer Charles Patin in 1697, in his book describing his travels around Europe. "This country is more especially famous for its mines of copper, iron, silver and gold." By then the dwellings in the Lesser Quarter in which the medieval merchants had made their homes had evolved into elaborate Baroque palaces. Today these palaces, many of which serve as foreign embassies or government departments, form the most obvious architectural feature of the Lesser Quarter; a stroll around the area through quiet cobbled squares shaded by trees and lined with the statue-encrusted, pastel-painted façades of grandiose former dwellings provides the most tangible reminder of the wealth concentrated in the city through medieval commerce.

The buying and selling of the medieval merchants served as a backdrop to the everyday bustle of city markets that heaved under a constant throng of people, such as the one in the Old Town Square. When Charles IV founded the Nové Město (New Town) district in the late Middle Ages he purposely created vast market squares where various commodities would be traded. What is now Wenceslas Square was originally the horse market while Charles Square served as the cattle market and also sold fish, wheat, and charcoal. The seventeenth-century maps adorning the walls of the chateau at Mělník, north of Prague, indicate just how dominant these squares were in the urban geography of Prague at that time: they were huge rectangular spaces around which dwellings and churches pressed in tight huddles.

Commerce also dominated the day-to-day economic life of the tangle of streets around the Old Town Square, as it does to this day. The plots nowadays occupied by souvenir shops, banks, cafés, and bookshops were in the past home to skilled craftsmen such as bakers, butchers, and silversmiths. In the late Middle Ages these traders formed powerful guilds that set prices and organized production, earning their members jealously guarded privileges. Tailors were the first to be allowed to form a guild, in 1348; they were quickly followed by goldsmiths, butchers, and millers. In 1648 the butchers of the Old Town were given their own chapel in the Church of Sv. Jakub (St. James) in recognition of their influence in town affairs, and specifically because they had helped defend the city from the Swedish army right at the end of the Thirty Years War. It was the butchers who, soon after being given their own chapel, cut off the arm of a thief who had already (supposedly) been apprehended by the Madonna while trying to steal some jewels from the church's high altar; the thief's highly decomposed forearm, carbon-black and with its hand curled into something resembling a claw, has hung on a chain in the church ever since, and can be seen high up on the wall just inside the main entrance.

Aside from the great markets of the Old Town Square, Charles Square, and Wenceslas Square, other, smaller markets once thrived amidst the huddle of buildings in the Old and New Towns. Their former existence is recorded in the names of streets and squares such as Ovocný trh beside the Estates Theatre, which was once the fruit market. As late as 1930 the American writer Marcia Davenport experienced a visit to the coal market where by chance a goose market was also in full session, the geese "dressed and very much alive" and creating a "pandemonium of honks and hisses." But these markets, like the larger ones that filled the city's great squares, are now long gone. Although German-style Christmas markets set up in many city center squares in December, serving hot sausage and beer to those browsing in the winter chill for gifts, the only permanent open air city-center market still operating today is the one that spreads along Havelská in the Old Town. Like many others, this market was in the hands of German speakers for much of its long history, specializing in selling flowers and vegetables. Nowadays it still does a brisk trade in these products, but its position immediately off one of the main Old Town thoroughfares leading from the bottom end of Wenceslas Square to the Old Town Square ensures an ample trade from passing tourists, who browse along its single row of wooden stalls for knick-knacks, souvenirs, and wooden toys.

From Tuzex to Tesco

By the turn of the twentieth century the center of Prague was crammed with fashionable emporia selling clothes, shoes, consumer goods, and provisions. The commercial center had shifted to Wenceslas Square, long since divested of its role as a horse market, and the new tramway network brought shoppers here from the fast-growing suburbs by the thousand. In her novel *A Stricken Field* the American writer and journalist Martha Gellhorn, who knew Prague well during the 1930s, describes Wenceslas Square as a neon-lit arena of commerce whose most famous shop was the Bat'a shoe shop (which is still there today), the flagship store of the chain established by philanthropic shoemaker Tomáš Bat'a in the 1890s. According to Gellhorn, the front windows of the Bat'a shop were "clogged with homely inexpensive shoes," while the rest of the street was similarly busy with

> flower vendors on the corner, and the bookstores and the jewellers and the place where you got fine Czech stockings cheap, and the wonderful mayonnaise hors d'oeuvres on trays in the Automat windows, and the newspaper stalls with papers from everywhere, full of effort and excitement and fury, all of them loud in such various prints and languages... a pleasant, bustling street, and the people on it had always seemed contented, attending respectably to their business.

Over seventy years later Wenceslas Square is still much the same, with busy bookstores, restaurants, and kiosks selling the *Times*, the *International Herald Tribune*, the *Corriere della Sera*, and the *Frankfurter Allgemeine*. The neon is probably more garish, though, and the classy clothes stores that Gellhorn knew have now been replaced by branches of Marks & Spencer and Debenhams; trams cross the square these days but do not rumble up and down it, while the upper half of the square is cluttered with exhaust-belching traffic. But Gellhorn would have recognized many aspects of today's Wenceslas Square, particularly the *art nouveau pasáže*, gloomily lit but extravagantly decorated shopping arcades dating from the

1920s and 1930s lined with coffee shops, clothing boutiques, and movie theaters. The most famous of these arcades is the Lucerna pasáž, accessed from Wenceslas Square and roads leading off it (such as Štěpánská), which features ornate chandeliers, florid sculptural embellishments, and advertisements fashioned from mosaics of colored glass. At the bottom of Wenceslas Square is the marble-tiled Koruna pasáž, which seems even more of a throwback to the stylish and confident inter-war years of the Republic, although the huge Bontonland DVD and CD store in the basement reminds you that Prague's city-center shopping scene is nowadays not much different to that of any other European capital.

The *pasáže* were there during communist times but Debenhams and Marks & Spencer certainly were not. Shopping in communist Prague meant coping with rude assistants and precious little on the shelves—unless, of course, you were a party *apparatchik* or a tourist or diplomat with money to blow, in which case you could shop at one of the department stores, which were inevitably pale imitations of grand stores in western cities. The best-known of these was Dům Módy on Wenceslas Square, which had entire floors reserved for shopping by communist party loyalists. Another store, Máj (meaning "May"), built in the 1970s next to Narodní třída underground station, came complete with glass-covered external escalators—which was the only part of it that ordinary Czechs ever got to see. (One department store, the Swedish-built Kotva, has survived from communist days. Its exterior faces Náměstí Republiky and is still adorned with 1970s glass and aluminum panels set at various arty angles, while inside shoppers busy themselves buying everything from luggage to wine.)

Tuzex shops, like the old department stores, are another feature of the communist shopping scene in Prague that has long since bitten the dust. Once there were Tuzex shops in every large town in Czechoslovakia, selling imported goods such as cameras, clothes, and cosmetics for anyone with "Tuzex crowns," coupons issued in exchange for hard currency. Everyone from prostitutes (who had been paid in dollars or deutschmarks by their clients) to visiting tourists shopped with them, and goods purchased were not subject to export duty if they were taken out of the country; the shops were established in 1957 and were killed off by the currency reforms that followed the Velvet Revolution in 1989.

The British food retailing giant Tesco opened its first store in the Czech Republic in 1996 and now maintains 84 branches throughout the country. In Prague its presence is felt in the city center (with a big store next to Národní třída metro), in the suburbs (with a colossal outlet in Smíchov, beside Anděl metro), and also on the fringes of the city, where a number of out-of-town shopping centers are focused around a Tesco superstore. The biggest of these is at Letňany, situated beside a highway interchange in the northern fringes of Prague, a retail mall that takes its cue from similar shopping centers in North America or Western Europe: dozens of shops can be found in one hermetically sealed, chromium-plated retail paradise along with restaurants, movie theaters, water parks, and bowling alleys, the whole place surrounded by acres of windswept parking lots. The aim is to provide a whole day out for families under one roof.

How Czechs have adapted to this new kind of shopping experience is explored in detail in the 2004 film *Czech Dream*. Made by two students at the Prague film academy, it describes how the students established what appeared to be a new superstore in Letňany—but in fact all they built was a façade behind which there was nothing but fields. Advertising jingles were composed, posters went up around the city, and there was a publicity campaign on television and radio. Hundreds turned up at the opening of the new store, enticed by the prospect of huge savings—only to discover that they were the victim of an elaborately staged practical joke. Tesco was used as a model for what customers wanted from a superstore, and the film provides intriguing insights into how modern retailing depends on focus groups and shrewd marketing to draw in customers. While the film succeeds in highlighting the bogus emptiness of advertising, it is the phlegmatic and stoical response of those who were hoodwinked that provides for its most surprising scenes: these are clearly a people who have been lied to before and are used to having their hopes dashed. At the end of the film many would-be shoppers leave the Letňany site shaking their heads in sadness after realizing that they have been the victims of a hoax, wondering how their country could ever be taken seriously as a member of the European Union.

The trip out to Letňany requires a journey right to the very end of metro Line C and then a short bus ride from a shabby suburban terminal. Few tourists go there, or to the other out-of-town shopping centers on the fringes of the city as they are little different from what is available at home. But shops in the center of town do well out of visitors: shopping today is focused (as it has been for a century or more) on the "golden cross," the intersection of the busy streets Na příkopé, Národní třída, Na můstku, and Wenceslas Square, which is served by perpetually busy Můstek metro. A more exclusive shopping experience can be found four hundred yards to the north-west, along a street in the Old Town named Pařížská linking the Old Town Square and the Vltava. Appropriately for a street whose name translates as "Paris Avenue" this is where internationally recognized designer boutiques cluster, and consequently this is the place to be seen shopping, with Louis Vuitton, Hermes, and other designer labels all sporting their wares in the windows. Away from the department stores, the bookshops, and the boutiques much of what is on sale in the very center of Prague is limited to tourist staples such as Kafka T-shirts and reproduction marionettes, and it takes a hunt around the back streets of the Lesser Quarter or the Old Town to turn up anything more idiosyncratic: the selection here includes anything from Bohemian crystal and wooden toys to antiques, junk, CDs, records, and bric-a-brac. Formerly it was possible to buy large quantities of uniforms left behind by the Soviet army after its personnel left Czechoslovakia in 1990—leaving behind their gear "like an army pillaging in reverse," according to David Brierley in his novel *On Leaving a Prague Window*—but there is less military memorabilia around nowadays than there was twenty years ago. Instead the large expatriate community of English-speakers has ensured the flourishing of a number of English-language bookstores of which two of the best are Anagram and the Globe, the latter (situated on Pštrossova, near Karlovo náměstí metro) something of a social center hosting regular events in its trendy café.

Trade Fairs

Prague's hosting of numerous trade fairs is a hark back to its role as a mercantile center in the Middle Ages. It is also something of a Central European tradition, seen most particularly in Frankfurt with its famous annual book fair, and Hannover, with its huge *Messe* (trade fair) grounds. These events serve as a forum where manufacturers and buyers can meet and trade, eye up the competition, and discuss the latest trends in their fields.

The first Prague trade fairs were held in the district of Holešovice in 1891 as a side-show to the grander Prague Exhibition of that year. Today a strange collection of buildings still form the Výstaviště (Exhibition Grounds) situated around two miles north of the center of Prague. At the center of this complex, which includes an ugly ice hockey stadium, a funfair, fountains, and an aquarium, all built in widely different and incongruous styles, is the Průmyslový palác, a wrought-iron structure that looks like a flamboyant nineteenth-century railway terminus. For over a hundred years this building has hosted trade fairs within its cavernous central space: in 2011 the building welcomed industry insiders from the world of books, kitchen furniture, jewelry, bodybuilding machines, nursery supplies, toys, and buses, all of whom were sniffing out the latest trends and making contacts within their particular industry, as have trade fair participants for the last century or more. (The exhibitions tend not to be open to the public.)

In 1928 another venue was created for trade fairs to the south of here in the form of the Veletržní palác, a seven-story purpose-built exhibition hall; although part of this building is now Prague's main modern art gallery trade fairs are still held in a vast central space that is regarded as a masterpiece of functionalist architecture. In 1998 new exhibition grounds, the PVA, were opened at Letňany in the northern fringes of Prague, close to busy arterial roads, a small airfield, and the largest of Prague's out-of-town shopping malls. However, none of Prague's trade fair exhibition sites can compete with those in Brno, the Czech Republic's second city, which were opened in 1928 and today are nearly three times bigger than even the ones at Letňany.

11 | The Dark Side
Murder, Madness, and Persecution

Many say that it would be hard to find a city whose history is as strange, hidden, and melancholic as that of Prague. This, after all, is a city whose political destiny has been shaped by successive defenestrations and whose most eccentric monarch kept a pet lion and provided a livelihood to alchemists and magicians. It is also the city of the golem, an artificial man made from mud who ran amok in a famous Jewish legend, and of Kafka, with his tales of labyrinthine, oppressive, and unseen bureaucracies. This sense of other-worldliness is deep rooted: as long ago as the early sixteenth century it was examined by the writer Jan Bechyňka in an essay entitled *Praga Mystica*, and in 1973 an Italian professor of the Czech language, Angelo Maria Ripellino, published *Magic Prague* which told of the mystery and hidden fascination of a city that was then frozen into Cold War gloom behind the Iron Curtain. Shortly afterwards Patrick Leigh Fermor published his classic travel book *A Time of Gifts* in which he maintained that Prague is "not only one of the most beautiful places in the world, but also one of the strangest… There were moments when every [architectural] detail seemed the tip of a phalanx of inexplicable phantoms." To Leigh Fermor, the city was pervaded by a "slightly sinister feeling" brought on by a history dominated by "fear, pity, zeal, strife and pride… haunted by [the] enormous shadows [of the Slavic and Teutonic worlds]." In his novel *Utz* Bruce Chatwin takes up the baton, describing Prague, the home of the secretive porcelain collector Kaspar Utz, as "still the most mysterious of European cities, where the supernatural was always a possibility," and where the pervasive Czech view of life is "metaphysical."

Yet the Czech-American writer Peter Demetz, the author of *Prague in Black and Gold*, the most heartfelt and thorough biography of the city, condemns all this. "The new travel industry lovingly cherishes the mystical aura for market reasons… it is difficult to discover any sustained traces of Prague's alleged mysticism

Memorial to the children of Lidice, the village near Prague destroyed by
the Nazis as a reprisal for the murder of Reinhard Heydrich

in historical documents," he maintains. "Magic Prague," according to Demetz, is a myth propagated by British and American writers (and by Ripellino, who according to Demetz "should know better"), and given the aforementioned quotations from Chatwin and Leigh Fermor, perhaps he is right.

Two myth-spreaders specifically mentioned by Demetz are George Eliot, whose 1859 story *The Lifted Veil* concerns strange visions experienced by an ageing would-be English poet who travels to Prague, and the American author Francis Marion Crawford, whose 1890 novel *The Witch of Prague* is full of séances and occult happenings. This chapter, however, begs to contradict Demetz: the hidden and mystical history of Prague runs deep, and it can be found in the tales of alchemists and astrologers at the court of Rudolf II, in the long, dark history of Prague's Jewish community, in the violence inflicted on the people of Prague during the Nazi occupation, in the prostitutes who have touted for trade in the city since the Middle Ages and in the overgrown tracts of the city's vast and forbidding cemeteries.

Magicians and Alchemists

It is in the figure of Rudolf II, the Habsburg ruler of Bohemia from 1576 to 1611, that Prague's strangeness and melancholy is writ large. He is one of a select group of personalities that includes Franz Kafka, Jan Hus, Charles IV, and Václav Havel whose lives have been inseparably bound up with Prague. Yet Rudolf was not a native of the city. The future emperor was born and brought up in Madrid, a scion of the Spanish branch of the Habsburg family, and the heritage of his birthplace never left him: when the English envoy Sir Philip Sidney visited Rudolf in Vienna in 1577 he reported back to Queen Elizabeth I that the emperor was "extremely Spaniolated." Rudolf assumed the title of Holy Roman Emperor in 1576 and seven years later responded to the Turkish threat to Vienna by moving the imperial capital to Prague.

Much has been written by contemporaries and historians regarding the emperor's bizarre personality. According to R. J. W. Evans in *Rudolf II and his World* he was "attractive and repulsive by

Evans in *Rudolf II and his World* he was "attractive and repulsive by turns… a notorious patron of occult learning, who trod the paths of secret knowledge with an obsession bordering on madness." The madness was well documented and might have been inherited from Joanna the Mad, Rudolf's great grandmother on both his mother's and his father's side. It was also something of a Habsburg trait, arising from the tendency of members of the dynasty to marry their cousins.

Rudolf's madness revealed itself in his mania for collecting, in his rejection of the worldly and his immersion in the arcane, the obscure, and the supernatural. His hated brother (and eventual successor) Matthias catalogued his eccentricities in a set of revengeful propositions issued in Vienna in 1606 to a group of Austrian archdukes. According to Matthias, "his Majesty is interested only in wizards, alchemists, cabbalists, and the like, sparing no expense to find all kinds of treasures, learn secrets and use scandalous ways of harming his enemies… he also has a whole library of magic books. He strives all the time to eliminate God completely so that he may in future serve a different master." The image is much repeated. In Jiří Karásek ze Lvovic's 1916 drama *Král Rudolf* (*King Rudolf*) the monarch's mistress Gelchossa characterizes the monarch as a "dreamer whose nature is deception of the senses, a dreamer to whom only the stars and faraway voices speak," while his chamberlain complains that Rudolf only walks along corridors whose windows are walled up, and that "there is no sadder and lonelier creature on earth" than his master. In *Utz* Chatwin describes Rudolf as "a secretive bachelor, who spoke Italian to his mistresses, Spanish to his God, German to his courtiers, and Czech, seldom, to his rebellious peasants… as the crises of his reign intensified, [he imagined] himself a hermit in the mountains."

The emperor-hermit often preferred the company of animals to people: Rudolf kept a menagerie of strange creatures within the walls of Prague Castle and he died heartbroken three days after the death of his beloved pet lion (named Otakar). By the end of his life he had become so withdrawn from public life that rumors spread that he had died. By then Rudolf's fame was well-known throughout Europe: in 1607 he even appeared in a satirical novel, *Euphormionis Lusinini,* by the Scottish author John Scot Barclay, in which he is portrayed as a lonely figure sitting at a table surrounded by celestial globes and astrology books while his alchemy experiments bubble away in the background.

Soon after his arrival in Prague Rudolf initiated the building of a major new wing of the castle (much of which is closed to the public today and used for official business of the Czech president). There he established his *Kunstkammer,* his collection of bizarre artifacts that was the outcome of a lifetime of collecting. To Rudolf, the collection was a *theatrum mundi*—a theater of the world—that would allow him to unlock the secrets of nature. Reality, he believed, could be glimpsed only through the extreme, the strange, the odd, and the rare. His collection was extraordinarily diverse. Chatwin describes the emperor treasuring "his mandragoras, his basilisk, his bezoar stone, his unicorn cup, his gold-mounted coco-de-mer, his homunculus in alcohol, his nails from Noah's ark and the phial of dust from which God created Adam." Other items in Rudolf's hoard included bizarre foetuses, parrot feathers, corals, fossils, ancient stones with indecipherable markings, whales' teeth, rhino horns, and gallstones from the stomachs of animals that were thought to be an antidote to poison. There were more arcane items too, such as feathers from a phoenix and demons imprisoned in blocks of glass. One of his most prized possessions was a bowl of precious agate, found in 1204 by Crusaders during the conquest of Constantinople, which bore the name of Christ in the vein of the stone and was thought the be the Holy Grail itself.

Even more notorious than Rudolf's *Kunstkammer* collection was his obsession with alchemy. In Renaissance Europe astrology, astronomy, medicine, and alchemy blended into a proto-science that Rudolf embraced completely in his quest for a "one-ness" that would help him understand the universe. One of his most famous alchemists was an Englishman named Edward Kelley, who first came to Prague in 1589. Kelley's alchemical career had apparently begun when he had unearthed a red powder possessing the properties of the Philosopher's Stone from a bishop's grave in Glastonbury Abbey in the west of England; he had also found a book by St. Dunstan in the same grave that explained how to manufacture the powder. No wonder he caught the attention of Rudolf when he pitched up in Prague. Kelley set up home in a house on Charles Square in the New Town that is now known as the Fastův dům or "Faust House" because of the stories that later became attached to it. Alois Jirásek, in *Old Bohemian Tales*, recounts how the Devil once flew out of the house through a hole in the ceiling with the soul of Faust. Later a student sheltering in the house is tempted into the room by the discovery of silver coins; he disappears and when his friends come looking for him they find blood on the ceiling around the original hole and realize that the Devil has claimed a second victim from the house. The building, situated on the corner of U nemocnice and Vyšehradská on the square's southern side, was originally a Renaissance Palace but is now a fairly ordinary Baroque building (with a pharmacy on the ground floor, which at least provides some sort of continuity with Kelley's alchemical experiments).

It is likely, however, that Rudolf's main alchemical laboratories were up in the castle. The Powder Tower in the North Wall probably served as one, and more alchemists sweated over their furnaces in Rudolf's own private laboratory under the *Kunstkammer*. It is also said that the narrow street known as the Golden Lane (Zlatá ulička), situated behind St. Vitus' Cathedral, was home to yet more of Rudolf's alchemists, whose quest to turn base metal into gold gave the street its name. (Other stories suggest that it was simply where Rudolf's goldsmiths lived—and another maintains that it was so-named because of the urine that flowed in the streets during Rudolf's time, when the soldiers barracked here were provided with no access to toilets.) Nowadays Golden Lane is a row of pastel-colored cottages that house gift shops and fancy cafés, crammed with tourists looking for any lingering evidence of Renaissance Europe's most notorious scientific quest.

Edward Kelley was not the only purveyor of magic attracted to Rudolf's court. Even more notorious was another Englishman, John Dee, formerly court astrologer to Elizabeth I, who was Kelley's inseparable companion. They made an extraordinary pair as they wandered Europe, constantly on the run from persecution for heresy from both Church and state. Kelley had no ears: they had been cut off as punishment for his forging of a document he had been working on during the period he served as a notary in Worcester. He wore a black cap with flaps to hide the mutilation. Dee had a long white beard and was obsessed with symbols and numerical codes; already he had impressed credulous noblemen in castles throughout Germany and Poland with his incantations during a European tour that had been forced on him after he was stripped of his Cambridge fellowship. Both men arrived in Prague together from Cracow. Kelley claimed to Rudolf that he was able to communicate with angels in a language called Enochian, while Dee conversed with his own spirit, a young girl named Madimi, and prophesied to Rudolf that the monarch would defeat the Turks in battle. No wonder that it was rumored that Dee was an Elizabethan agent who had come to Prague to plot the downfall of Catholicism in Europe. Rudolf threw the pair out of Prague at least once, on the advice of his Catholic advisers, but Kelley for one later returned, and possibly died in Rudolf's custody.

The Danish astronomer Tycho Brahe was another Renaissance man of learning attracted to Rudolf's court. He was no charlatan but like Edward Kelley he had suffered bodily mutilation—in his case it was his nose that was missing rather than his ears, lopped off in Denmark during a duel. Brahe arrived in Prague in 1599 to serve as Rudolf's court astronomer. But he was interested in astrology and alchemy too, referring to the latter as "terrestrial astronomy." His advice, garnered from the movements of the heavens, was used by Rudolf in matters concerning everything from government appointments to military campaigns; quickly the stargazer earned the moniker "the evil spirit of the Emperor" as a result. Brahe famously died from a burst bladder after not wanting to get up to relieve himself during a banquet, and is buried in the Týn Church in the Old Town. He was succeeded by another great Renaissance astronomer, Johannes Kepler, whose *Astronomia Nova* of 1609 is dedicated to Rudolf. After crossing the Charles Bridge in a snowstorm one night, Kepler also wrote a short treatise entitled *The Six-Cornered Snowflake* in which he pondered the six-sided nature of snowflakes. It turned out to be one of the first attempts at a mathematical theory of the origin of organic and inorganic shapes, and its composition was just one more instance of Rudolf's Prague being the foremost center of learning and endeavor in late Renaissance Europe.

The Jewish Community

Much of Prague's darkest history revolves around the changing fortunes of the Jewish community. Jews often achieved positions of authority in the city during periods of religious tolerance—but these were interspersed with vicious pogroms and expulsions that culminated, of course, in the catastrophe of the Holocaust. In the late nineteenth century the author of a Baedeker guide to Prague maintained that the history of the city's Jews was "one uninterrupted narrative of tyranny, extortion, and blood on one side, and of long-suffering on the other," and that Charles IV, Rudolf II, and Joseph II had been the only rulers who protected what the author calls "the devoted race." The vilification of Prague's Jews was deeply rooted: in the twelfth century the chronicler Cosmas of Prague described with relish a Jew called Jacob whose hands made dirty everything he touched, who threw Christian holy relics into his cesspool and whose breath killed by poison. And yet in the time of Cosmas Prague was a vitally important center of Jewish teaching and thought, and later on in 1500 the city saw the establishment of the first Hebrew printing press in Central Europe.

The earliest recorded mass persecution and expulsion of Jews came in 1096 and coincided with the First Crusade. But the situation regarding Prague's Jewry during the late Middle Ages was never stable: in 1262, inspired by freedom offered to Jews in Hungary, Otakar II passed the *Statuta Judaeorum* granting the Jews of Prague his full protection. Moreover, he proclaimed the superstition that Jews used human blood for ritual purposes to be untrue, and forbade any disturbance of Jewish festivals and the desecration of cemeteries and synagogues. Seventy years later, in 1336, this tolerance turned to persecution when John of Luxembourg seized property from synagogues. The bloodiest and most wretched medieval pogrom occurred later in the same century, on April 18 1389, when Easter Day and the last day of the festival of Passover happened to coincide. According to later (and not particularly trustworthy) commentators, the pogrom was sparked off when a priest carrying the Host to a dying man was stopped in the streets by some Jews, whereupon a brawl erupted. Clerics delivered anti-Jewish sermons and a Christian mob ran riot through the ghetto. Three thousand inhabitants of Josefov were slaughtered and blood stains could be seen on the walls of the Old-New Synagogue for centuries after. The poet (later rabbi) Avigdor Kara survived the pogrom and his prayer is recited in the Old-New Synagogue at Yom Kippur to this day. He wrote that murdered Jews "were robbed of their garments, and in the dirt of streets the bloody corpses of babies, men young and old, boys and virgins, were wildly heaped together."

The precariousness of the Jews' position in Prague continued beyond the Middle Ages. In 1502, 1507, and again in 1509 the burghers of the Old Town insisted the Jews should be expelled. Vladislav II's response was to issue the Edict of Olomouc in 1510, which confirmed the ancient privileges of the Jewish community. In 1541 a Jewish man confessed under torture to starting the fire that engulfed much of the Lesser Quarter, and the Emperor Ferdinand I ordered the Jews should be expelled; yet the order was carried out half-heartedly, thanks to the prominence that Jews held in the business life of the city.

It was around this time that the darkest legend of Prague's Jewish community—that of the monster known as the golem—began to gain currency. The golem (Hebrew for "unformed matter") was a living servant fashioned from the mud of the Vltava by a rabbi named Judah Löw. The rabbi brought the creature to life by placing a *shem* (a tablet with a magic Hebrew inscription) across its forehead or under its tongue. The tablet was inscribed with the Hebrew word *emeth* or "Truth of God"; when the rabbi wished to destroy the golem he would strike out the first letter so *emeth* read *meth*, meaning "death." (The legend has clear origins in the creation of Adam by God: Genesis 2:7 recalls how "The Lord God formed man of dust from the ground, and breathed into his nostrils the breath of life; and man became a living being.") Alois Jirásek maintains that the golem was a tireless servant. "He fetched water, chopped wood, scrubbed and swept, and performed all sorts of hard labour," he wrote in *Old Bohemian Tales*. "At the same time he did not eat or drink, and never needed any rest."

One day the rabbi forgot to remove the tablet from the creature's mouth, whereupon it rampaged through the ghetto causing havoc. When the creature was cornered Rabbi Löw was forced to confront him. "The rabbi stretched forth his arms, and walked right up to him, staring him fixedly in the face," Jirásek wrote. "Golem stood still, staring at his master. The rabbi reached in Golem's mouth and with a single twist took out the magic plug. Golem toppled over, as though felled, and lay there powerless, as inert as a clay puppet. The onlookers, young and old, gave a shout of relief." The golem was then taken to the attic of a synagogue, and left to decay back into the mud from which he had been fashioned.

Not surprisingly the legend of the golem has provided fertile material for novelists and filmmakers through the ages, most notoriously in a novel of 1915 by Gustav Meyrink, which Peter Demetz dismisses as "a highly effective but kitschy melodrama," and which Meyrink himself turned into a silent film in 1920. In his novel Meyrink describes the Jewish ghetto as "a demonic underworld, a place of anguish... whose eeriness seems to have spread and led to paralysis."

Although the golem is fantasy, Rabbi Löw actually existed: he was born in 1520 in the German city of Worms, was Chief Rabbi of Moravia and then Bohemia, and is buried beneath the grandest tomb in the Old Jewish Cemetery. He was also steeped in the Jewish mystical tradition known as the Cabala. But many legends surround him, one of which was that he lived to be a hundred, and even Death himself was wary of approaching him as the old man studied at his scholarly books; Death had to resort to hiding in a rose bush that was offered to Löw by his unsuspecting granddaughter before finally bringing the rabbi into his clutches.

Changing fortunes continued to beset the Jewish community during the sixteenth, seventeenth, and eighteenth centuries. In 1567 the Emperor Maximilian confirmed the ancient privileges of Prague Jews and four years later visited Josefov with his wife, duly receiving a blessing from the Chief Rabbi. His successor Rudolf II appointed the mayor of Josefov, Mordecai Maisel, as his finance minister. By then the Jewish community of Prague numbered twelve thousand, a third of the population, and formed the largest Ashkenazi Jewish community in the world and the third largest Jewish population in Europe after Amsterdam and Thessaloniki.

Two hundred years later the old persecution was back. In 1744 the Empress Maria Theresa blamed the Jews for the conduct of her disastrous war on Prussia and expelled them; true to historical form the Jews were invited back four years later after shopkeepers complained about the lack of custom and diplomatic pressure was exerted by Britain and the Netherlands. Finally, in 1781, the Emperor Joseph II opened the gates of the ghetto, allowing Jews free passage throughout the city—which is why Prague's Jewish Quarter is named Josefov in his honor. Yet Joseph also ordered Prague's Czech-speaking Jews to Germanize their names and banned Hebrew and Yiddish in business transactions. In Joseph II's time most Prague Jews were German-speakers, as they had been in the Middle Ages, but the immigration into the city of many Jews from other parts of Bohemia meant that many spoke Czech by 1938—the year that catastrophe struck.

The Holocaust in Prague

In the year of the Nazi annexation of Czechoslovakia 56,000 Jews were living in Prague. Many, fearing the worst, immediately left the city for Britain or America—or Palestine. Those who were left faced an increasing tide of persecution. Initially Jewish property was confiscated and Jews were excluded from practicing in law and medicine and working for the civil service; later on they were barred from receiving education, from using public transport, and from attending restaurants and theaters. From September 1941 the Nazis forced Jews to wear a yellow Star of David with the inscription *Jude*, and stamped a yellow "J" on their identity cards.

According to Jiří Weil in his novel *Mendelssohn is on the Roof*, the persecution was coordinated by the Central Bureau, a division of the Security Police that took its orders direct from Berlin, and occupied a villa on the edge of Prague with its own garden and garage. "People crossed the street to avoid [the villa]," he wrote,

> [where] death was lurking in hundreds of documents, in file folders, in property deeds, in photographs of houses, villas, and factories. It dwelled in signatures and symbols, abbreviations, and initials, rubber stamps and graphs. It was neat and orderly, perfectly typed on fine paper, on file cards of various colours. It was everywhere and it filled the house with fear.

But Weil also described the grimly comic side of the persecution: in his novel an SS officer is ordered to remove a statue of Mendelssohn from the roof of the Rudolfinum concert hall on the grounds that the composer was Jewish. But the bemused officer does not know which one of the statues is of Mendelssohn, until he thinks to "go round the statues again and look carefully at their noses. Whichever one has the biggest nose, that's the Jew." In the end the statue that he ordered to be pulled down was that of the Nazis' most esteemed composer, Wagner.

The deportations began in October 1939. The year before, Goebbels had written in his diary that Hitler was of the opinion that "the Jews have eventually to be removed from the whole of Germany. The first cities to be made Jew-free are Berlin, Vienna and Prague." The first deportations were to the Lublin region of south-eastern Poland, where the sealed trains were met personally by Adolf Eichmann. The leading Nazi told those who had survived the journey that they had to build houses if they wanted shelter and dig wells if they wanted water free of typhus. In subsequent months transports left Prague for the newly-established ghettoes in Polish cities such as Łódź, where Jews suffered terrible deprivations and disease. Jiří Weil, who survived the Holocaust in Prague by hiding in an apartment owned by a niece of Franz

Kafka, described the transports in another of his novels, *Life with a Star*.

> Travelling with fifty kilos to an unknown destination was the order of the day. Nobody wanted to guess what happened at the end of this journey. They tried to talk about preparations instead— money sewn into the linings of jackets, jars of lard disguised as marmalade, fake toothpaste tubes with money hidden in them… I heard how on the way east jewellery was traded for lemons. It was good to have a sleeping bag, a metal bowl for food, a long-sleeved sweater, ski boots, vitamin pills, a pocket knife with various instruments, a razor, and a supply of razor blades. And one's luggage should be prepared in advance, ready any time of day or night, because sometimes transports were called up suddenly… when a train departed for the fortress town or for the east, nobody noticed, because it was an entirely ordinary freight train moving slowly along the tracks with closed cars that might have carried cement or gun mounts.

The "fortress town" Weil mentions was Terezín in northern Bohemia, a former Habsburg army town that the Nazis transformed into a ghetto for the displaced Jews of Prague. At the end of 1941 three thousand Czechs were evicted from Terezín and the place was made ready to receive its first consignment of Jews. Over the next three years 140,000 Jews passed through Theresienstadt, as the Nazis renamed the place; they were brought here from all over Czechoslovakia before being sent on to the extermination camps in Poland. The conditions were appalling: around 34,000 died in the camp due to hunger and disease. In *Life with a Star* Weil likened the place to a grim circus where "one had to walk a tightrope without a safety net and jump over high hurdles… But it was a town that lay in the middle of the country. A river flowed through it and meadows were close by. The wind would bring the fragrance of apricots in bloom… It was a good thing to enter with hope, since there was the possibility that some would stay in the town, if only to tend the dead."

In 1943 the Nazis allowed inspectors from the Red Cross to visit Terezín and cynically beautified the place beforehand, allowing the inspectors to experience a week of cultural events that even included opera performances. The visit was portrayed afterwards in an extraordinarily warped propaganda film entitled *Hitler Gives the Jews a Town*.

Terezín today is a grim ghost of a town. Its enormous main square—actually, the old parade ground for the Habsburg army—is lined with blank-walled and lifeless buildings, while walls of dour red-brick fortifications lie at the end of every street. An excellent clutch of museums has been established across the town in recent years, while to the south of it, over the River Ohře, is a military prison dating from the 1780s that was later used by the Gestapo for housing political prisoners. Its cells are open to visitors (Gavrilo Princip, who assassinated the Archduke Franz Ferdinand in 1914, was its most famous prisoner) and its requisitioning by the Nazis can be seen in the grim endorsement *Arbeit macht frei* above one of the archways. Access to the former prison is through a huge cemetery where 2,300 victims of the prison's brutal regime are buried. Memorials are scattered through Terezín too, with a huge concrete menorah overlooking the site of the former crematoria, and a stark memorial by the quiet reach of the Ohře where the ashes of 22,000 people who died in the ghetto were thrown.

Back in Prague, a wing of the Pinkas Synagogue in Josefov displays drawings made by the children in Terezín—often simple pencil representations of life in stark dormitories on plank beds, but also pictures of trees, animals, and trains that any child might draw. That the Pinkas Synagogue itself, together with all the other monuments of Josefov, was not destroyed in the war is thanks to a strange twist of fate, namely that Hitler himself specifically asked for the district to be preserved as a "monument to an extinct race." The novelist Jiří Weil was a director of the museum and wrote in *Mendelssohn on the Roof* that it "collected confiscated objects from the defunct synagogues, everything to do with religious ceremonies. It was to be a storehouse of trophies commemorating the Reich's victory over its enemy... The Museum was supposed to be a victory memorial, for the objects displayed here belonged to a race scheduled for annihilation. Nothing would remain of that race but these dead things."

The ancient cemetery, the synagogues, and the Town Hall of the district remain to this day, picked over daily by tourists and reverentially looked after by present-day members of the slowly recovering Jewish community of Prague. The memory of those who perished in the Holocaust is ever-present: the Pinkas Synagogue, originally built for a powerful local Jewish family in the 1530s, houses a memorial to all 77,297 Czech Jews who were murdered. The name of each victim is carved on the wall—and the names cover a huge area, with around half coming from Prague.

Compounding the tragedy of the Holocaust was the anti-Semitism of the early communist era. Artur London, Czechoslovak Deputy Minister of Foreign Affairs at that time, wrote of the "naked anti-Semitism, purely Hitlerite" of the Gottwald years (1948-53) and of the notorious purge of Communist Party officials in 1952. "As soon as a new name would come up [in investigations of government members] the investigator demanded to know whether the person was Jewish," he went on. (The main defendant, Rudolf Slánský, was charged under the name Salzmann.) The anti-Semitism spread from Moscow and according to Arkadiai Vaksberg in his book *Stalin and the Jews*, it stemmed from the allegiance of the newly-founded state of Israel towards the United States and its turning away from Moscow. As a result, Stalinist propaganda promoted the notion that "the Jews had perverted the ideas of Stalin's socialist paradise instead of promoting it." Although the situation eased somewhat as the communist period progressed it was not until after the Velvet Revolution that the Jewish community of Prague was able to fully begin the process of healing itself after the tragedy of Holocaust.

The Heydrich Assassination and the Tragedy of Lidice

In Prague's humdrum northern suburb of Libeň, close to the spread of dockyards and industry along the banks of the River Vltava, traffic on a busy highway called V Holešovičkách screeches past a tall, stark, rust-colored monument that towers above the road. The monument takes the form of a giant Toblerone box standing on its end, and is utterly unadorned except for the three figures that surmount it cast from bronze and gazing over the highway with arms outstretched as if frozen in a moment of freefall from its summit. As it sweeps northeastwards V Holešovičkách soon becomes Liberecká, the main road linking Prague with northern Bohemia and Dresden; it is one of the busiest traffic arteries into and out of the city. Yards away vehicles on a minor road called Zenklova slow as they round a bend and then feed into the city-bound streams of traffic tearing along V Holešovičkách. And it is the slowing of the traffic that is important, for it was at this exact spot that Reinhard Heydrich's car had to slow down on the morning of 27 May 1942, as the Acting Reichsprotektor of Nazi-occupied Bohemia and Moravia was being driven from his country home to his offices in Prague Castle.

Heydrich was one of the most ruthless and ambitious men in the Third Reich. He had been appointed by Hitler to turn the occupied Czech lands into a police state run by the SS, and was seen by many as the Führer's eventual successor. But Heydrich's ambitions were to remain unfulfilled. As the driver of his Mercedes slowed to negotiate the tight bend, a man casually standing by the side of the road walked in front of the slowing car, drew a Sten gun from under his jacket, pointed it at Heydrich, and pulled the trigger. The gun's mechanism jammed. As the would-be assassin wrestled desperately with the weapon a second man leapt forward and lobbed a grenade at the car. The grenade exploded under the rear fender, sending shards of metal into Heydrich's body but leaving him conscious enough to draw a pistol and fire at the assassins who were escaping from the scene by bicycle. Heydrich had only enough energy to fire a couple of rounds. Within moments the most powerful man in Bohemia and Moravia had collapsed by the side of the road, onlookers pressing round him from all sides. A truck that had been delivering floor polish was commandeered to take Heydrich to hospital, where he was operated on immediately. Although at first his injuries did not seem life-threatening, over the course of the next few days the fragments of upholstery embedded in Heydrich's spleen caused an infection to spread in his blood, and nine days after his admission to the Bulovka hospital, he was dead from septicaemia.

A state funeral—the most grotesquely elaborate ever staged by the Third Reich—was held in both Prague Castle and in the Reichschancellery in Berlin, where Hitler and Himmler both spoke in glowing terms of the man who had sown fear throughout the Czech lands. Hitler called Heydrich "One of the best National Socialists… the man with the iron heart," while Himmler eulogized that Heydrich's example was "an ideal always to be emulated, but perhaps never again to be achieved" before maintaining that "it is our holy duty to avenge him and to destroy the enemies of our Fatherland." That revenge came very soon afterwards. It was swift and brutal and took the form of one of the most wanton acts of barbarism in the history of the Second World War—and the wounds from it remain very raw to this day.

Hitler's man in Prague—only 37 years old when he was appointed Acting Reichsprotektor—had been born to a Catholic family in Halle an der Saale near Leipzig. Heydrich's father was a minor-league composer of operas and chamber music named Bruno; his maternal grandfather had founded the Dresden Conservatory. (A childhood home shaped by music resulted in Reinhard Tristan Heydrich—the middle name honors one of Wagner's most famous operatic heroes—becoming a proficient violinist: the day before his assassination he was present at a concert of his father's chamber music given in Prague Castle to open the Spring Music Festival.)

Photographs of Heydrich as a child show a fair-haired, blue-eyed youth, an Aryan poster-boy for the Nazi movement, and Heydrich retained his charismatic good looks into adulthood. His rise through the ranks of the Nazi party was swift; he had already proved himself an ultra-efficient administrator and schemer by the time Himmler appointed him head of the Gestapo in 1934. In fact Himmler transformed his protégé into a cult figure within the SS, whose cadets plastered the walls of their notorious training school in Bad Tölz with photographs of this virtual Nazi demi-god. By the outbreak of war Heydrich, with his vast collection of obsessively cross-referenced index cards, had gained control of the entire

Nazi security apparatus, and it was his skills as an organizer that prompted his appointment in the occupied Czech lands.

In Prague Heydrich imposed a totalitarian rule that was ruthless, murderous, impulsive, and arbitrary; it was exacted through the deliberate spread of terror and by the annihilation of anyone perceived to be an enemy of the state. Hand in hand with this came a vicious and unswerving racism that possibly stemmed from persistent rumors that Heydrich had Jewish ancestry. The Acting Reichsprotektor made it his stated aim to rid Bohemia and Moravia of Jews and murder, deport or "Germanize" those Czechs who remained—after they had worked for the Germans by manufacturing arms in Bohemia's industrial plants. (During Heydrich's brief rule the city of Plzeň became the largest German manufacturing center outside the Ruhr, the Škoda works there churning out tanks and weaponry for the Nazi war machine.) There is a compelling portrayal of Heydrich—the ambitious schemer, the meticulous bureaucrat, the vicious racist, the full-blooded Nazi—in *Mendelssohn is on the Roof* by Jiří Weil, in which the Reichsprotektor's thoughts are often presented in the first person. "The air was bad here and it penetrated even the closed windows," Heydrich thinks to himself as he is being driven through the industrial suburbs of Prague.

> Smells of sulphur, smoke and sweat. Right now [the Nazis] needed these subhumans to slave in the factories for the Reich. But some day this too would be cleaned out. Great squares would be created here, and tree-lined boulevards. The robots would be herded into reservations behind barbed wire to live in their own dirt under the gaze of guards in towers with machine guns trained on them, to be there for as long as the Reich needed them.

Heydrich's vision of a rebuilt and Germanized Prague, articulated here by Weil, was a monumental one: whole sections of the city would be razed to allow colossal new buildings to rise, as they would in other great cities of the Reich such as Berlin and Linz. Among Heydrich's specific plans were a grand new opera house and the construction of a fast autobahn link to Berlin.

At the same time as Heydrich was consolidating his cruel regime in Prague the former Czechoslovak president Edvard Beneš was forming a government-in-exile in England. Its base at first was a house in Gwendolen Road in the south London suburb of Putney; the blitz later forced Beneš to move his operations to a requisitioned country house at Aston Abbotts near Aylesbury in Buckinghamshire. Beneš was a somewhat aloof man, intelligent and coldly logical, who used to remind his biographer Compton Mackenzie of a "well-preened chaffinch." As news of Heydrich's murderous rule began to reach England, Beneš resolved to have him assassinated. The ex-president's motives went beyond simple retaliation for Heydrich's wanton barbarism: Beneš wanted to give the Allies cause to recognize Czechoslovak independence when the war was over, and he knew that the coup of a political assassination would surely indicate that Czechoslovak forces had contributed to the war effort in a major way. In addition, Beneš wanted to prove that it was his government-in-exile in England, and not the rival exiled government led by Klement Gottwald in Moscow, that was the true bearer of Czechoslovak sovereignty during the occupation.

Beneš instructed Colonel František Moravec, the head of Czechoslovak intelligence in London, to plan the dangerous and complex task of assassinating Heydrich. Moravec worked alongside two highly secretive British agencies, the security service SIS (later MI6), who had given him a house on Rosendale Road in West Dulwich from which to conduct his operations, and the clandestine unit known as SOE (Special Operations Executive), formed by Churchill to fight the Nazis in highly secretive and dangerous missions deep within occupied territory. Once the logistics of the assassination had been worked out, Moravec approached two soldiers based in Britain with Czechoslovak fighting units with the task of carrying it out. They were 29-year-old Josef Gabčík and 28-year-old Jan Kubiš, and when they agreed Moravec sent them on an intensive training course at a commando school in Mallaig in the Scottish Highlands to get them physically and psychologically fit for the daring assault. When their training was over both men were parachuted into the countryside near Prague on the night of

December 28, 1941, the time of year dictated by the long hours of darkness that allowed an RAF Halifax aircraft to fly to Bohemia and back from Tangmere airfield near London.

On landing, the two parachutists linked up with members of the Czechoslovak resistance and with other parachutists dropped on the same night but in different locations who carried radio and communications equipment. Operation Anthropoid was under way. All Gabčík and Kubiš had to do now was to go to ground, to keep in contact with London and with the Resistance and find a suitable time and location to kill Heydrich.

The eventual date of May 27—some six months after the parachute drop—was chosen because by then time seemed to be running out. Heydrich was clearly destined for higher tasks than running the Protectorate and Gabčík and Kubiš feared that he was about to be posted elsewhere. Weeks of surveillance work by the two men indicated that Heydrich always took the same route to Prague Castle every morning from Panenské Břežany, his home in a requisitioned country house some eleven miles (eighteen kilometers) outside Prague. Heydrich was confident of his mastery over his subjugated people, and wanted to show Czechs that he did not fear them: he dispensed with bodyguards and armored cars and did not alter the routes he took around the city. On the morning of his assassination he was even traveling in his Mercedes with the roof down. His arrogance was his undoing: armor plating in the car would have prevented the fragments of horsehair upholstery from the car seats from entering his body. And it was the single piece of good fortune that came the assassins' way; a maelstrom of bad luck had previously beset the operation including the initial parachute drop that left the men far from their intended destination and the jammed Sten gun, which probably malfunctioned because its mechanism was filled with grass, which Gabčik had used to conceal the weapon in his briefcase (his choice was not so unusual: citizens of Prague often picked grass in parks and used it to feed goats they kept in their gardens).

Following the assassination, as Heydrich lay bleeding beside his car and shocked onlookers gazed at the scene from a halted tram, Gabčik and Kubiš escaped on bicycles to a pre-arranged safe house, convinced that their assassination attempt had failed. Within hours the biggest man hunt ever staged by the Nazis was raging around them: its opening salvo was the seizure of the assassins' bicycles and their display in the window of the Bat'a shoe shop in Wenceslas Square. Moving from house to house, and under continuous threat of denunciation by a cowed population, the assassins were eventually hunted down to the New Town's Church of St. Cyril and St. Methodius, where the lay preacher Vladimir Petřek had agreed to shelter the parachutists and their accomplices in the crypt.

It was one of the assassins' own number, Karel Čurda, who revealed their hideout—in an effort, he was to claim later, to end the Nazis' vicious series of reprisals for the killing of Heydrich. The end came in a six-hour battle fought during the early hours of June 18, during which the seven parachutists holed up in the crypt repelled a series of assaults by Waffen SS and Gestapo troops. In the end, the Germans resorted to calling the Prague fire brigade and forcing them to use one of their fire trucks to flood the crypt with water. The hoses were shoved through the window of the crypt that opened onto Resslova, the wide street that links Charles Square with the riverbank. Still the men inside fought back as the water rose around them. But as the Germans prepared to blow open the main entrance of the crypt with explosives, they heard a series of single shots from inside: the parachutists had killed themselves with their last bullets rather than lay themselves open to capture. Karel Čurda was then led inside the church to identify the bodies of his former comrades for the benefit of the Gestapo officials.

Hitler felt personally affronted by the assassination of Heydrich. The Acting Reichsprotektor had been one of his key lieutenants, and like Heydrich Hitler viewed the Czechs with vicious, racially-driven contempt. Retaliation was swift and ferocious: on June 10, the day after Heydrich's burial in the Invalidenfriedhof military cemetery in Berlin (the exact location of the grave is uncertain as the planned tomb over it was never constructed), the village of Lidice, situated in the countryside north-west of Prague, was chosen as the place where brutal, systematic retaliation would be realized. The choice was essentially a random one: some partisans associated with the raid had sheltered there, and the name of the village was found on a document belonging to one of the parachutists. Nothing more than these flimsy pieces of "evidence" linked Lidice with the assassination. But during a morning of brutality and butchery the likes of which were seen nowhere else in Nazi-occupied Europe, all 173 male inhabitants of Lidice aged fifteen and over were executed row by row outside the farm in the center of the village. The women were rounded up and sent to Ravensbrück concentration camp, and the children were sent to other camps or handed over to German-speaking families to be "Aryanized." The village was then burned to the ground, its more substantial buildings such as the seventeenth-century church detonated with explosives. The next day thirty Jews from the ghetto at Theresienstadt were forced at gunpoint to bury the victims, working non-stop for thirty-six hours. Over the next few days residents of the village who were not present on that fateful morning were shot in military barracks in Prague. Yet even then the Nazis had not finished. Three days after the shoot-out in the church crypt in Prague the inhabitants of another village, Ležáky, were murdered after it was found that one of the agents had concealed radio equipment there, while "Operation Reinhard" saw several hundred Jews shot in Sachsenhausen concentration camp and arrested in Berlin, and three thousand deported from Prague and Theresienstadt direct to newly-established death camps in Poland.

Nazi reprisals for the death of Heydrich were widely covered and reviled abroad, particularly in Britain and the United States. Typical of comments were those of Frank Knox, the US Secretary of the Navy, who proclaimed, "If future generations ask what we are fighting for in this war we will tell them the story of Lidice." In 1943, the year after the assassination, three separate films were made about the tragedy, two in America and one in Britain, which helped to spread the story of Lidice as an example of Nazi barbarity in occupied Europe. The oddest of these was *The Silent Village*, directed by the British documentary maker Humphrey Jennings, in which the story of Lidice is transposed onto a small mining village in Wales, with miners playing the role of villagers— emphasizing Lidice's own former role as a mining village. The film was a joint production of the Crown Film Unit and the London-based Czechoslovak Ministry of Foreign Affairs.

In the same year came *Hitler's Madmen*, an American film directed by the German-born director Douglas Sirk and based on a poem by Edna St. Vincent Millay, and *Hangmen Also Die*, directed by the Austrian-born director Fritz Lang and adapted for the screen in part by the German playwright Bertolt Brecht. The three films were the first of many made in subsequent decades that told the story of the Heydrich assassination and its terrible aftermath. The tragedy is still inspiring filmmakers today: in the summer of 2011 a new Czech-made film about the Lidice tragedy was showing in Prague cinemas, entitled simple *Lidice*. It focuses on the tragedy of the villagers rather than on the Heydrich's assassins, who have been the subject of many of the other films such as the 1975 Hollywood account, *Operation Daybreak*, which covers the Lidice tragedy only sketchily.

Those terrible events of 1942 cast a long shadow that still hangs over Prague and Central Bohemia to this day. Monuments and memorials abound, in the Czech Republic, in England, and all over the world. The monument overlooking the place where the assassination took place is perhaps the least visited. The scene it overlooks has changed much in seventy years. The highway has been widened, curling feeder roads have virtually obliterated the junction as it originally looked, buildings have been extended and tram lines have been removed. (The street Zenklova was known as Kirchmayerova třída in Heydrich's time.) In the center of Prague the crypt of the Church of St. Cyril and St. Methodius is home to a somber memorial to the seven men who died there in the final shoot-out, their busts lined up beside the coffin-sized niches in the walls in which they sought refuge. Another memorial plaque is fixed to the outside wall of the church above the window through which the fire hoses were shoved; the masonry around the window is still visibly scarred by deep craters from Nazi bullets. In a park in the slightly unlikely setting of Royal Leamington Spa in the English Midlands is a memorial to the parachutists stationed near the town in the form of a mushroom-shaped fountain resembling an open parachute, and a tiny garden that includes stands of heather taken from Lidice.

It is, of course, in Lidice itself that reminders of events are the most poignant. Of the 203 Lidice women who were sent to concentration camps some 143 returned, while only seventeen out of 105 children returned to Lidice after the war, the rest having perished in the death camp at Chelmno. Today the fold in the hills where Lidice stood is sprinkled with monuments: the outline of the church is picked out in ankle-high remains, a high wooden cross watches over the communal graves and sculptures in bronze and stone stand where the houses once were. The foundation walls of the farm in the center of the village where the men were shot have been preserved too.

Among the sculptures and memorials is an intensely moving work by Marie Vchytilova overlooking part of the site that depicts a group of Lidice children, resigned and haggard, the younger ones with faces raised as if something might save them, the older ones downcast as if they know their fate is sealed. Fresh flowers and children's toys sit by the base of the monument; new ones are added each day. Overlooking the fold in the hills—it can hardly be called a valley—is the memorial and museum to the Lidice tragedy, with splashing fountains and arcaded walkways and one of Europe's largest rose gardens. The museum includes film footage the Nazis took of the destruction of the village, and a picture of every single Lidice resident who perished—some of whom were young enough to still be alive today, were it not for the atrocity of the destruction of their village.

Immediately after the war tens of thousands of people gathered at the site to create a new village, and the red roofs of the houses of the modern village of Lidice overlook the memorial site from a discreet distance, full of all the normal things like bus stops and convenience stores and schools. (This is part of Prague's commuter belt countryside now: buses take only thirty minutes to reach Dejvická station on the Prague metro, and fifteen minutes to reach the city's airport.) It is now one of dozens of villages named "Lidice" all over the world in commemoration of the tragedy.

The impact of Lidice still reverberates down the decades to this day. In March 2011 it was reported that Heider Heydrich, the 76-year-old son of the Nazi Reichsprotektor, wanted to be involved in the restoration of the chateau at Panenské Břežany where, on the morning of May 27, 1942, as an eight-year-old boy, he had bid his father goodbye for the last time. Heider is mostly known through the famous photograph taken at the gates of Prague Castle on June 7, 1942, where he stands suited and blond-haired beside Heinrich Himmler, waiting for his father's coffin to be brought out of the castle by a ceremonial troop of SS officers after the body had lain in state for three days. No wonder the news of Heider Heydrich's interest in Panenské Březány sparked consternation throughout the Czech Republic—even if, as he claims, he wants to restore the house so that it can be turned into a museum and memorial to the Czech resistance. Czechs of a more phlegmatic disposition commented that the son should not be judged for his father's crimes, but with the wound of the Lidice tragedy still very raw even after seventy years, it remains to be seen how far Heydrich Jr. will progress with his plans to become involved with his father's former property.

The End of Nazi Rule

Heydrich's successor as Nazi overlord in Bohemia and Moravia was his former deputy, Karl Hermann Frank. Under Frank's leadership the regime of terror intensified and the rounding up, imprisonment, and execution of those suspected of anti-Nazi activity became part of the daily routine of life in Prague. From 1942 until the end of the war a thousand Czechs were beheaded by the busy guillotine in Pankrác prison, with lists of those condemned to die pinned up all over the city on a weekly basis. In *Mendelssohn is on the Roof* Weil writes of the "Red decrees with long lists of names [that] hung on every street corner... Everyone could read the red decrees. They never said what it was that people had done, nor was it necessary, for the punishment for everything was death." In her memoir *Prague Farewell* Heda Margolius Kovály, who had escaped from one of the notorious death marches at the end of the war, also recalls the "pink posters plastered onto the walls with long columns listing the names of people who had been executed for 'crimes against the Reich.' Often, there were three or four people with the same surname: whole families murdered for trying to help someone like me." Those who dared, and who had access to radios, listened to the broadcasts given by Edvard Beneš from London. But the population, cowed by the terror, the daily executions, and by the response of the Nazis to the death of Heydrich, did not fight back with the subterfuge that Beneš hoped for. By the closing months of the war Nazi rule of Bohemia and Moravia was as secure as ever, with the factories at Plzeň building the V1 and V2 rockets that rained so much fear on the population of suburban London.

Jaroslav Stránský, the Czechoslovak Justice Minister in Exile, warned that the Nazis in Prague would be like "cornered rats" as the end of the war neared. And he was right: by the spring of 1945 an air of panic and desperation permeated the city as both the American Third Army, approaching Prague from the west under the command of General Patton, and two Soviet armies, liberating Czechoslovakia in stages from the east, set their sights on freeing the city from Nazi rule. Yet the Nazis planned that the fighting would last until the bitter end—and beyond. Himmler's "werewolf" divisions, squads of ideologically driven Nazis who would carry on the fighting after Germany's imminent defeat, were formed throughout Bohemia during the early months of 1945 and readied themselves for the final showdown. When Patton's eastward march was abruptly halted at Plzeň on specific instruction from Eisenhower, it soon became clear, however, that the Nazis' final battle would be with the Red Army rather than the Americans. Patton was incensed by the instruction from the supreme Allied commander, but Eisenhower wanted to honor the demarcation line agreed with the Soviets at Yalta, and he was also mindful of avoiding casualties so that American troops in Europe could be sent to fight the war in the Pacific that was still raging. So Patton was forced to relinquish the triumph of liberating the Czech capital to his Soviet counterpart Marshal Malinovski, and by the time of Hitler's suicide on April 30 Malinovsky's Ukrainian Second Front was poised to enter Prague—the only city in central Europe (apart from Berlin) still in German hands.

As the Red Army closed in, Beneš left London and based himself in Soviet-occupied Slovakia, ready to move into Prague once the final battle was won. "When the day comes," Beneš cried, "our nation will take up the old battle cry again: Cut them! Beat them! Save nobody! Everyone has to find a useful weapon to hit the nearest German!" With the inspirational words of Beneš sounding over the airwaves and the Soviet artillery already firing on German positions on its outskirts, the Czech resistance launched an uprising in the capital on May 5. Its opening salvo saw resistance leaders seize the radio station behind the National Museum and transmit a call to arms: *Smrt Němcům! Smrt všem okupantům!* came the battle cry: "Death to the Germans! Death to all occupiers!" Barricades appeared in the streets as more partisans gained control of the city's loudspeaker system (controlled from the Old Town Hall) and by the evening of the first day of the uprising much of the city was in Czech hands. The SS garrison retreated to their headquarters in the law faculty of Charles University and made plans to raze the city to the ground.

Mayhem and violence erupted as Soviet tanks finally entered the city. Rogue SS units looted and massacred at will, gouging out eyes and ripping open bodies. Hastily formed Czech brigades did the same, lynching Germans and burning some of them alive in the streets. In the confusion it was a renegade Russian force, the anti-communist Russian National Liberation Army or KONR, that finally brought order and discipline to the Czech troops engaged in the uprising. Initially these renegade Russians had fought with the Nazis against their invading comrades. But at the last minute their leader Andrei Vlassov swapped sides and joined forces with the Czech leaders of the uprising—only to have his men fired on by the Soviets, who still considered KONR forces traitors of the motherland. Vlassov's men found themselves vastly outnumbered and began streaming out of Prague westwards towards Plzeň, where they hoped to find refuge in the zone of American occupation. Behind them the fighting raged on: on May 7, the day when the Wehrmacht high command unconditionally surrendered to the Allies in Reims, SS units in Prague announced that they would fight on to the death. Another four days of vicious conflict raged through the city and it was not until May 11, with Nazi forces in full retreat and 800,000 German prisoners captured by the Soviets, that the guns in Prague finally fell silent.

Yet the Czechs believed that worse was to come, in the form of Nazi werewolf divisions that were now poised to unleash a new wave of terror. Czech resistance forces quickly organized themselves into two divisions, the RG (Revoluční Garda) and the special police (SNB or Sbor národní bezpečnosti), who roamed the streets, beating up and torturing any suspected werewolf members. In the lawless and chaotic atmosphere a mood of paranoia and retribution swept across the city. Tens of thousands of German-speakers were rounded up and imprisoned in the sports stadia on Letná plain above the Vltava, where they were forced to take part in macabre running races that saw hundreds killed in volleys of machine gun fire. Eventually the Germans who remained alive were moved to the former ghetto in Terezín (in advance of their eventual deportation to Germany), and order was restored. The werewolf threat did not materialize and Czechs breathed a collective sigh of relief: the occupation of Prague was over, and with it the last shots of the war in Europe.

The uprising that ended the occupation of Prague left 1,694 Czechs dead and some three thousand wounded. But the city itself emerged remarkably unscathed. The most obvious damage was to part of the Old Town Hall, which had been set on fire as an act of defiance by SS units. Thankfully the conflagration did not spread, but much of the building was destroyed and after the war the damaged part was demolished and a patch of grass now covers the spot where it stood. In *The Unbearable Lightness of Being* Milan Kundera suggests that Czechs had an inferiority complex compared to residents of Warsaw or Dresden as their city had not suffered as much—so the Old Town Hall "was left in ruins so that no Pole or German could accuse them [Praguers] of having suffered less than their share." The Old Town Hall carries another visible reminder of the battle for Prague: embedded into the wall of the building is an urn containing earth from the Dukla Pass where 80,000 Soviet and

Czech troops lost their lives during the westward Soviet push into occupied Czechoslovakia. The blood of Soviet troops was also shed in the streets of Prague during the uprising, and the dead from this final campaign of the war were eventually buried in the Soviet war cemetery in the suburb of Žižkov, where to this day a tiny Russian Orthodox church nestles amidst rows of fastidiously tended graves. (British and Commonwealth war graves can be seen in a neighboring part of the same cemetery.)

In the months after the war, as the cemeteries were filling and reconstructed buildings were rising from the rubble, the campaign against traitors began: Karel Čurda, the parachutist who had betrayed the hiding place of the Heydrich assassins, was hanged in 1946, as was Heydrich's successor Karl Hermann Frank, who was executed in Pankrác Prison in front of a crowd of over five thousand people, some of whom were survivors of the Lidice tragedy. Andrei Vlassov, the leader of the pro-Nazi battalion of Russian troops in Prague who had joined forces with the Czech resistance right at the last moment nonetheless suffered the grim indignity of being hanged with piano wire in a Moscow prison.

Perhaps the oddest memorial from the final days of the Second World War was a tank donated by the Soviets that not only commemorated their liberation of Prague but also served as a reminder of their political mastery over Czechoslovakia after the war. It originally stood on a plinth in a square in the Smíchov district of south-west Prague. The number on the side of the tank was 23, which belonged to the army division commanded by General Lelyushenko, the first to enter the city. After forty years of sitting on its plinth the tank was painted pink by the artist David Černý soon after the Velvet Revolution. Černý also painted a large phallic finger on its top—distinctly unhelpful at a time when Czechoslovakia was trying to negotiate the withdrawal of Soviet forces. Later still the label "Trojský kůn" or "Trojan Horse" was hung around the tank as a sardonic comment on Soviet involvement in Czechoslovakia. It was eventually removed in 1991, and nowadays not a trace of the tank, nor the concrete podium on which it sat, remains.

Communist Prague

The communist coup of February 1948—the "glorious February" as it was christened by the victors—merely exchanged one totalitarian regime ruling from Prague Castle for another. Soon after Klement Gottwald's seizure of power the cells in Pankrác Prison, once crammed with supposed enemies of the Nazi regime, began to fill with anti-communist dissidents. In *Utz* Bruce Chatwin describes the numbing climate of fear that pervaded Prague during those first months and years of communist rule. "It was almost impossible for ordinary citizens not to fall into one or other of the categories—bourgeois nationalist, traitor to the Party, cosmopolitan, Zionist, black-marketeer—that would land them in prison, or worse," he wrote. Those enemies of the state were interrogated in a grim building on Bartolomějská in the Old Town, which became home to the Státní bezpečnost (or StB), the feared secret police force who gained a reputation for being every bit as ruthless as the Stasi in neighboring East Germany.

During the Nazi occupation the same building had been used by the Gestapo for silencing dissenters: now the new terror machine simply took over the abandoned spaces of the old one. The workings of the StB first manifested themselves in the show trials of Milada Horáková, and then Rudolf Slánský and the former Politburo members (see Chapter 4). Away from politics the people of post-war Prague lived in a city where seediness and poverty co-existed with a *Mitteleuropa* sophistication that was a hangover from the great flourishing of culture in the 1920s and 1930s. The travel writer Jan Morris came to the city in the 1950s and saw the seedy side. In her 1997 book *Fifty Years of Europe: an Album* she remembered it as a place of "degraded servility, where everything seemed to smell of sausages. The slogans of Communist piety nagged from every hoarding, the drab emblems of State management were on every corner shop... Prague had seemed to me the most oppressive of the Communist capitals of Eastern Europe." In his memoir *Turnaround*, however, the film director Miloš Forman recalls a different side to Prague: he was struck by the "streetcars, beautiful women, foreigners, taxis, sports stars, the sleek black limos of the politicians... the classy prostitutes, cafés and theatres" that filled the city when he came here in the early 1950s to train as a theater director.

Initially the 1948 coup received considerable support from Czechs. Heda Margolius Kovály writes in *Prague Farewell*: "For many people in Czechoslovakia after the war, the Communist Revolution was just another attempt to find the way home, to fight their way back to humanity... a 'national road to socialism' was basic to our thinking... Marshal Tito, who had introduced a special brand of Communism in Yugoslavia, was still a hero at the time, and following his example in our own country seemed a real possibility." The Czechs, she maintained, would not be building socialism in a "backward society" but "in an industrially advanced country, with an intelligent, well-educated population."

Twenty years later the brutal crushing of the Prague Spring saw any remaining support for the socialist system drain away like snowmelt in April. As the Soviet tanks rumbled through the Old Town Square the Hus memorial was draped in black, as if the people of Prague wanted to spare the eyes of the fabled Czech revolutionary from the insult that had been inflicted on his countrymen. The events of that hot and often bloody August have been described extensively by writers, not least by the émigré novelist Milan Kundera who set much of *The Unbearable Lightness of Being* during the invasion. "Hatred for the Russians drugged people like alcohol," Kundera wrote. "It was a drunken carnival of hate." One character in his novel, a professional photographer named Tereza, takes "pictures of tanks, of threatening fists, of houses destroyed, of corpses covered with bloodstained red and white and blue Czech flags, of young men on motorcycles racing full speed around the tanks, waving Czech flags on long staffs." When Soviet tanks under the command of Marshal Grechko fired at the National Museum in the mistaken belief that it was the parliament building people joked grimly that the museum with its bullet scars was a recent work by "El Grechko."

Five months after the invasion, on January 16, 1969, a 21-year-old student at Charles University named Jan Palach set himself on fire at the top end of Wenceslas Square in protest against the continuing presence of Soviet troops in Czechoslovakia. His extraordinary act of courage and defiance made headlines around the world; when he died three days later Palach became an instant emblem of the Soviet stranglehold on his country. He was buried in the vast Olšanské hřbitovy in Prague's eastern suburbs, the largest cemetery in the city, and his grave immediately began to attract a steady stream of pilgrims. Alarmed at Palach's transformation into a political martyr, the authorities had the body reburied in his home town, but the stream of pilgrims kept on flowing—although now the pilgrims simply visited the grave of the woman who had been buried in the plot in the cemetery where Palach's body had originally lain.

That tenaciousness, that desire to make some sort of stand against the occupying forces, however seemingly futile, stemmed directly from the anger and disgust at the Soviet invasion that was felt by virtually every Czech; and over fifty years on from Palach's death another self-immolation—that of a Tunisian street vendor in Sidi Bouzid named Mohamed Bouazizi—is associated with yet another springtime of democracy, namely the Arab Spring, whose most revered martyr is as emblematic today in a Middle Eastern world slowly shedding itself of dictators as Palach's was in an Eastern Europe dominated by Moscow.

By the time of Jan Palach's martyrdom a period of so-called "normalization" had been imposed on Czechoslovakia by the ruling Communist Party. Legislation passed in 1969 creating the framework for this post-Dubček period of systematic repression denied defendants the right to a fair hearing in political trials and prepared the way for purges within bodies such as schools, universities, theaters, and the government. Over the next two years three quarters of a million people lost their jobs, were demoted, or were actively discriminated against. Included among them were scores of diplomats, government officials, journalists, and trade unionists, while thousands of teachers were dismissed or disqualified from teaching political subjects. Over one hundred writers (including Václav Havel) were placed on a blacklist and had their works removed from libraries and bookstores. By the end of 1969 Dubček's reform movement was a distant memory and the scene was set for the cold, grim, faceless years of the 1970s and 1980s, when a more or less permanent state of emergency was imposed throughout Czechoslovakia.

The regime began to extend its political tentacles into almost every aspect of life, from the planning of housing developments to the organization of television schedules. The party and the state, virtually inseparable and indistinguishable from one another, acted as employer, teacher, policeman, social worker, judge, and jailer, and retained monopolistic control of industrial and agricultural production. (There was no toleration of private business as there was in neighboring Hungary.) The system perpetuated itself through the dispensing of rewards to the party faithful, who then had no reason to press for any reforms. "Society became polarized between those who wielded power—a power that had become self-sufficient and independent of the will of the people—and all other mortals," Heda Margolius Kovály maintained. That power was wielded specifically through the crushing of dissent. In this regard the StB resorted to violence and imprisonment when necessary. But this was actually rare. "Only a few people were subjected to real violence," Ivan Klíma noted in his novel *No Saints or Angels*. "Just enough to ensure that everyone else lived in fear and submitted to control and humiliation as the only possible form of existence."

Instead of being imprisoned or being subjected to violence it was more usual for dissident writers and academics to be silenced by being forced to work in menial jobs, typically as janitors or boiler attendants, a fate that is covered in more detail in Chapter 5. Dissidents often had no idea which of their transgressions would land them in trouble and which would be apparently ignored (though actually continually monitored) by the authorities. And the memory of Jan Palach continued to inspire many during this time: Václav Havel received his last prison sentence in January 1989 for trying to lay flowers at the memorial site on Wenceslas Square where Palach had set fire to himself.

Ordinary people—the "community of the defeated," as they were christened by the novelist Ivan Klíma—were not necessarily required to believe in the system under which they were forced to live: they just had to keep their heads down and, outwardly at least, profess loyalty to it. Failings in the system were glossed over or hidden behind a welter of clichés and official jargon. "Socialism is a young, dynamic social order," maintained Gustav Husák, Czechoslovak president from 1975 to 1989. "It is seeking and testing in its stride ways of making even better use of its advantages, of organizing and controlling social development most efficiently."

Others saw through the hyperbole. "Prague wits [defined] socialism as a system designed to successfully resolve problems that could never arise under any other political system," wrote Heda Margolius Kovály. Around Husák the country trudged into the 1980s in a state of political torpor. By some measures the economy thrived: within the Eastern Bloc the standard of living in Czechoslovakia was second only to East Germany, consumer goods were relatively easy to obtain and industrial and agricultural production remained strong. (A 1968 tourist publication, *Your Guide to Czechoslovakia* by Nina Nelson, indicated, however, that British visitors to Prague would find chocolate five times dearer than back home.) But many people had to hold down two jobs to make ends meet. The pallbearers who carry Kaspar Utz's coffin in Chatwin's *Utz*, for example, worked night shifts at a rubber factory and day shifts at the undertakers— and their fate was shared by thousands of real rather than fictional Czechoslovak citizens. According to Kovály, "Almost everyone was moonlighting for an often semi-legal second income and put in an appearance at his regular place of work just to rest up."

Small-scale corruption was endemic. The authorities turned a blind eye to minor bending of the rules such as trading on the black market or the use of bribes to obtain goods and services, if they felt that rule-benders could in turn be recruited as informants. Among the network of informers were the female concierges in Prague's apartment blocks whose "lives became an intoxicating orgy of spying and informing, which sometimes involved outright blackmail," according to Kovály, who later maintains that that "lying and play acting became a way of life; indifference and apathy became its essence." In his New Year's Address of 1990 the newly inaugurated President Havel touched on similar themes, talking of the "devastated moral environment" caused by four decades of living under the old system. "We are all morally sick," he went on, "because we all got used to saying one thing and thinking another." The intense paranoia instilled in the political establishment during the show trials of the 1950s remained present up until the final days of communism. During the 1980s the belfry of St. Nicholas' Church in Prague's Lesser Quarter was used to observe the comings and goings from foreign embassies, while StB agents kept a watch over the riverside apartment where Václav Havel lived from the top of the sixteenth-century Šitek water tower.

Any visitors to communist Prague could treat themselves to the rose-tinted view of the socialist system propagated by three museums scattered across the capital, namely the Police Museum, the Gottwald Museum, and the Lenin Museum. Bizarrely these places managed to remain open while other museums and galleries slowly moldered away or closed their doors to visitors for long periods of "renovation." The exhibits in the Muzeum Policie included Bob Dylan records and printed editions of Václav Havel's plays that had been seized from dissidents, along with a stuffed German shepherd dog named Brek that once patrolled Czechoslovakia's iron curtain borders with Germany and Austria. The museum is still in existence today—housed, as it always has been, in a former Augustinian monastery overlooking the Botič valley and Vyšehrad—but these days its exhibits provide a mundane account of the type of crime that police in any European country have to deal with, from drug trafficking and forgery to road traffic offences and street robbery.

The museum dedicated to Klement Gottwald, the mastermind of the 1948 communist coup, could be visited on Rytířská near the Estates Theatre, where the great man's pipes and overcoats were placed on reverential display together with rows of photos of him with Stalin and Communist Party cronies. Time and changing political fashions did not seem to dim the reputation of this vile and cynical man. As late as 1988, the official Olympia guide to Prague was referring to Gottwald as "an outstanding representative of the Communist Party of Czechoslovakia"—but two years and one Velvet Revolution later the museum was no more and the building that housed it had become a bank. Finally, the Lenin Museum was situated close to the main railway station at Hybernská 7, where in 1912 Vladimir Ilych had chaired a conference that led to the formation of the Russian Bolshevist Party. After the Velvet Revolution this building became the headquarters of the Social Democratic Party and for a time a terse note in the window informed people that the nearest Lenin museum was now in Moscow.

These days, instead of the Lenin and Gottwald Museums there is a Museum of Communism in the Old Town and a smaller museum dedicated to the operations of the Soviet KGB in the Lesser Quarter. The latter, along a quiet backstreet off Nerudova, is full of antiquated listening and bugging equipment crammed into rooms whose walls are lined with photos of KGB officials taken during the crushing of the 1968 reform movement, in which the subjects look for all the world as if they are taking a weekend break in Prague. The much larger and hugely popular Museum of Communism has become one of the unmissable museums of Prague. Here are mock-ups of a communist-era classroom (with poems on the wall extolling the virtues of tractors), a food shop (with only two types of canned food on its virtually empty shelves), and an interrogation room (with ancient typewriter and appropriately sinister-looking angle-poise lamp). Propaganda posters line the walls while in a separate room an extraordinary film of the demonstrations in Prague in November 1989 is shown on a giant television screen. The museum was established in 2002 by an American business entrepreneur who scoured junk shops and internet auction sites to obtain the memorabilia, and then engaged the formerly exiled Czechoslovak documentary film maker Jan Kaplan to design the exhibition spaces. The museum occupies a prime site on Na příkopě, a few steps away from the Můstek end of Wenceslas Square, and its position could not be more ironic: it is situated above a McDonald's and in the same building as a casino.

Apart from the communist kitsch on sale in some markets and on display in these museums, there are few reminders in Prague that hark back to the period between 1948 and 1989. Understandably the mood of the city since the Velvet Revolution has been to move on and not spend too long looking back. But here and there acknowledgment of those days can be seen in the form of subdued memorials. In the Lesser Quarter, at the foot of Petřín hill, statues of naked men cast from bronze and standing on a series of steps form the city's official memorial to the victims of communism; the bodies become progressively disintegrated as the steps rise, with the uppermost man lacking the side of his head and much of his torso. The statues are self-portraits by the memorial's sculptor, Olbram Zubek, who has placed an inscription below it that recounts the toll of victims of the regime: the 205,486 who were imprisoned, the 248 who were executed, the 4,500 who died in prison, the 327 who were killed trying to cross the border, the 170,938 who emigrated.

Six hundred and fifty yards (six hundred meters) to the east of the memorial, across the river in the Old Town, Bartolomějská, where the secret police maintained their headquarters, retains an eerily silent quality to it: a block away from busy Národní and the National Theatre, it is devoid of bars and souvenir shops and is one of the few streets in the Old Town almost completely shunned by tourists. One of the cold, austere buildings lining the street is the current headquarters of the Prague police, while next door the old StB building has been turned into a swish hotel, the Unitas, which betrays few traces of its former role apart from a collection of photos along the walls of a plushly carpeted corridor; the cell in which Václav Havel was once imprisoned, P6, is usually kept locked, a change from the days when this place was a cheap hostel run by Franciscan nuns and the room could be slept in by guests. But the memory of Jan Palach remains as tangible as it always has been. In 1990 his body was reburied in the Olšanské hřbitovy and his grave once again attracts a stream of pilgrims: it now serves as a shrine both to his memory and to all the victims of communism, as does the memorial site on Wenceslas Square marking the spot of his sacrifice, which is also marked with flowers and photographs.

The Cemeteries

It is in its cemeteries that Prague's strangeness, its sense of melancholy and mystery, come most poignantly and most acutely to the fore. By far the most expansive is the Olšanské hřbitovy, whose perimeter wall stretches for half a mile (nearly a kilometer) along Vinohradská, the main traffic artery heading east out of the city. In the seventeenth century the land here lay well beyond the edge of Prague and provided an ideal location for the burial of plague victims, the first of whom were interred in 1680. Since then over 37,000 people have been buried here, creating a city of the dead within the living metropolis whose suburbs steadily grew up around it. Streets are laid out between the rows of elaborate tombs, mausoleums, and more modest headstones; maps are provided at each of the entrances where bunches of flowers can also be purchased from ramshackle shops; and below the thick covering of trees, the few mourners the cemetery draws are often paying their respects to distant ancestors they never knew. Disorientation among the crisscrossing streets is all too easy, and an intended brief visit can, after a few twists and turns, become a melancholic amble along endless streets lined with all-too-similar funerary monuments that have become overgrown by foliage and are crumbling into the dust with age.

Immediately to the east of the Olšanské cemetery are two more cemeteries, the Nový židovský hřbitov and the Vojenský hřbitov, respectively the New Jewish Cemetery and the Military Cemetery. The walls of the adjacent burial grounds stretch for more than a quarter mile (five hundred meters) along Jana Želivského, which itself separates these two cemeteries from the Olšanské cemetery—the three spaces together creating a somber necropolis that dominates this eastern district of Prague. The former cemetery has been active since the 1890s and is chronologically the third Jewish burial ground in Prague, opened when the first two—the Old Jewish Cemetery in the city center, and then a replacement one in Žižkov—had filled up. It was intended to last a hundred years and on its opening had room for a hundred thousand graves. But thousands of the intended incumbents died in the Holocaust, and today, over a hundred and twenty years since its foundation, the cemetery has large empty tracts of the land within its walls, abandoned to straggling clumps of trees or the odd surprising patch of overgrown meadow. At its entrance is an ornate Ritual Hall, built in neo-Renaissance style and intended for cleansing the bodies of the recently deceased, and a quarter mile (four

hundred meters) away is the grave many visitors have come specifically to see: that of Franz Kafka. The writer's parents are buried in the
same plot and there is a memorial to his sisters, both of whom died
in Nazi concentration camps. Many other prominent members of the
Jewish community are laid to rest in the cemetery, often in ornate
tombs in functionalist or *art nouveau* styles decorated with Hebrew
inscriptions and emblems such as lions.

Next door, a major part of the Military Cemetery is taken up
by the graves of Soviet soldiers who died during the liberation of
Prague in 1945. A whitewashed, onion-domed Orthodox church
stands amidst the graves, while in another part of the cemetery a
monument portraying an armed solider beneath a hammer and
sickle emblem overlooks neat rows of graves marked by reliefs of
rifles and communist stars. Not far away is a small plot in the care
of the Commonwealth War Graves commission, where British and
Commonwealth prisoners of war who died in captivity in Central
Europe are buried under rather less bombastic headstones.

Many capital cities honor their dead artists, writers, and intellectuals within their great cathedrals but this was never a tradition in
Bohemia. There are exceptions such as the Danish astronomer Tycho
Brahe, a major figure in the court of Rudolf II who is buried in the
Týn Church in the Old Town. But the lowly status of the Czech
language within this part of the Habsburg and then Austrian Empire
assured that few important cultural figures were allowed to flourish
before the nineteenth century. When at last a national reawakening
came its instigators—writers, artists, composers, and architects—had
to be afforded a suitable burial place. This came in the form of the
Vyšehradský hřbitov, which was founded within the grounds of the
old Vyšehrad fortress, south of the center of Prague. At the time of
the cemetery's foundation the site of the old fortress was occupied
by an abandoned Austrian barracks; but the hill had an extraordinary
mythical significance, for it was here that Libuše had supposedly
founded the city of Prague some thousand years before. Its significance continued into the twentieth century: on November 17, 1989
a crowd fifty thousand strong assembled here to march on Wenceslas
Square in the first days of the Velvet Revolution.

The grave of the Romantic poet Karel Hynek Mácha, the creator of modern Czech poetry, was the focus for the leaders of the march. His name is unfamiliar to most non-Czechs, as are those of most of the other composers, writers, intellectuals, and artists whose carefully tended graves lie along paved avenues behind the high perimeter walls. (The odd sports star has also earned a place here.) Words such as *sochař* (sculptor) or *umělec* (artist) adorn the headstones, and the inscription *zasloužilý* (honored) frequently appears. Many headstones were designed by leading sculptors such as František Bílek, and Karel Hladik even designed his own headstone whose title is *Cathedral*.

The graves that foreigners come to see are those of the composer Antonín Dvořák, whose fabulously fussy tombstone is inscribed with a mosaic of gold tiles that spell out his surname, and Bedřich Smetana, whose grave is a simpler affair consisting of a plain stele topped by a pyramid. The tomb of the writer Karel Čapek (see Chapter 5) is marked by an open book carved from stone—and by the occasional model robot left there by a well-wishers. At the cemetery's eastern end is the Slavín monument, built between 1889 and 1893, a grandiose affair reached by flights of stone steps and topped by a statue representing genius. This fancy necropolis is adorned with commemorative plaques for yet more artists including the sculptor Ladislav Šaloun (who designed many of the tombstones in the main part of the cemetery), the architect Josef Gočár, who was a leading figure in the Cubist movement, and Alfons Mucha, who introduced the *art nouveau* style to Prague's art scene and was, with Gočar, one of the leading figures in the great flowering of art and culture in the opening years of the twentieth century.

The Vyšehrad and Olšanské cemeteries are all situated beyond the center of Prague, creating splashes of green at the edge of standard tourist-oriented maps of the city. But Prague's most famous cemetery lies right in the heart of the city, between the Old Town Square and the banks of the Vltava. The Old Jewish Cemetery (Starý židovský hřbitov) is also the oldest and smallest of Prague's cemeteries and the burial ground that is most replete with legends. This extraordinary necropolis was founded in the fifteenth century at the heart of Josefov, the city's Jewish quarter. The earliest grave is that of the poet Avigdor Karo, who died in 1439. Over the next three and a half centuries—the last grave dates from 1787—over a hundred thousand people were buried within this tiny, tight-walled space. To pack all the bodies in, burials were often twelve deep, with the space between bodies fixed at the width of six palms. Despite the jumbled profusion of stone stelae at the surface, most of the older burials are unmarked, the wooden gravestones having long rotted into the earth. The oldest graves are marked with oblong or square tombstone made from stone, while later burials from the end of the sixteenth century are marked with tombstones fashioned from white and red marble, marking the zenith of the fortunes of the Jewish community in Prague.

The collection of haphazard headstones shaded amidst trees and sealed in from the city behind a high wall now forms one of the most remarkable monuments in all of Prague—and one that has caught the attention of many writers. In his novel *Prague Orgy* Philip Roth describes the cemetery as a "jumble of crooked, eroded markers that looks less like a place of eternal rest than something a cyclone has torn apart," before remarking that the site covers an area that "in New York would be a small parking lot." In Bruce Chatwin's *Utz* the cemetery is lit on a late summer's evening by "sunbeams, falling through sycamores" that land "on mossy tombstones, which headed one upon the other, resembled seaweed-covered rocks at low tide." Headstones on the graves include not only the names of the deceased and the date of their death but also a note of their moral qualities, their education and their scholarship; professions are often represented in the form of symbols (scissors for tailors, books for scholars, surgical instruments for doctors), while carvings of lions, deer, wolves, bears, and fishes symbolize family names (a dove for Jonah, a goose for Gans, a mouse for Maisel). Only one tomb marks the burial place of a woman: she was named Hendel Bassevi and was noted for the charity and support she provided for the poor who lived in the ghetto in the seventeenth century.

The most popular tomb is that of Rabbi Löw, according to legend the creator of the golem; his tomb is decorated with reliefs of grapes (the symbol of fertility) and surmounted by a realistic-looking pine cone. Believers, often clad in the long black cloaks that are the hallmark of Hassidic Jews, still like to gather here and place small pebbles on the ornate tombstone, a tradition dating back to the time of the Exodus when rocks were used to mark graves in the desert. The pebbles often secure small slips of paper on which are inscribed wishes or prayers. To one side of the cemetery, lining the eastern wall of the Klausen Synagogue, is a mound marking the burial ground for still-born babies or those who died within a month of their birth, to whom different burial rules applied; it is the most poignant part of a cemetery whose silence, sealed off from the rest of the city, and best experienced in the early morning or at dusk, exemplifies to best effect all the secrecy and the melancholy of Prague.

Today's Hidden City

Many argue that Prague's melancholy and mystery have, in the past two decades, been subsumed beneath its post-communist commercial drive and its swarms of tourists. This may be the case, but commercialism and visitors have also resulted in a new "hidden" side to the city that has only been visible since 1990. Pickpockets prey on newly-arrived and unsuspecting tourists in the metro and particularly on the number 22 tram, which plies the "classic" route from the New Town through the Lesser Quarter to the castle. Another scam is illegal money changing on the street resulting in tourists being ripped off by the sleight-of-hand of con merchants. Such black market transactions are rare these days, although plenty of public notices in multiple languages still warn against them.

Away from tourist scams, the most hidden aspect of Prague—and by late evening it is not so hidden—is the flourishing sex industry. There have always been prostitutes in Prague—in 1372 the eccentric religious reformer Jan Milíč acquired a house in the Old Town that offered a Christian haven to prostitutes—and now there are thought to be over two hundred brothels, which for health and other reasons were eventually licensed by the government in 2010. The red light district centers on Perlova, just south-west of Můstek, but strip clubs and dingy "Herna" bars, full of slot machines and low life, can also be found in the streets off Wenceslas Square.

The situation is far more tucked away now than it was in the years immediately following the Velvet Revolution, when an unrestrained free market and a new influx of visitors brought thousands of prostitutes to Prague, and a flourishing pornography industry too meant that poorly produced soft-core porn magazines were available at seemingly every corner. These were presumably examples of the "smouldering layers of sleaze and squalor" that according to Jan Morris flooded Prague in the wake of the collapse of the Soviet Empire. One notoriously squalid aspect of Prague at this time was the scourge of underage prostitution. In 1994 this uncomfortable topic was highlighted by a remarkable documentary film entitled *Not Angels but Angels*, which largely consists of teenage male prostitutes talking about their experiences in the wretched clubs that festered in those days around the city's main railway station. (The film, though controversial, was passed for legal video and cinema distribution in the UK by the British Board of Film Classification.) The teenagers in the film talk frankly about their experiences; most have been driven to prostitution through economic necessity and come across as real people, driven by poverty into making their choices. The film makes for compelling if deeply unsettling viewing, underscored as it is by lush snatches of Mozart as the camera pans over familiarly beautiful views of Prague.

Five years after the film was made the sexual exploitation of children in Prague received international attention when Chris Denning, a former BBC Radio 1 DJ, was given a prison sentence of four and a half years by a Prague court following a conviction for sex offences involving underage boys. In the last decade, however, the police have thankfully cracked down on this particular aspect of Prague's sex industry, which seems now to be on a much more even footing; these days the red light district even maintains its own website; although by late evening on most days all the metro stations in central Prague have at least a couple of women plying for trade.

For over a hundred years a visit to Karlštejn Castle, deep in the Bohemian countryside, has been a popular way of escaping the bustle of the city

12 | **Surroundings**
The Hinterland

Much of the Bohemian countryside, particularly to the west and south of Prague, is a beguiling blend of dark forests and rolling hills cut through by ribbons of shimmering water and scattered with villages of red-roofed houses that cluster in hollows around onion-domed churches. The pace of life is visibly slower here than in Prague: villagers still maintain small-holdings, drivers out from the city can become stuck behind donkey carts while the typical one-story dwellings that form the heart of these settlements nestle in a time warp, gently peeling in the sun during the hot summers. The illusion can occasionally be shattered by the sudden appearance of clunking industrial plants from the communist period or by the shabby tenement blocks that blight the outskirts of most medium-sized towns; but not even these can spoil Bohemia's reputation as one of the most beautiful areas of Central Europe. Much of the province is deserted, too. Its population, much reduced by war and by the expulsion of German-speakers in the late 1940s, is scattered thinly over a beautiful landscape redolent in legend and history, and it is amidst these landscapes that many Czechs maintain weekend homes and where many foreign visitors to Prague come to seek a glimpse of provincial Bohemia.

Castles, Countryside, and Spa Towns
The chief magnet for coach party excursions from the capital is Karlštejn Castle, a picturesque fortress that glowers splendidly from a wooded hillside some thirty kilometers south-west of Prague. With its steep grey roofs, lines of crenulated walls that drape themselves fluidly across the hillside, conical turrets and whitewashed walls punctuated by arrow-slit windows, this is everyone's idea of a perfect medieval castle, and the setting overlooking a craggy gorge cut by a swift-flowing river only adds to the appeal. But Karlštejn

is no great secret. Even in communist days the place was one of the few locations in Czechoslovakia that could be described as "touristy" and these days visiting Karlštejn is something of an endurance test, with the road leading up through the village to the castle a continuous ribbon of souvenir shops, Bohemian crystal showrooms, and busy food stalls, while the castle itself is populated by guides and musicians dressed in cod-medieval outfits spouting their spiel in eight different languages. There is even a waxworks museum, an exhibition of Christmas nativity cribs that were once so popular in Central Europe, and a nineteen-hole golf course, to keep visitors amused once they have tired of the castle. Road access to the village from Prague is quick and easy, and the pretty country station that serves the village of Karlštejn, with its manned signal box and cream-colored nineteenth-century buildings, is a stop for the "City Elefant" double-decker commuter trains that glide down the valley of the Berounka river twice an hour, taking forty minutes to cover the distance from the main railway station in the capital. In summer each train disgorges another load of tourists who wend their way through the village and up to the castle in a straggly line; and yet the castle is genuinely set in deep countryside, and for those willing to give the place more time there is a multitude of marked paths that can guide walkers into the silent forests surrounding it. A quarter of a million people visit Karlštejn each year but with the use of a hiking map getting away from the crowds is surprisingly easy.

Karlštejn was built on the orders of Charles IV, the builder of the Charles Bridge and the founder of St. Vitus' Cathedral, as a repository for the Bohemian crown jewels and for the various saintly relics that Charles had accumulated over the course of his devoutly Christian life. These included part of the whip used in Christ's passion, the bones of Abraham, Isaac, and Jacob (a gift from the Emperor of Byzantium), Aaron's staff, one of Mary Magdalene's breasts, and the tablecloth used in the last supper. The designer of the castle was Matthias of Arras, brought over from France by Charles to create a building that was to serve as both a country retreat and a fortified strong box. Matthias fulfilled his brief well: the castle successfully withstood onslaughts by the Hussites and the

Swedes, while the ascetic Charles often used to hole himself up in his apartments in the castle for days on end, with important business matters being passed to him on parchments through the hole in the wall of a tiny chapel.

The castle's current appearance, inside and out, owes as much to the neo-Gothic restoration carried out by Joseph Mocker in the nineteenth century as it does to Charles and his architect. Mocker successfully prettified the exterior of the building but could do little with the sullen heaviness of the interior. The guided tours of the place are disappointing, and take the form of a dutiful shuffle through barely-furnished rooms lined with dour paintings and other artifacts ("this is a replica of Charles' bed—the original is in Vienna; this is a replica of the crown jewels of Bohemia—the originals are in Prague"). The most remarkable space inside the building is Charles' own Chapel of the Holy Cross, whose twenty-foot- (six-meter-) thick walls are inlaid with over two thousand precious stones, and which is lined with beautiful fourteenth-century panel paintings by Charles' favorite artist, Master Theodoric. But the chapel can only be seen by those who book a longer tour in advance in Prague rather than just turn up at the castle. In the end, though, it is the castle's spectacular setting in a radiant Bohemian landscape that leaves the greatest impression, rather than anything that can be seen inside it.

The castle—or to be more precise the heavily restored Renaissance château—at Konopiště, some thirty miles (fifty kilometers) to the southeast of Prague, is in many ways a more satisfying destination than Karlštejn. The whitewashed and turreted *Schloss* has its origins in the Middle Ages but nowadays its appearance dates from extensive and successive bouts of rebuilding, particularly a thorough makeover just before the turn of the twentieth century. Its historical resonance is wrapped up almost exclusively in the figure of the Archduke Franz Ferdinand, the last heir to the throne of Austro-Hungary, who lived here with his wife Sophie Chotek and whose assassination in Sarajevo in 1914 sparked off the First World War. His legacy is a vast (bordering on the fetishistic) collection of weapons and stuffed animals that visitors to Konopiště troop past, the legacy of years of hunting in the thick forests around the castle and in other parts of the world such as Ceylon and East Africa. In fact, between 1880 and 1906 Franz Ferdinand killed 171,537 birds and animals, all of which were lovingly dated and catalogued; no animal was safe from a cartridge fired from one of his ivory-inlaid rifles, as the elephant's foot ashtray in one of the rooms admirably demonstrates.

Alongside the displays of hunting paraphernalia are rooms brimming with period furniture and Meissen porcelain, while the archduke's collection of chivalric statues of St. George, and his shooting range complete with mechanical moving targets, can be visited for a few crowns. But as with Karlštejn it is the setting rather than the rooms that is the real draw. Below the castle is a beautiful terraced rose garden, while the Baroque statuary in the grounds and the sight of the castle's shimmering reflection in the adjacent lake form an attractive backdrop to strolls through Franz Ferdinand's former hunting grounds. A quiet path through woodland links the castle with the nearby town of Benešov u Prahy, a stop for trains on the main line south from Prague to České Budějovice.

More multi-turreted castles set amidst fine countryside await discovery by those who want to press on beyond Konopiště and Karlštejn. Between those two castles—around twelve miles (twenty kilometers) from both of them—a hydro-electric dam has turned the Vltava into an elongated lake named Slapy which is lined with campsites and resorts and is hugely popular with vacationing Czechs (though not so much with foreigners). Two more castles are perched attractively above another hydro lake, to the south—a mock-Gothic pile named Orlík, stuffed full of yet more weaponry and Empire-style furniture, and Zvíkov, further south again, which retains more of its medieval appearance. Like most castles in Bohemia the setting of these castles is more attractive than the interiors, and it is the summer boat trips along the swollen Vltava (or the walk through the adjacent forests) that appeal more than traipsing round the buildings themselves.

Then there are the regions of West and South Bohemia themselves, distinctive and separate from the area around the capital. Those heading further into western Bohemia from Karlštejn will inevitably pass through Plzeň, a steel-making and brewing city famous as the home of Škoda cars and Pilsner beer, and two hours by train from Prague; a similar distance further on are the world-renowned spa towns of Mariánské Lázně (Marienbad) and Karlovy Vary (Karlsbad), both absorbing places to visit but, with traveling times from Prague anything from two to four hours by road or rail (respectively), only viable as day-trips by those who can tolerate the general slowness of Czech trains or the comparatively poor quality of the roads.

České Budějovice, the main urban center of South Bohemia, is also a brewing town, famous for Budvar beer, and thirty kilometers to its south the picture-perfect town of Český Krumlov draws visitors by the bus load who come primarily to see the medieval castle that watches over a knot of narrow lanes from a cliff-top eyrie above River Vltava. Beyond Český Krumlov lie the gloomily beautiful, thickly forested and eerily deserted Šumava hills stretching along the German border. But visitors to South Bohemia are once again up against the problem of distance: a day excursion to Český Krumlov from Prague involves a fair few hours of traveling, and, as is the case with the West Bohemian excursions, a more fulfilling visit would entail staying in the region itself rather than day-tripping there from the capital.

North of Prague: the Elbe

The scenery to the north of Prague is flatter and less immediately appealing than that to the west and south. Only the Krkonoše Mountains along the Polish border, and the attractive area of sandstone gorges and natural rock arches known as "Bohemian Switzerland" hard up by the German border, can compete with the rest of Bohemia in terms of scenery. But they really are too far from Prague to make for viable day trips. Rising amidst the skiing grounds of the Krkonoše, and creating the gorge at the heart of Bohemian Switzerland, is the River Elbe—Labe to Czechs—whose north-westward journey out of Bohemia takes the great river through Dresden and Magdeburg and on to the North Sea at Hamburg. As it loops luxuriously through northern Bohemia the Elbe flows through two small market towns that make for ideal excursions from the capital: these are Mělník, where the Vltava merges with the Elbe, and Litoměřice, another thirty kilometers downstream, where the Ohře, Karlovy Vary's river, swells the Elbe still further. Both towns have a history of wine-making—indeed, they are the only wine-making towns in Bohemia and together they lie at the heart of the most northerly grape-growing area in continental Europe. Their viticultural tradition dates from the patronage of Charles IV, the great ruler of Bohemia in the Middle Ages; his preferred variety of grape came from Burgundy, where he was also king, and in the case of Litoměřice the town was forced to start cultivating vineyards as a condition of accepting a gift from the ruler in the form of a hill known as Radobýl, which overlooks the town (and to this day can be reached by a popular marked trail from the center). With rapid bus links to Prague (and slower rail ones), and occasional cruise and passenger ships that make it to Litoměřice and Mělník from Prague or even Dresden, these two towns easily form the best way of escaping into northern Bohemia from the capital.

Mělník is closer to Prague than Litoměřice but marginally less appealing. However it carries a greater historical significance, as it was here in the early decades of the tenth century that Queen Ludmila converted her young grandson Václav to Christianity. The boy grew up to rule as Václav I and entered Czech legend as St. Wenceslas, the first Christian ruler of Bohemia. It was Ludmila and Václav together who established the tradition of Mělník being the royal seat of widowed Queens of Bohemia, a succession of whom lived out their widowhoods in a grandiose medieval palace built on a high bluff above the confluence of the Elbe and the Vltava. Today, a Renaissance château stands where the old palace was situated, and the building is back in the hands of the Lobkowicz family from whom the communists purloined it in 1948. Now the place is used for weddings, concerts, and conferences, while visitors amble through rooms stuffed with period furniture before sampling local wines in the cellars (the most popular is a rosé appropriately named Ludmila). As with many a Bohemian castle the setting is the most compelling feature: its exterior walls are built hard up against a steep vineyard-covered slope that drops down to the Vltava, and the views from the ramparts stretch away almost as far as the suburbs of Prague. After sampling the wines and the view most visitors head for the adjacent church, with its gruesome ossuary made from ten thousand bones of medieval plague victims, and finally drift into the town's arcaded main square lined with bars and eateries where the local wines can be imbibed long into the night, perhaps as an accompaniment to a traditional Czech meal of pork and dumplings.

According to the twelfth-century chronicler Cosmas of Prague, Litoměřice was named after the Ludoměřic people, a Slavic tribe who settled in the region in the very early Middle Ages. The first written mention of the town came in 993 and shortly afterwards Litoměřice was home to a sizeable community of German-speaking merchants and craftsmen. The town's heyday came in the thirteenth and fourteenth centuries, when it was the third largest settlement in Bohemia, controlling an important stone bridge over the Elbe, the Tyrš, which was later lined with statues in the same manner as the Charles Bridge in Prague. Then came the familiar cycle of war, plague, and fire, and a disastrous flood that destroyed the great medieval bridge. Rebirth began in the late seventeenth century when the town received a Baroque makeover masterminded by Giovanni and Ottavio Broggio, a father and son architectural team from Italy. They are buried in one of the town's many churches, the Kostel Všech Svatých, which Ottavio himself remodeled in 1718. But the prettification, and the elevation of the town to a bishopric, was not enough. Litoměřice gives the impression of having dozed its way through recent centuries, and in 1945 most of its population was uprooted and deported to Germany for the simple reason that as the descendents of the craftsmen and merchants who settled here a thousand years ago, they spoke German. In November 1989, during the Velvet Revolution, the town was chosen as a slightly unlikely place for a communist counter-demonstration to those in Prague, where eighteen hundred faithful members of the Party gathered in the vast main square to futilely proclaim "Long Live Socialism" and "Long Live the Party!" Nowadays Litoměřice seems prosperous enough, buoyed up by its visitors and its wine production, and despite its pretty main square, its churches, and its beautiful setting beside the Elbe it does not seem as overwhelmed by tourists as other centers in Bohemia.

At the heart of the town is Mírové náměsti, one of the most luxuriously expansive squares in the Czech Republic. It was created in 1228 during the town's medieval remodeling, but its current appearance dates largely from the eighteenth century. Arcaded façades colored pastel shades of mint and mustard-yellow line the square; there is an extensive wash of sgraffito illustration on the exterior of one building named the House at the Black Eagle, while next door the town's wine-making tradition is celebrated by a copper chalice, green with oxidation, that adorns the roof of a mustard-colored building now housing the tourist office. Close by on the southeastern corner of the square the Renaissance Town Hall, with its panelled council chamber from 1542, accommodates a somewhat mundane regional museum, while in the center of the square is a plague column from 1680 by Giovanni Broggio. Alongside the Broggios' tombs the Kostel Všech Svatých contains a valuable panel painting from the late fifteenth century, The Agony in the Garden, which is the work of a nameless artist known simply as the Master of Litoměřice. Another of that master's works, an important altarpiece thought to have been commissioned by Vladislav Jagiello for his chapel in Prague Castle, can be seen in the town's worthwhile art gallery on a side street leading from the square.

Away from the area immediately around Mírové náměsti the attractions of Litoměřice lie in three different directions. To the south-west of the square overlooking its own carefully tended patch of greenery is the cathedral dedicated to St. Stephen, founded in 1057 and rebuilt in the eighteenth century with a free-standing bell tower next door that is later still. This area, known as Cathedral Hill and centered on Dómské náměstí, was the first part of the town to be settled and was once the location of a fort. No trace of that building remains now, and today the pink-and-cream façade of the Bishop's Palace overlooking the tree-lined banks of the river (and another work of Giovanni Broggio) provides one of the town's most distinctive photo opportunities.

To the northeast of Mírové námesti the shell of the castle built by Charles IV now houses a congress center, a restaurant, and a museum of wine-making. To the southeast of the center of town, beyond the Jesuit Church of Our Lady and the former Jesuit college, is the Tyršův most, an elegant nineteenth-century bridge built to replace the flood-damaged medieval structure that formerly spanned the Elbe here. A mile (one and a half kilometers) beyond the bridge, set back from the Elbe but on the banks of its tributary the Ohře, is Terezín, the grim Habsburg-era garrison town that was turned into a Jewish ghetto by the Nazis during their occupation of Bohemia (see Chapter 11). The place can be coupled with Litoměřice as a day trip from the capital—indeed most buses that make the run to Litoměřice from the depot outside Holešovice station in Prague also stop outside the main memorial and museum in Terezín.

Kutná Hora

During the reign of Charles IV Prague was such an ostentatiously wealthy city that parts of it must have actually glinted when the sun shone. The wealth of the so-called "golden age" came not from gold but from silver traded by the city's merchants and mined at Kutná Hora, these days a small town an hour's train journey east of Prague, but back in the late Middle Ages a place almost literally built on money whose size of population at one time rivaled that of medieval London. Silver dinars were being struck in Malín close to Kutná Hora a thousand years ago, but the exploitation of the town's extensive silver deposits did not begin in earnest until the year 1260.

The first pioneering miners to head underground in Kutná Hora spoke German and came from Jihlava in Moravia, where silver had already been mined for a generation. Within thirty years a gold rush—or to be more specific a silver rush—was in full swing in Kutná Hora (or Kuttenberg as those first miners knew it). Within the short space of a decade clusters of ramshackle buildings that had sprouted around the tops of mine shafts grew into a proper town, and in 1300 Václav II brought the mining industry under royal control and established the Bohemian Royal Mint in Kutná Hora. By then the town's mines produced a third of Europe's silver and the currency minted here, the Prague *groschen*, quickly became the most stable currency in Europe, acquiring the status of the modern-day Swiss franc.

Not surprisingly the town's wealth excited envy and interest both within and outside Bohemia. In the same year that Kutná Hora began minting *groschen* for the King of Bohemia, the Holy Roman Emperor demanded an annual tax payment of 80,000 talents of silver from the town (one talent being about half a pound/253g of metal), making his request clear by besieging the place. But the miners remained loyal to the King of Bohemia and responded by constructing fortifications around Kutná Hora, which ensured that the emperor went away empty handed. The loyalty of the miners to the Bohemian crown continued intact at the start of the Hussite wars, when in 1420 the Catholic claimant to the Bohemian throne, the Emperor Sigismund, received hospitality from the town's burghers after losing the Battle of Vítkov. For a time following this decisive battle Kutná Hora gained a reputation for being a center of virulent anti-Hussite activism. The Smíškovský hymn book, produced in the town in 1490, includes a colorful illustration depicting white-clad Hussites being hurled down a mine shaft as the town's burghers look smugly on. The heretical Hussites were of course not just being thrown down a mine: they were being cast into hell in the same manner depicted in hundreds of gory medieval paintings. Their fate was a common one in Kutná Hora at the beginning of the Hussite conflict, when hundreds of Hussites starved to death at the bottom of abandoned mine shafts. Yet the Hussite forces led by Jan Žižka soon prevailed in East Bohemia and for much of the remaining conflict the town was a Hussite stronghold. The fighting took its toll, however: by the time the embers of the conflict had died down Kutná Hora's great monastery at Sedlec was in ruins, its mines were flooded and its great municipal buildings had been torched by armies from both sides. Still, the town retained an important political role in the latter part of the fifteenth century. It was in Kutná Hora in 1471 that members of the Bohemian diet elected Vladislav Jagellon as king, and it was also here that Valdislav organized the important meetings that led to the reconciliation between Catholics and the moderate Hussites (known as Utraquists). At around the same time a new generation of Czech-speaking miners began to repopulate Kutná Hora and begin mining again. Slowly the town began to recover some—although not all—of its former glory.

Before Kutná Hora could reclaim its status as Europe's greatest silver mining center the miners came face to face with another problem—one that eventually affects mining settlements all over the world: the seams of ore were becoming exhausted. In 1547 the Osel Mine, the deepest in the world at that time (at an astonishing 550 yards/500 meters), was abandoned, and in the same year the town stopped minting the Prague *groschen*. The final blow came during the following century when the town was still important enough to be burned and plundered by both the Swedish and the Imperial armies during the Thirty Years War. By the turn of the eighteenth century Kutná Hora had become a dozy backwater, albeit one with a significant religious role, thanks to the enormous cathedral built during the heyday of mining, and the Jesuit college constructed right next door to it.

During the Nazi occupation of Czechoslovakia in the 1940s the town again became a mining center—this time of zinc and lead—but these deposits were worked out by 1991, just in time for the town to begin living off the influx of tourists who descend on the place in summer to see the glorious buildings that form the legacy of the town's mining past. These days it is the income from tourism (together with an enormous Philip Morris cigarette factory) that prevent the town from slowly sinking into an East Bohemian obscurity.

The building that everyone wants to see in Kutná Hora is the extraordinary Cathedral of St. Barbara, the town's trademark and one of the most impressive Gothic buildings in Central Europe. It is distinguished (and immediately recognizable) by the curving rows of flying buttresses that support the roof, which itself consists of three spires of unequal height shaped like giant witch's hats and appearing from some angles as if they are actually floating above the cathedral. The whole building bristles with such an array of spires and turrets that from a distance it has the appearance of a giant porcupine. Construction work on this remarkable building, dedicated to the patron saint of miners, began in 1388 and the builders intended that it would rival St. Vitus' in Prague. In fact, the first architect who worked on the cathedral was Jan Parler, son of Peter Parler who endowed the Bohemian capital with its extraordinary Gothic splendor. But after the initial enthusiasm of the first building phase at the turn of the fifteenth century progress slowed somewhat. As Kutná Hora's fortunes ebbed and the money ran out, the building's planned dimensions were slashed, which is why today the cathedral seems so out of proportion, with a nave that is far too high and broad for its comparatively short length.

There was enough money, though, to pay Benedikt Ried, who designed Vladislav Hall in Prague Castle, for his splendid ribbed vaulting, which loops and curls itself around the ceiling of the cathedral into an exhilarating array of flower and petal forms. Above the chancel the curls of Ried's vaulting embrace a clutch of colorful shields that are heraldic emblems of the town's various mining guilds. Also striking are the late Gothic frescoes that adorn the walls of the cathedral, depicting miners and minters going about their day-to-day work—striking coins, selling ore, or working winches that lift miners with their bulging sacks from the sweaty depths up to the surface. The activity depicted on the frescoes is similar to that shown on a page in the Kuttenberg hymn book of 1490, which was generously illustrated by an artist named Matthew the Illuminator. The bottom third of this illustration depicts miners underground chipping at the rock, crawling through tunnels, and hauling bags of rock up ladders, while the middle third is awash with other miners operating winches and machinery and washing themselves in their underwear in a stream; at the top of the page sacks of ore are sorted, mainly by women, while traders haul off bags of freshly minted coins. The whole illustration is awash with color: the miners are clad in white, the womenfolk in orange, and the underground seams that the miners are cutting through appear a vivid but unlikely blue. It is clear from this remarkable illustration and from the frescoes in St. Barbara's that mining defined the entire community of Kutná Hora, just as it did in towns in northeast England or Pennsylvania up until the 1980s.

Away from St. Barbara's further reminders of the former wealth and importance of Kutná Hora sprinkle the town like a dusting of silver. The Jesuits established their presence here in 1667, in the conspicuous form of an enormous college whose high walls tower over the streams of tourists heading for the cathedral. Softening the bluntness of the college is the row of Charles Bridge-style statues of saints across from its façade, which in turn watch over the deep wooded valley of the Vrchlice river. Facing the same valley is the Hradek, once the home of a late medieval mine entrepreneur and social climber named Jan Smíšek, who was rumored to own and operate a private mint within its thick walls. Nowadays the Italian-style Renaissance ceilings that Smíšek installed overlook the exhibits of the town's museum, and the courtyard of his fortress-style home allows access to the entrance to a section of mine workings that reach a depth of one hundred and sixty feet (fifty meters). Edging on past the all-too-predictable array of cafés and souvenir shops one reaches the town's second church, smaller and older than St. Barbara's, a hulking, graceless soot-blackened late Gothic affair dedicated to St. James and built between 1350 and 1420 to serve the needs of the fast-expanding mining community. The north tower, which soars confidently to a height of about 95 yards (85 meters), tilts visibly from the vertical, wrenched askew by the collapsing mine workings on top of which the whole church was unfortunately constructed. Builders feared the same would happen to the south tower, which as a result was never completed, and which is capped today by a squat pyramid roof barely higher than that over the main church.

Inside the church are the usual Baroque embellishments—but sadly none of the unique frescoes that so mark out St. Barbara's as a miner's church. Things do not get much cheerier next door, where the Vlašsky dvůr (Italian Court), home of the royal mint and the officials who looked after it, is now home to an unimaginative museum of mining, which its curators imagine is enlivened by a display of medieval torture instruments. The courtyard is not much better—only a fourteenth-century oriel window remains from the original medieval construction—and the one memorable thing about the place where Florentine minters were brought over to supervise the production of the Prague *groshen* is the view across the Vrchlice valley to the cathedral, its buttresses appearing from this angle to be about to launch the great building and its trio of witch's hats straight into the Bohemian sky.

But Kutná Hora's historic interest does not end with the cathedral and the clutch of buildings around it. Nor, indeed, does it end at the main square close by, an irregularly shaped expanse of cobbles and greenery surrounded by the familiar Bohemian rows of pastel-colored buildings flanked by arcades. Little more than half a mile (a kilometer) to the northeast of the town center, close to the main railway station and the cigarette factory, is the great abbey church of the former Cistercian monastery of Sedlec. The abbey was founded in 1142 under the auspices of the Bishop of Olomouc in Moravia, who personally knew Bernard of Clairvaux, the founder of the Cistercian order. The first community of monks turned Sedlec into a rich and productive agricultural settlement a full century before any mines were dug in neighboring Kutná Hora—whose name in fact derives from Kuntha Antiqua, or Old Monk's Habit, the name given to one of the original settlements established near the monastery. The monks could never have guessed that they had founded their monastery on a silver mine: when mining started most of the mines were dug on monastic land, and the monastery grew rich from the taxes it imposed on miners—only to fall into poverty when loans the monks made to the Czech aristocracy were never repaid.

In later centuries the monastery found itself the victim of a familiar chain of catastrophes—destruction in Hussite and Thirty Years Wars, and then closure in 1784 when the Emperor Joseph II dissolved all the Austrian monasteries. The Convent Church of the Virgin Mary survives, its Gothic architectural heritage easily traced back to medieval France, where the practice of ending the church with a ring of chapels around the presbytery was common-place but at the time unheard of in Bohemia. The vaulting, dating from Baroque times, was inspired by Ried's work in St. Barbara's Cathedral, and these days forms the centerpiece of a color scheme that contrasts brilliant white with pale yellow. The church receives a steady stream of visitors, but most ignore it in favor of what is certainly Kutná Hora's—and arguably Bohemia's—goriest tourist attraction. A minute's walk away from the abbey is a tiny cemetery chapel where, in the thirteenth century, the Abbot of Sedlec sprinkled some earth that had been brought here from Jerusalem. At once the cemetery earth became part of the Holy Land and the well-to-do from all over Central Europe paid enough to the monastery to be buried here. It is the interior of the chapel that draws the bus tours now, for it is decorated entirely with human bones. Lines of leg bones are suspended between pillars like macabre Christmas decorations; there are chandeliers made from skulls; but the most surprising ornament is the coat of arms of the Schwartzenberg family, constructed from everything from shoulder blades to dozens of ankle bones all carefully lined up in parallel. The origins of the ossuary date back to 1511 when blind monks filled their time by piling up human bones into a pyramid. In the late eighteenth century, when the Schwartzenberg family of South Bohemia purchased the property of Sedlec Abbey following its dissolution, they commissioned wood carver František Rint to create the monstrosity that can be seen today. It is reckoned that Rint used the remains of 40,000 people to create this bizarre reminder of the transience of human life: he even used some of the bones to form his own signature, which hangs on the wall beside the steps that these days groan with the lines of the curious.

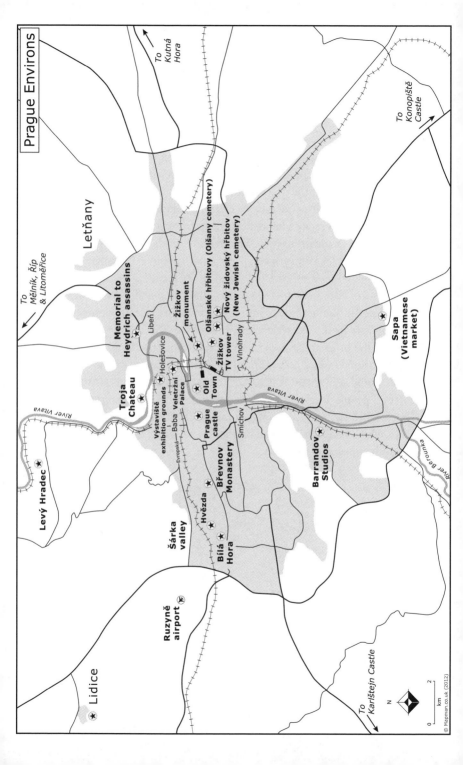

Further Reading and Useful Websites

The following section comprises a list of books that have been consulted in the preparation of this book. In addition to the titles listed, a number of websites have also been consulted, and I would particularly like to acknowledge those belonging to religious groups and expatriate groups in Prague. The main website for tourists visiting the city is www.praguewelcome.cz/en though others exist such as www.pragueexperience.com. Sites aimed at English-speaking residents in the Czech Republic such as www.expats.cz offer more than the usual advice about restaurants, hotels, and what to see and do. Many other website scan be identified by using any search-engine and it seems pointless to list them all here.

Legends

Jirásek, Alois, *Old Bohemian Tales* (1894). Indiana: Forest Books/ Paris: UNESCO, 1992 (this edition is published as *Old Czech Legends*)

Cultural, Architectural, and Literary History; and the History of Prague before 1900

Andel, Jaroslav *et al*, *Czech Modernism 1900-1945*. New York: Bulfinch Press, 1990

Birgis, Vladimir, *Czech Photographic Avant-Garde 1918-1948*. Cambridge, MA: MIT Press, 2002

Brook, Stephen, *The Double Eagle: Vienna, Budapest, Prague*. London: Hamish Hamilton, 1988

Burton, Richard, *Prague: a Cultural History*. Northampton: Interlink Books, 2003

Demetz, Peter, *Prague in Black and Gold*. London: Penguin Books, 1998

Evans, R. J. W., *Rudolf II and his World* (1973). London: Thames and Hudson, 1997

Kaplan, Jan, *A Traveller's Companion to Prague*. London: Constable and Robinson, 2005

Margolius, Ivan, *Prague: a Guide to Twentieth Century Architecture*. London: Ellipsis, 1994.

Marshall, Peter, *The Theatre of the World: Alchemy, Astrology and Magic in Renaissance Prague*.   London: Harvill Secker, 2006

Murray, Nicholas, *Kafka*. London: Abacus, 2005

Ripellino, Angelo Maria, *Magic Prague*. London: Picador, 1995

Salfellner, Harald, *Franz Kafka and Prague*. Prague: Vitalis, 2007 (abridged edition 2010)

Wagenbach, Klaus, *Kafka's Prague: A Travel Reader*. New York: Overlook Press 1998

Wilson, Paul, (ed.) *Prague: A Traveller's Literary Companion*. Berkeley, CA: Whereabouts Press, 1995

Twentieth-Century History

Bryant, Chad, *Prague in Black: Nazi Rule and Czech Nationalism*. Cambridge, MA: Harvard University Press, 2007

Garton Ash, Timothy, *We the People*. London: Granta Books, 1990

Gerwarth, Robert, *Hitler's Hangman: The Life of Heydrich*. New Haven CT: Yale University Press, 2011

Kaplan, Karel, *The Report on the Murder of the General Secretary*. London: I. B. Tauris, 1990

Keane, John, *Václav Havel: A Political Tragedy in Six Acts*. London: Bloomsbury Publishing, 2000

MacDonald, Callum, and Kaplan, Jan, *Prague in the Shadow of the Swastika*. London: Quartet Books, 1995

MacDonald, Callum, *The Assassination of Reinhard Heydrich* (1990). Edinburgh: Birlinn, 2007

Guidebooks

Humphreys, Rob, *The Rough Guide to Prague* (eighth edition).
  London: Rough Guides, 2011
Wilson, Neil, *Prague City Guide* (ninth edition). Melbourne:
  Lonely Planet Publications, 2010
Turp, Craig, *Eyewitness Travel Guide: Prague* (eighteenth edition).
  London: DK Publishing, 2012
Various authors, *Time Out: Prague* (eighth edition) London: Time
  Out Guides, 2009

Travel Books

Baker, James, *Pictures from Bohemia* (1897). London: The British
  Library, 2010
Leigh Fermor, Patrick, *A Time of Gifts* (1979). London: John Mur-
  ray, 2004

Memoirs and Essays

Forman, Miloš, *Turnaround*. London: Faber and Faber, 1994
Havel, Václav, *Letters to Olga*. London: Faber and Faber, 1990
Havel, Václav, *Disturbing the Peace*. London: Faber and Faber, 1990
Havel, Václav, *The Art of the Impossible: Politics and Morality in
  Practice*. New York: Knopf, 1997
Havel, Václav, *To the Castle and Back*. London: Portobello Books,
  2009
Margolius Kovály, Heda. Her 1973 memoir is variously published
  in English as *Prague Farewell, I Do Not Want to Remember* and
  The Victors and the Vanquished. It is most recently published as
  Under a Cruel Star, London: Granta Books, 2012
Weiss, Rachel, *Me, Myself and Prague*. London: Orion Publishing,
  2009

Poetry

Mácha, Karel Hynek, *May.* Prague: Twisted Spoon Press, 2005
Nezval, Vítězslav, *Prague with Fingers of Rain* (1936). Tarset,
    Northumberland: Bloodaxe Books, 2009
Seifert, Jaroslav, *The Poetry of Jaroslav Seifert.* New Haven, CT:
    Catbird Press, 1998

Fiction (originally in Czech)

Hašek, Jaroslav, *The Good Soldier Švejk* (1923). London: Penguin
    Books, 2000.
Hrabal, Bohumil, *Too Loud a Solitude* (1976). London: Abacus,
    1993.
Klíma, Ivan, *Waiting for the Dark, Waiting for the Light.* London:
    Granta Books, 1994
Klíma, Ivan, *No Saints or Angels,* London: Granta Books, 2001
Kohout, Pavel, *The Widow Killer,* New York: Picador, 1995
Kundera, Milan, *Life is Elsewhere* (1973). London: Faber and
    Faber, 2000
Kundera, Milan, *The Book of Laughter and Forgetting* (1978).
    London: Faber and Faber, 1996
Kundera, Milan, *The Unbearable Lightness of Being* (1985).
    London: Faber and Faber, 2000
Neruda, Jan, *Prague Tales.* Budapest: Central European University
    Press, 2001
Weil, Jiří, *Life with a Star* (1949). London: Daunt Books, 2012
Weil, Jiří, *Mendelssohn is on the Roof* (1960). London: Daunt Books,
    2011

Fiction (originally in English)

Brierley, David, *On Leaving a Prague Window.* London: Warner
    Books, 1996
Burgess, Alan, *Seven Men at Daybreak.* London: Companion
    Books, 1961

Chatwin, Bruce, *Utz* (1988). London: Vintage Classics, 2008

Crawford, Francis Marion, *The Witch of Prague* (1891). New York: Cornell University Library, 2009

Gee, Sue, *Letters from Prague*. London: Arrow, 1995

Gellhorn, Martha, *A Stricken Field* (1940). Chicago: University of Chicago Press, 2011

Roth, Philip, *Prague Orgy* (1996). London: Vintage, 2006

Fiction (originally in German)

Kafka, Franz, *The Castle* (1926). London: Penguin, 2000

Kafka, Franz, *The Trial* (1925). Oxford: Oxford University Press, 2009

Meyrink, Gustav, *The Golem* (1914). Mineola, NY: Dover Publications, 2003

Rilke, Rainer Maria, *King Bohusch* and *The Siblings* (published together as *Two Prague Stories*). Prague: Vitalis, 2005

Plays

Havel, Václav, *Selected Plays 1963-1983* and *Selected Plays 1984-1987*. London: Faber and Faber, 1992 and 1994 respectively.

Havel, Václav, *The Garden Party and Other Plays*. New York: Grove Press, 1993

Stoppard, Tom, *Dogg's Hamlet/Cahoot's Macbeth, Professional Foul* and *Rock 'n' Roll* are all published singly and in collected editions by Faber and Faber (London).

Index